More Than We Have Ever Known About Discipline and Discharge in Labor Arbitration: An Empirical Study

More Than We Have Ever Known About Discipline and Discharge in Labor Arbitration: An Empirical Study

Laura J. Cooper

Mario F. Bognanno

Stephen F. Befort

VANDEPLAS PUBLISHING, LLC

UNITED STATES OF AMERICA

More Than We Have Ever Known About Discipline and Discharge in Labor Arbitration: An Empirical Study

Cooper, Laura J.
Bognanno, Mario F.
Befort, Stephen F.

Published by:

Vandeplas Publishing, LLC – May 2015

801 International Parkway, 5th Floor
Lake Mary, FL. 32746
USA

www.vandeplaspublishing.com

ISBN 978-1-60042-242-3

Dedication

To the National Academy of Arbitrators and its Research and Education Foundation for their enduring commitment to expanding knowledge and understanding of workplace dispute resolution

L.J.C.

M.F.B.

S.F.B.

More Than We Have Ever Known About Discipline and Discharge in Labor Arbitration: An Empirical Study

Table of Contents

List of Tables and Figures

Chapter 1: Twenty-Four Years of Discharge and Discipline Arbitration Awards

Tables

Chapter 2: Overview of the Survey's Data

Tables

Chapter 3: Wins, Losses and Split Decisions in Discharge and Discipline Awards

Tables

Figures

Chapter 4: Offenses

Tables

Figures

Chapter 5: How Arbitrators Assess Proof

Tables

Figures

Chapter 6: The Seven Tests of Just Cause

Tables

Foreword

Labor arbitration in America is chronicled in numerous seminal books, such as, *Elkouri & Elkouri, How Arbitration Works, The Common Law of the Workplace, and Discipline and Discharge in Arbitration.* These and kindred scholarly works often recite conventional beliefs about the field, many of which lack foundational support. In discussions among ourselves, we reached the obvious conclusion that the origin of these deficiencies is the paucity of data about labor arbitration and its outcomes. The idea for this book was inspired by this realization.

Our book is based on the analysis of a vast amount of empirical information about the content of 2,055 discipline and discharge arbitration awards, including, for example, each award's outcome, grieving party, the parties' advocates, and the arbitrator who issued that award. Since our unit of analysis was the arbitration award, we spent significant time and resources in compiling these awards, carefully reading and coding each award for critical items of content, and coding independently gathered information about the individual arbitrator who issued each award. Such research undertaking required the help of many people and institutions, and it gives us great pleasure to acknowledge them.

First, as academics, we wish to acknowledge and thank our many graduate students and second- and third-year law students who served as research assistants for varying periods. Graduate students Jonathan Booth, Kristen Munday and Thomas Norman assisted us in designing the computerized survey instrument used to code each arbitration award, and they undertook the statistical analyses of data presented throughout the chapters of the book. Law students Deborah Broderson, Tana Dietzler, Angela Lam, Jessica Marsh, Mike Pangborn and Jeff Vockrodt performed the vital tasks of reading and coding each award in our survey for the precise content we required.

Second, without the considerable help and assistance we received from the Minnesota Bureau of Mediation Services the empirical information required by this undertaking could not have been gathered. For assistance and facilitating access to the Bureau's arbitration case files, we wish to thank Commissioners James A.

Cunningham, Steven G. Hoffmeyer, and Josh L. Tilsen. In particular, we extend a special note of appreciation to Carol S. Clifford, Assistant to the Commissioner, for her help that went well beyond the call of duty.

Finally, the research that resulted in this book would not have been possible without the generous financial support of the Research and Education Foundation of the National Academy of Arbitrators, and from the encouragement we received from National Academy colleagues. In addition, a special note of thanks is due the University of Minnesota's Law School and Center for Human Resources and Labor Studies, Carlson School of Management, for augmented financial support and investigative critique.

Laura J. Cooper
Mario F. Bognanno
Stephen F. Befort

Minneapolis, Minnesota
June 2014

CHAPTER 1

TWENTY-FOUR YEARS OF DISCHARGE AND DISCIPLINE ARBITRATION AWARDS

Introduction

This book analyzes the largest and possibly the most representative collection of labor arbitration awards ever assembled to provide insights into the private and somewhat hidden process that is labor arbitration: a process on which the job security of millions of Americans depends. Most American workers have little recourse when discharged or disciplined by employers. Generally, an employee not represented by a union can challenge an employer's decision only through litigation and can prevail only upon proof of specific discriminatory intent or violation of some very limited common law right.[1] The 17.7 million workers covered by labor contracts, however, have vastly greater protection.[2] They can have their employers' disciplinary decisions reviewed by private arbitrators who have the power to, and regularly do, overturn the employers' decisions. For more than 50 years, employers and unions have increasingly relied upon private arbitration to resolve their disputes. Nevertheless, until this study, knowledge about the exercise of arbitral power has been limited to commentaries and small empirical studies.

For workers represented by unions, the right to challenge employers' discharge and disciplinary decisions in labor arbitration is ubiquitous. Ninety-nine percent of private and public sector labor contracts include binding arbitration as the final step in a grievance resolution process. That processes begins with grievances first being considered by progressively higher levels of employer and union authority.[3] When grievance resolution

---

[1] See Stephen F. Befort & John W. Budd, *Invisible Hands, Invisible Objectives: Bringing Workplace Law and Public Policy into Focus* (Stanford, CA: Stanford University Press, 2009), 61-64, 87-88.

[2] The workers covered estimate is for the year 2008. See U.S. Bureau of Labor Statistics, Household Data Annual Averages, ftp://ftp.bls.gov/pub/special.requests/lf/aat40.txt (reported on October 15, 2009).

[3] Laura J. Cooper, Dennis R. Nolan, Richard A. Bales, & Stephen F. Befort, *ADR in the Workplace* (St. Paul, MN: West Academic Publishing, 3d ed. 2014), 20.

fails at the highest level of employer and union authority, the dissatisfied party may bring the grievance to arbitration. In arbitration, the parties jointly select a neutral labor arbitrator whom they empower to issue a binding award or decision.[4] It has been estimated that 1.2 million written grievances were filed in 1986[5] and, in that same year, labor arbitrators issued 64,000 awards.[6] Decided arbitration cases like these have a multiplying effect because they become part of an informal system of precedent the parties use for guidance in resolving grievances that are settled annually without resorting to arbitration.

Collective bargaining agreements, in addition to including arbitration provisions, uniformly prohibit employers from discharging or disciplining employees except for "just cause."[7] Grievances alleging that employers have violated such "just cause" provisions constitute the largest single category of cases heard each year by labor arbitrators.[8]

The labor arbitration of such disputes, in addition to providing valuable substantive and procedural rights for union-represented workers, also performs an important social and economic function. As the U.S. Supreme Court noted in 1960, when unions and employers agree to arbitrate contract grievances they are implicitly agreeing to forego strikes and

---

[4] *Id.* at 22-24, 28-29.

[5] David Lewin & R. B. Peterson, *The Modern Grievance Procedure in the United States* (New York, NY: Quorum Books, 1988), 200.

[6] *Labor Arbitration in America* (New York, NY: Praeger Publishers, Mario F. Bognanno & Charles J. Coleman, eds., 1992), 92.

[7] Arbitrators and courts consider protection from unjust dismissal so basic an element of the collective bargaining relationship that they find it exists even in those rare contracts that contain no explicit "just cause" provision. See, for example, SFIC Properties, Inc. v. Machinists, District Lodge 94, 103 F.3d 923 (9th Cir. 1996); Superior Products, 116 LA 1623 (Hockenberry 2002).

[8] The Federal Mediation and Conciliation Service reported that discipline and discharge cases constituted more than 37 percent of contract grievances arbitrated in fiscal 2008 The next largest category, wage disputes, represented less than six percent of the cases. Federal Mediation and Conciliation Service, Arbitration Statistics Fiscal Year 2008, *available at* http://www.fmcs.gov/assets/files/Arbitration/FY2008%20Statistics/Issues_Arbitrated.doc.

lockouts as alternative means of grievance resolution.[9] Thus, arbitration increases not only private welfare, but social and economic welfare as well.

Despite the importance of labor arbitration for the nation and its workers, our knowledge of the arbitration process is remarkably limited. Generally, both labor arbitration hearings and their resulting awards are private. The privacy of the process leaves the public and even participants in the process with relatively little accurate information about the nature of grievances that are arbitrated, the workers who submit the grievances, the arbitrators who decide them, and the outcomes of the cases.

This book pierces labor arbitration's veil of privacy. It reports in extraordinary detail on more than two thousand discharge and discipline awards issued over a twenty-four year period in a single state. The presented analysis is based on an extensive coding of the content of each of those awards and related records, providing information on numerous and diverse aspects of arbitral decision-making. Using discharge and discipline awards, we can make comparisons across awards because, in each case, the arbitrator's task is the same. In every case, the arbitrator is interpreting and applying the "just cause" provision, answering the same two-part issue statement: Was the grievant discharged or disciplined for "just cause"? If not, what is the appropriate remedy?[10]

Previous studies of disciplinary arbitration awards have often focused on narrow issues and usually have been based on small numbers of non-representative published decisions. This book, however, offers a comprehensive analysis of the largest data set ever assembled of published and unpublished discharge and discipline decisions. Thus, enabling it to offer vital information and analysis never before available about the arbitration process and the awards arbitrators issue.

In this chapter, we explain the purposes of our research and describe our research methods. We also explain why we believe that our Minnesota findings may be guardedly generalized to the nation as a whole. The chapter concludes with an overview of the book's

---

[9] Steelworkers v. Warrior & Gulf Navigation Co., 363 U.S. 574, 578, 581 (1960); Steelworkers v. American Manufacturing Co., 363 U.S. 564, 567 (1960).

[10] *Elkouri & Elkouri, How Arbitration Works* (Washington, D.C.: Bureau of National Affairs, Kenneth May, ed., 7th ed. 2012), 15-23.

remaining chapters.

Purpose

The book has three purposes: (1) to present new information about the arbitration process, the parties to the arbitration hearing and arbitral outcomes; (2) to test statements about the "conventional wisdom" of disciplinary arbitration, articulated in commentaries and arbitration awards; and (3) to test newly constructed hypotheses about arbitration as well as to re-test empirical relationships reported in the literature. Each of these purposes is discussed below.

Information

The courts, legislatures, and other policymaking bodies have long endorsed labor arbitration, but their continued endorsement relies, in part, on the availability of information about the arbitration process and what it is that arbitrators do. To continue to have faith in arbitration and to renew their agreements to arbitrate grievance disputes, the parties require information about arbitration. Moreover, arbitrators themselves desire information about how other arbitrators address common substantive and procedural issues so they may benefit from their peers' wisdom as they confront new and challenging questions.

For these reasons, foremost among the book's purposes is to present information that the courts, policymakers, the parties and arbitrators need to better understand disciplinary arbitration. To satisfy this need, a great deal of information is required about the arbitration process, the arbitrators who decide disciplinary grievances, the grievants, and the decisions or awards that arbitrators ultimately issue. This book presents that information.

Validation

The book's second purpose is to scrutinize empirically numerous assertions found in the arbitration literature about how "most," "many" or "some" arbitrators decide discharge and discipline cases. The *Elkouri & Elkouri* treatise makes innumerable generalizations, many of which are used in classrooms and cited in briefs and awards.[11] A second source of such generalizations is *The Common Law of the Workplace*, a compilation written by respected arbitrators and members of the National Academy of Arbitrators (NAA).[12] That work includes the following assertions, among others:

A. *Last-Chance Agreements*

Generally, arbitrators will enforce last-chance agreements.[13]

B. *Retention of Jurisdiction*

Once it is determined that a back pay award is appropriate, an arbitrator may remand the task of computation to the parties. Such a remedy is *usually*, but not always, accompanied by retention of jurisdiction by the arbitrator in the event that there is a subsequent dispute over the amount.[14]

C. *Quantum of Proof*

(1) For *most* arbitrators, the normal quantum of proof required in disciplinary cases is "preponderance of the evidence." For a *minority*, it is "clear and convincing evidence."

(2) When the employee's alleged offense would constitute a serious breach of law or would be viewed as moral turpitude sufficient to damage an employee's reputation, *most* arbitrators require a higher quantum of proof, typically expressed as "clear and convincing evidence." *Some* require proof "beyond a reasonable doubt" but, absent an express contractual provision to the contrary, *most* hold that the criminal-law standard of beyond a reasonable doubt" has no place in an informal dispute mechanism like arbitration.[15]

Sweeping statements like these seem to be consistent with conventional wisdom, which may explain why they are usually offered without attribution or empirical support.[16]

---

[11] *How Arbitration Works*.

[12] *The Common Law of the Workplace: The Views of Arbitrators* (Washington, D.C.: Bureau of National Affairs, Theodore J. St. Antoine, ed., 2d ed. 2005).

[13] *Common Law of the Workplace*, § 6.29 Comment c (emphasis added).

[14] *Common Law of the Workplace*, § 10.14 (emphasis added).

[15] *Common Law of the Workplace*, § 6.10 (emphasis added).

[16] Assertions about last chance agreements and retention of jurisdiction by arbitrators are tested in Chapter 7. The quantum of proof assertion is evaluated in Chapter 5. Also, Chapter 3 addresses the effects of last chance agreements and the quantum standard on arbitration outcomes. These and other

In this book, we attempt to determine whether these and other assertions can withstand empirical scrutiny.

Hypothesis Testing

The book's third purpose is to test new hypotheses, and to re-evaluate a range of empirical conclusions about discharge and discipline arbitration as reported by other analysts. Sometimes our findings contradict previous research findings. Consider the following examples of hypotheses that we examine. First, we test for the effects of arbitrator and grievant characteristics, like gender, on arbitration outcomes. Assuming that we could design a controlled experiment where the alleged type of employee offense, the degree to which the grievant was forthcoming and contrite about his or her transgression, as well as all the other factors that go into an arbitrator's decision, then the gender of the arbitrator and/or the gender of the grievant should not matter to arbitrator decision-making. This hypothesis rests on the assumption that arbitrators decide cases based on their *merits* and, thus, variables like these should not affect decision making. But do they?

One idea that is empirically tested for the first time is the extent to which arbitrators who adjudicate employee discharge and discipline cases apply the rubric of "The Seven Tests of Just Cause," as first articulated by Arbitrator Carroll R. Daugherty.[17] The Seven Tests are widely presented to students, employer and union practitioners and practicing arbitrators as *the* basis for determining just cause. Implicitly, our null hypothesis is that the Daugherty framework is the standard by which arbitrators make just cause adjudications. We then proceed to scrutinize this assumption empirically. Our findings were unexpected and readers should find them interesting, if not surprising.

As another example, we reevaluate the relationship between arbitration outcomes and *delay* (i.e., the time lapse between the date of the employer's discharge decision and the date of the arbitrator's award). The competing hypotheses about delay are (a) delay and

---

generalizations regarding arbitrator practices are tested in this book. Some generalizations pass these tests, while others are relegated to "myth" status.

[17] The Seven Tests were first enumerated in Grief Bros. Cooperage Corp., 42 LA 359 (Daugherty 1964).

reinstatement without back pay are positively correlated *versus* (b) delay and employer win outcomes are positively correlated. The validity of both hypotheses is called into question in Chapters 3 and 7.

Methodology

Survey and Source Material

In mid-2004, the Research and Education Foundation of the NAA awarded a grant to support research for this book, which was generously augmented by the University of Minnesota Law School and the Carlson School of Management's Human Resources and Labor Studies Center. For the next two years, our survey team read 2,055 published and unpublished discharge and discipline arbitration awards concerning Minnesota workplaces issued between February 12, 1982 and July 15, 2005—nearly 24 years of awards.

We coded 36 survey items for each award and we later merged information garnered about the deciding arbitrator's state of residence, age, education, gender, occupation and NAA membership status. Our 2,055 awards were decided by 81 different arbitrators. Considering that some of our survey items included multiple response categories, we collected data on more than 100 variables per award. For example, with respect to the "alleged offense" committed by the discharged or disciplined employee, we coded 43 different offense categories, which we later clustered into 9 categories for analysis.[18]

In addition to the authors, our survey team included two Ph.D. graduate students who assisted in data analysis and in creating our computerized—*Microsoft Access*—survey instrument, and four second- and third-year law students who used the survey instrument to code the individual awards. Subsequently, we transferred our *Access* data files to *Excel* and *Stata* software packages for analysis, which was conducted with the assistance of an additional Ph.D. graduate student and two additional law students.

---

[18] Similar offenses were clustered into the following nine categories: Violence & Aggression (467 cases); Attendance & Absenteeism (352 cases); Dishonesty (377); Drug & Alcohol Use (96); On-the-Job Misconduct (175); Off-the-Job Misconduct (94); Insubordination (469); Performance Issues (370); and Other (24).

To ensure consistent coding of awards, we cross-checked each other's work. Initially, for example, the authors and our legal assistants read and coded several specimen awards. We then matched our codes on an item-by-item basis, checking for differences. Where they existed, we agreed on a protocol to regulate the future coding of that item and, on several occasions, we honed the phrasing of that item in our survey instrument. A copy of the survey instrument appears as Appendix A.

In 1939, the Minnesota legislature established a labor relations agency, presently known as the Bureau of Mediation Services (BMS). Among its services, the BMS maintains a roster of experienced, neutral labor arbitrators for referral to requesting parties. Sometime in 1980 or 1981, the BMS began to require the arbitrators on its roster to file their Minnesota decisions with the BMS regardless of the source of the arbitrator's appointment (e.g., BMS, Federal Mediation and Conciliation Service (FMCS), American Arbitration Association (AAA) or permanent panel).[19] Accordingly, this study's 2,055 awards are the awards filed by arbitrators on the BMS roster.

In 1982, the BMS and its vendor, LRP Publications, began preparing written summaries of each arbitration decision it received, cataloging each summary in loose-leaf binders entitled *Minnesota Labor Arbitration Awards Summaries.* Each case summary is given an identification number and "Key Classification Index" (KCI) number. Our legal assistants retrieved from the BMS case files the hard copy of each decision with the KCI numbers 37 (discipline), 109 (suspension) and 112 (termination of employment).

Early in the coding process we decided to omit discharge and discipline cases that involved multiple grievants because of coding complexities. On the other hand, while going through the BMS case files we unearthed numerous veterans' preference and teacher tenure

[19] Minnesota Rules, Chapter 5530.08, subpart 9, requires arbitrators to file their public and private sector awards with the Commissioner of the BMS. Specifically, the rule states: "Unless one or both private sector parties have specifically requested that an award not be provided to the commissioner, arbitrators shall submit copies of all awards involving Minnesota work sites to the commissioner regardless of the source of appointment or selection. Awards filed with the commissioner are public documents."

termination awards that had not been indexed. Because these statutory-based decisions are governed by similar "just cause" standards, we added them to our sample.[20]

Survey Representativeness

We cannot assert that our survey of 2,055 Minnesota-workplace discharge and discipline arbitration awards, involving a single grievant, is a representative sample of the population of comparable awards. Nevertheless, the specific features of our data set make it the most representative to date.

Published and Unpublished Awards

In addition to its size, our survey is unique because it is not limited to awards published by the Bureau of National Affairs (BNA) and Commerce Clearing House, Inc. (CCH). For several reasons, the awards published by these organizations are not representative of awards generally, the immense majority of which are not published. First, some parties permit their awards to be published, while others do so only occasionally or never. Second, with approval from the parties, some arbitrators submit some or all of their awards for publication, while others never do. Finally, it is the BNA and CCH who decide on the awards that should be published from among the awards submitted and received; their selection criteria are not intended to ensure that awards they publish are representative.[21] As an example, one study found that discharge awards published by the BNA and CCH were not representative of unpublished Michigan discharge decisions, at least not during the 1979-

---

[20] The Minnesota Veterans Preference Act provides that veterans who are employed in the public sector may be discharged for "incompetency" and "misconduct" grounds that are equivalent to "just cause" standards. See Minn. Stat. § 197.46 (2009) and AFSCME Council 96 v. Arrowhead Reg'l Corrs. Bd., 356 N.W.2d 295, 297-298 (Minn. 1984). The Teacher Tenure Act and Continuing Contract Act similarly provide procedural and substantive protections for Minnesota public sector teachers in employment termination. See Minn. Stat. § 122A.41 (2009), and Minn. Stat. § 122A.40 (2009), respectively. A discussion of these statutes and their implications is taken up in Chapter 10.

[21] Merton C. Bernstein, "Proper Prepublication Procedures: An Arbitrator's Comment," *Arbitration 1984: Absenteeism, Recent Law, Panels, and Published Decisions, Proceedings of the 37th Annual Meeting of the National Academy of Arbitrators* (Washington, D.C.: Bureau of National Affairs, Walter J. Gershenfeld, ed., 1985), 192-199.

1982 timeframe.[22] Yet, published BNA and CCH awards are the principal source materials upon which most field studies of disciplinary arbitration rely. In addition, none of these studies suggest that the awards they analyze are drawn from a random sample of all discharge and discipline awards. The fact that the present study is based on a survey of both published and unpublished awards certainly does not detract from the prospect that it could be—but not necessarily is—a representative sample of *all* similar awards. However, we are more certain that our survey of 2,055 awards approximate the universe of single-grievant discharge and discipline awards rendered in Minnesota during the above-referenced time period. Thus, we argue, with a hint of caution, that our sample is representative at the Minnesota level of generality.

Public and Private Sector Awards

Approximately 60 percent of our awards involve public sector cases. This percentage seems high, which causes us to question, "Can we be sure that public sector cases are not over-represented by our survey?"

For technical reasons, public sector awards may be over-represented in our survey because some of Minnesota's private sector parties surely have exercised their right *not* to have their awards submitted to the BMS, either all or some of the time.[23] In addition, during the period covered by our survey, out-of-state arbitrators who were *not* on the BMS roster of arbitrators, but were on the rosters of the FMCS or AAA, for example, were not obligated to send a copy of their decisions to the BMS.[24] For these reasons, some unidentified number of private sector awards is *not* included in our survey, implying that public sector awards may be over-represented in our survey.

Further, the total number of employees on non-farm payrolls in Minnesota was about

---

[22] Jack Steiber, Richard N. Block & Leslie Corbitt, "How Representative Are Published Decisions?" *Arbitration 1984: Absenteeism, Recent Law, Panels, and Published Decisions, Proceedings of the 37th Annual Meeting of the National Academy of Arbitrators* (Washington, D.C.: Bureau of National Affairs, Walter J. Gershenfeld, ed., 1985), 172-192.

[23] See *supra* note 19, Minnesota Rules, Chapter 5530.08, subpart 9.

[24] *Id.*

2.8 million in 2004, approximately 85 percent of whom worked in the private sector and 15 percent who worked in federal, state and local government jobs.[25] These private-public employment shares have been fairly constant over the years. The difference in the absolute size of Minnesota's private and public sector workforces also suggests that we should have a larger, not smaller, share of private sector awards represented in our data set. However, because the difference in private-public employment shares was largely offset by the difference in private-public union member density shares, this source of over-representation may not be as ominous as it appears. To demonstrate this point, note that in 2004, the share of Minnesota non-farm wage and salary employees who were union members was 17.1 percent, which disaggregates into a private sector density of 11.1 percent and a public sector density of 53 percent, a differential that has grown over the years.[26] Hence, by multiplying Minnesota's 2004 workforce of 2.8 million by each of its 2004 private-public employment shares, and further multiplying each of the resulting products by their respective 2004 union density share, we estimate that in 2004 there were about 261,000 union members in Minnesota's private sector and 217,000 in its public sector.

In addition, the relatively large share of public sector *versus* private sector union members in Minnesota can be partly explained by differences in the statutes that regulate public and private sector collective bargaining. Moreover, statutory differences help explain the 60:40 ratio of public to private sector single-grievant discharge and discipline awards in

---

[25] See Minnesota Department of Employment and Economic Development, Current Employment Statistics, http://www.deed.state.mn.us/lmi/tools/ces/Results.aspz; Minnesota Department of Employment and Economic Development, Data Center, http://www.deed.state.mn.us/lmi/publications/trends/0406/wages.htm. The 2004 statistics appearing in the text are not that dissimilar from comparable May 2009 statistics. In addition, the 2004 private-public employment shares appearing in the text approximates the comparable 2000 shares.

[26] See U.S. Bureau of Labor Statistics, Economic News Release-Union Members Summary http://www.bls.gov/news.release/union2.nr0.htm (January 28, 2009); Public and Private Sector Data By State and Occupation, http://www.law.harvard.edu/programs/lwp/Public%20and%20Private%20Sector%20Data%20by%20State%20and%20Occupation%201988-2004.xls. In 1992, Minnesota's overall union density was 22.2 percent. The latter figure disaggregates into a private sector density of 15.6 percent and a public sector density of 54.5 percent. In 2008, the overall union member density in Minnesota was 16.1 percent.

Minnesota. This ratio results from the fact that while the discharge awards in our data set are almost evenly divided between public and private sector cases,[27] there are nearly five non-discharge discipline awards in the public sector for every private sector discipline award.[28] It would be interesting to know *why* Minnesota's public sector unions and employers exhibit a greater propensity to arbitrate non-discharge discipline cases than do their private sector counterparts. In any event, a detailed discussion about the specific statutes and their effects on Minnesota's public and private union densities, and on differential public and private propensities to arbitrate is deferred to Chapter 10.

To summarize, the number of public sector union members in Minnesota is large relative to private sector union members, and this is particularly so in light of the huge difference in the number of private-over-public employees in its workforce. As we elaborate in Chapter 10, statutory nuances partly explain why the number of public sector union members in Minnesota is so large relative to the size of private sector union membership. In addition, we explain in that chapter why the inclination to arbitrate workplace disputes is greater in Minnesota's public sector relative to the private sector. For these reasons, we are not overly concerned that our survey of awards over-represents public sector cases at the Minnesota level of generalization.

Minnesota and U.S. Arbitration Profiles

The profile of industrial relations is different in each state and profiles change in different ways over time. Thus, the Minnesota survey of single-grievant discharge and discipline arbitration awards that were issued from 1982 to 2005 may not be representative of the population-based sample of *all* like awards. However, we may never know definitively because a nationwide random sample of awards has never been taken. Nevertheless, some data are available that can be used to compare, albeit imperfectly, industrial relations and arbitration in Minnesota and nationally.

---

[27] See Chapter 3, Table 3.14.

[28] *Id.*

Minnesota and U.S. Union Density

Presently, Minnesota ranks among the upper echelon of states in terms of both the percent of employees who are union members and the percent of employees who are covered by union contracts. On a national level, union members and covered workers accounted for 12.4 percent and 13.7 percent of employed wage and salary workers in 2008, respectively.[29] In comparison, 16.1 percent of such employees in Minnesota belonged to unions in 2008, and 17 percent of Minnesota employees were covered by a union contract in 2008.[30] Only twelve states—Alaska, California, Connecticut, Hawaii, Illinois, Michigan, Nevada, New Jersey, New York, Oregon, Rhode Island and Washington—had a higher percentage of union membership or representation than Minnesota.[31]

Nationally, in 2008, public sector employees were over four times more likely to be members of a union (40.7 percent) than were employees in private industry (8.4 percent).[32] This discrepancy, as suggested earlier using 2004 data, is even more pronounced in Minnesota, where the public sector union density rate was more than five times higher than in the private sector. In 2006, 52.1 percent of public sector employees in Minnesota belonged to a union as compared to 9.7 percent of their private sector counterparts. Only six states—Connecticut, Michigan, New Jersey, New York, Oregon, and Rhode Island—had a higher percent of unionized public sector workers.[33]

The public sector union membership density rate in Minnesota far exceeds that of

---

[29] See U.S. Bureau of Labor Statistics, http://www.bls.gov/news.release/archives/union2_01282009.pdf at Tbl 1. As has been well-documented, union membership in the United States peaked at 34.5 percent of the workforce in 1954 and since has experienced a long and continuous decline. See Michael Goldfield, *The Decline of Organized Labor in the United States* (Chicago, Il: University of Chicago Press, 1987), 10 Tbl. 1; Stephen F. Befort, "Labor and Employment Law at the Millennium: A Historical Review and Critical Assessment," 43 *Boston College Law* Review 351, 361-362 (2002).

[30] See U.S. Bureau of Labor Statistics, http://www.bls.gov/news.release/archives/union2_01282009.pdf at Tbl 5.

[31] *Id.*

[32] *Id.* at Tbl. 2.

[33] Barry T. Hirsch & David A. Macpherson, *Union Membership Density 2006, available at* http://www.trinity.edu.bhirsch/unionstats.content.htm (last accessed Aug. 20, 2008).

the United States—a fact that leads us to conclude that our survey is more heavily weighted with disputes arising out of the public sector than may have been the case *nationally*.

Minnesota and U.S. Workforce Characteristics

In general, Minnesota's workforce is less racially and ethnically diverse than is the national norm.[34] Minnesota workers also are better educated[35] and earn a higher income as compared nationally.[36] Also, Minnesota's unemployment rate generally is lower than the national unemployment rate. In May 2009, Minnesota's seasonally adjusted unemployment rate was 8.2 percent and the comparable national rate was 9.4 percent—a 1.2 percentage point difference.[37] How these differences affect the number and type of discharge and discipline cases in Minnesota and nationally is unknown. Moreover, we do not know if or how these workforce differences affect arbitrator decision-making.

Minnesota and U.S. Arbitrator Characteristics

There is information about the demographic characteristics of arbitrators in the United States that we can compare to the characteristics of the arbitrators who decided the awards in our survey. However, it is important to note that these comparisons are of questionable value to the discussion of reprensentation since we surveyed single-grievant discharge and discipline *awards* and not *arbitrators*. Thus, the comparisons are not *apples-to-apples*.

Based on a national sample of arbitrators, one study estimated that in 1987 the mean age of U.S. arbitrators was about 58 years. It also estimated that 56 percent of these

---

[34] U.S. Census Bureau, State & County QuickFacts-Minnesota, http://quickfacts.census.gov/qfd/states/27000.html (white, non-Hispanic persons constitute 85.9 percent of Minnesota's population as compared to 66.4 percent nationally).

[35] *Id.* (87.9 percent of Minnesotans over the age of 25 are high school graduates as compared to 80.4 percent nationally).

[36] *Id.* (in 2004 median household income in Minnesota was $51,202 as compared to $44,334 nationally).

[37] See Minnesota Department of Employment and Economic Development, Data Center, http://www.deed.state.mn.us/lmi/home.htm.

arbitrators had J.D. degrees and 23 percent had Ph.D. degrees. Further, it reported that 17 percent of *all* labor arbitrators were members of the NAA.[38] The arbitrators in our survey had a mean age of 57, which was computed on the basis of each arbitrator's age at the time he or she issued an award. The percent of our arbitrators with J.D. and Ph.D. degrees is about 65 percent and 12 percent, respectively.

The arbitrator age characteristic is almost identical, as between the national study and our study. However, the J.D. comparison presents a remote match, at best, and the Minneosta *versus* national Ph.D. comparison misses the mark altogether—12 percent *versus* 23 percent, respectively. Finally, the percent of arbitrators who were NAA members are different by a wide margin—32 percent in Minnesota *versus* 17 percent nationally.

The difference in the Ph.D. degree comparison is a puzzle. But the NAA difference can be explained by considering a combination of two facts: first, we surveyed discharge and discipline awards; and, second, NAA members decide about three and one-half times more grievance cases than do non-NAA members, nationally.[39] Therefore, because NAA members have much heavier caseloads than do non-NAA members, the odds are that any survey of decisions—including our own—will have been decided by NAA members in numbers that are relatively greater than their numbers in the population of *all* of the nation's arbitrators, NAA plus non-NAA members.[40] To demonstrate this point, consider a 1998 study by Nelson and Uddin.[41] Their analysis was based on 170 discharge awards published in select volumes of *Labor Arbitration Awards* (a CCH publication). They found that NAA members issued about 54 percent of these awards.[42] Remarkably, 53.91 percent of our discharge awards were issued by NAA members, as we show in Chapter 3, Table 3.8.

---

[38] *Labor Arbitration in America,* 7, 10.

[39] *Id.* at 54.

[40] Chapter 2, Table 2.1 shows that NAA members issued 70.61 percent of our survey's discharge and discipline decisions.

[41] Nels E. Nelson & A.N.M. Meshquat Uddin, "The Impact of Delay on Arbitrators' Decisions in Discharge Cases," *Labor Studies Journal* 3, 20 (Summer 1998).

[42] *Id.* at 13.

The average age of arbitrators in Minnesota and the United States is nearly identical, but large comparative differences exist among their NAA, J.D. and Ph.D. demographic characteristics. However, for the *apples-to-apples* comparison reason mentioned above, it is difficult to say whether these differences in arbitrator characteristics will affect the representativeness of our survey of single-grievant discharge and discipline awards *vis a vis* a comparable national sample of awards.

Minnesota and U.S. Arbitration Outcomes

Whether the information gleaned from our survey can be used to make statistical inferences that apply generally, may, in the view of some readers, turn on the answer to the question, "How well does the distribution of our survey's arbitration awards across possible discharge and discipline outcomes compare to similar national distributions?" The data in Table 1.1 address that question.

Four studies are referenced in this table, with three based on samples of (multi-state) discharge and discipline awards published by the BNA and/or CCH. The last row in the table reports award data based on our study. As the table shows, the time periods and number of awards that were sampled varies from study to study. All four studies reflect that management won the largest share of disciplinary arbitrations, yet the four studies are equally divided between union wins and split decisions as the second largest share of arbitration outcomes. The distribution of awards based on our survey of single-grievant, published and unpublished discharge and discipline awards closely corresponds to the Zirkel and Breslin sample of published awards. But as previously observed, there is nothing representative about the Zirkel and Breslin study, nor any of the other studies that are based on published awards.

We know that our survey over-represents the share of public sector awards rendered generally. Too, our comparative analyses of both workforce and arbitrator characteristics added little to this discussion. However, given the absence of any studies based on national samples of discharge and discipline awards, we may never know whether our sample is an approximate representation of the national scene. Thus, since our results are based on such a large sample of both published and unpublished awards, we conclude that it is no more risky to generalize them beyond the borders of Minnesota than it is to make generalizations based on published awards.

Table 1.1 Discharge and Discipline Award Outcomes by Study
(N-size and row % are the top and bottom value, respectively)

Study	Management Win	Union Win	Split Decision	Total
1986 Data Zirkel and Breslin[1]	108 46.8	43 18.6	80 34.6	231 100.00
1988-1990 Data Mesch and Dalton[2]	193 44.6	128 29.5	112 25.9	433 100.00
1987-1993 Data Mesch[3]	1,888 47.8	1,282 32.5	779 19.7	3,949 100.00
1982-2005 Data Present Study	1,022 49.73	441 21.46	592 28.81	2,055 100.00

[1] Perry A. Zirkel & Phillip H. Breslin, "Correlates of Grievance Arbitration Awards," 24(1) *Journal of Collective Negotiations* (1995), 45 (data from designated 1986 volumes of BNA, *Labor Arbitration Reports* & CCH, *Labor Arbitration Awards*).
[2] Debra J. Mesch & Dan R. Dalton, "Arbitration in Practice: Win, Lose, or Draw?" 4 *The Human Resources Professional* (Spring 1992), 37 (data from BNA, *Labor Arbitration Reports*, 1988-1990).
[3] Debra J. Mesch, "Grievance Arbitration in the Public Sector: A Conceptual Framework and Empirical Analysis of Public and Private Sector Arbitration Cases," 15 *Review of Public Personal Administration* (Fall 1995), 22 (data from BNA, *Labor Arbitration Reports*, 1987-1993).

With the above-discussed caveats in mind, we, nevertheless, assume that our survey approximates a randomly drawn sample from the population of single-grievant discharge and discipline awards issued during the timeframe in question. Under this assumption, the mean and percent estimates, and the measures of inter-variable associations that are presented in this book are treated as reliable measures of the values and associations present in *all* single-grievant discipline and discharge cases. Thus, to determine whether our empirical results are random occurrences, we report chi-square tests of dependency between categorical variables and t-test results to discern whether the differences between means and percentages are statistically significant.

Outline of the Book

A general description of the data underlying the remaining parts of the book is presented in Chapter 2, with sections on the characteristics of the arbitrators who decided our awards, characteristics of the grievants who were the subjects of our cases and characteristics of the arbitration awards themselves. Chapter 3 is our first analytical chapter. Therein, we categorize award outcomes as decisions where the arbitrator: (1) fully sustained management's disciplinary actions; (2) fully upheld the union's grievance; or (3) issued a split decision. This chapter describes the distribution of arbitration outcomes across these categories. Mainly, however, it identifies the determinants of the arbitrator awards, using a host of arbitrator, grievant and case characteristics as plausible explanatory variables. Chapter 4 identifies the offenses employers alleged as the basis for their decisions to discipline and fire workers. Moreover, it analyzes these allegations *vis a vis* employer disciplinary decisions and arbitration outcomes.

Chapter 5 explores the amount of proof that arbitrators require in reaching decisions in the face of conflicting evidence. "Burden of proof" is distinguished from "quantum of proof" and data pertaining to the latter concept are empirically evaluated, possibly the first analysis of its kind. Chapter 6 is devoted to a careful examination of the "The Seven Tests of Just Cause." Therein, we challenge the widespread belief of the pre-eminence of this analytical tool for evaluating whether the employer's disciplinary action was for "just cause."

Chapter 7 addresses the full range of remedies arbitrators render in discharge cases, including split decision remedies. This chapter presents new information about the relationship between discharge remedies and the nature of the grievant's alleged offense. It offers new insights into whether arbitrators reduce back pay awards when reinstating discharged workers because of wages earned through interim employment and/or because the worker failed to mitigate losses by seeking alternative employment. It also analyzes the effect of delay on arbitration outcomes. Among other things, it takes a second look at whether the sector—public or private—from which the grievance arose affects arbitration outcomes, and it evaluates often reported generalizations, such as, those quoted above about the Last Chance Agreements and Retention of Jurisdiction

Chapter 8 presents and analyzes data on discipline short of discharge, namely, reprimands and suspensions. The analysis of these outcomes is unique to the literature. Moreover, this chapter examines how reprimand and suspension disciplinary actions are related to variables like offense categories, whether the arbitrator is trained as an attorney, and whether the arbitrator is a member of the National Academy of Arbitrators—an often used measure of arbitral "experience."

Chapter 9 partially answers the question, "Why do arbitrators modify the disciplinary actions taken by employers?" The three-part answer is: (1) the evidence does not support the alleged factual basis for discipline; (2) procedural failings in the employer's disciplinary process; and (3) mitigating factors. The information we gleaned from our survey of discharge and discipline awards uniquely allows us to examine answers (2) and (3)—procedural failings and mitigating factors for reducing employer penalties.

In Chapter 10, we compare contract-based and statute-based arbitration systems. We discuss the effects the Minnesota Public Employment Labor Relations Act (PELRA) and the private sector's National Labor Relation Act have on union membership levels, and on the propensity to arbitrate in Minnesota. More generally, however, we discuss Minnesota's public sector and, specifically, the arbitration of just cause grievances brought under Minnesota's PELRA, Veterans Preference Act, Teacher Tenure Act, and [Teacher] Continuing Contract Act.

The book's major findings are summarized in Chapter 11.

CHAPTER 2

OVERVIEW OF THE SURVEY DATA

Introduction

Given the multitude of factors that arbitrators consider in reaching decisions, can we explain "why" they decide cases the way they do. We believe we can and, in doing so, we hope we will have improved on the literature's efforts to do so. On several counts, the current literature about arbitral decision-making can be strengthened. First, most of the field's empirical studies rely exclusively on published decisions, which are not representative of *all* arbitration awards.[1] To avoid this shortcoming, our data base is made up of both published and unpublished decisions.[2] Second, the samples used in many published studies are small relative to our sample of 2,055 discharge and discipline awards. Finally, most prior studies focused on discrete issues and coded few variables. We, on the other hand, coded each award for many more prospective correlates to arbitration outcomes and other variables of interest, allowing for a more comprehensive analysis of the arbitration process and its outcomes.

This chapter briefly introduces the study's data. Our intent is to offer a glimpse at the empirical foundation upon which this inquiry rests: a foundation that is rich and reliable. We avoid replicating the data arrays and accompanying discussions that appear in substantive chapters of the book. This chapter is organized around the topics we analyzed—arbitrator characteristics, case characteristics and grievant characteristics.

Arbitrator Characteristics

This study's 2,055 decisions were issued by 81 different arbitrators, over a 24-year period. Select characteristics of these arbitrators are presented in Table 2.1. Based on the arbitrator's age at the time he or she issued each award in our survey, the mean age of

---

[1] Jack Steiber, Richard N. Block & Leslie Corbitt, "How Representative Are Published Decisions?" *Arbitration 1984: Absenteeism, Recent Law, and Published Decisions, Proceedings of the 37th Annual Meetings of the National Academy of Arbitrators* (Washington, D.C.: Bureau of National Affairs, Walter J. Gershenfeld, ed., 1985), 172-192.

[2] See *supra* Chapter 1.

arbitrators was about 57 years. Slightly more than 17 percent of our 81 arbitrators were women, and they decided a roughly equivalent share (17.03 percent) of the 2,055 awards.

Table 2.1 Select Characteristics of Arbitrators

Characteristic	Mean/Percent	Percent of Decisions Decided
Mean Age	57.21	--
Percent Female	17.28	17.03
Percent with J.D.	64.20	61.75
Percent with Ph.D.	12.35	19.42
Percent who are Professors	27.16	40.05
Percent NAA Members	32.09	70.61

Approximately 65 percent and 12 percent of our arbitrators held J.D. and Ph.D. degrees, respectively. The arbitrators with J.D. degrees were slightly underrepresented with respect to the share of awards they issued (61.75 percent), and arbitrators with Ph.D.s were overrepresented (19.42 percent). Table 2.1 shows that the share of decisions issued by arbitrator-professors and arbitrators who also were members of the National Academy of Arbitrators (NAA) far exceeded their relative numbers among the 81 arbitrators in our data base. When viewed from the parties' perspective, these results reveal a relative preference to select arbitrator-professors and arbitrators who are members of the NAA—characteristics that are not mutually exclusive—to hear their disciplinary disputes. Finally, nearly 69 percent of the awards we surveyed were decided by arbitrators who were selected *via* the Minnesota Bureau of Mediation Services (BMS), Federal Mediation and Conciliation Service (FMCS) and American Arbitration Association (AAA) appointing agencies.

Within our data set, the typical arbitrator decided about 25 cases over the 24-year period of the survey, with the number of decisions rendered *per* arbitrator ranging from 1 to 247. The first column in Table 2.2 indexes the percent of our 2,055 awards that were issued by the number of arbitrators indicated in the table's second column. For example, the first numerical row in this table indicates that 56 (or 69.14 percent) of our 81 arbitrators decided less than one percent of the 2,055 awards under consideration. These data suggest that a large proportion of awards we surveyed were decided by relatively few arbitrators. At the extreme, there were 56 arbitrators each of whom decided less than one percent of our 2,055 cases, while 4 arbitrators decided at least five percent each.

Table 2.2 <u>Distribution of Arbitrators by Relative Caseload</u>*

Percent of Awards Issued per Arbitrator	Number of Arbitrators	Percent of 81 Arbitrators in Survey	Cumulative Percent
< 1%	56	69.14[1]	69.14
1% < 2%	10	12.35[2]	81.49
2% < 3%	5	6.17	87.66
3% < 4%	3	3.70	91.36
4% < 5%	3	3.70	95.06
≥ 5%	4	4.94	100.00
Column Totals	81	--	--

* The numeric indexes 1, 2, 3, 4, 5 and 6 indicate that the percentages in row 1 and row 2, row 2 and row 3, row 3 and row 4, row 4 and row 5, row 5 and row 6, and row 6 and row 1, respectively, are statistically different at the .05 level or lower.

The fact that a handful of arbitrators decided a disproportionately large share of awards is also made in Table 2.3 and 2.4, implying, of course, that the caseloads of some arbitrators were heavier than others. In Table 2.3, we define "caseload" as the *percent* of our 2,055 awards that were issued by each arbitrator; whereas, in Table 3.4, "caseload" is defined as the *absolute number* of awards issued by each arbitrator. Focusing on the intersection of the column labeled "Row Totals" and the last numerical row in Tables 2.3 and 2.4, we note, respectively, 32.65 percent (or 671) of awards were issued by only 4 (or 4.94 percent of) arbitrators, each of whom decided at least 5 percent of all awards in our data set; and 59.22 percent (or 1,217) of awards were issued by 11 (or 13.67 percent of) arbitrators, each of whom decided at least 50 awards. Thus, regardless of definition, it is clear that the caseload distribution among arbitrators is skewed, which leads to an intriguing question, "Does this skewing affect arbitration outcomes?" The information in Tables 2.3 and 2.4 suggests an answer to this question. In both tables, awards are classified into three mutually exclusive outcome categories: management win; union win; and split decision. The arbitrator caseload and award outcome cross-tabulations in Tables 2.3 and 2.4 enable us to test whether there is an association between the skewed distribution of arbitrator caseloads and decisions rendered. The computed chi-square in Table 2.3 is 41.7719 with 10 degrees of freedom, which suggests that the odds are less than 1 in 1,000 (i.e., $p = 0.000$) that arbitrator caseloads and the awards they issued are independent. In other words, in all likelihood there is a dependency relationship between our caseload and award outcome categories. However, the chi-square test in Table 2.4 yields the opposite result. In this case, there is nearly a 9 percent chance (i.e., $p = 0.086$) that caseloads and awards are independent, implying that the skewed distribution of arbitrator caseloads may not affect the distribution of award outcomes.[3] So what is the answer to our skewed distribution question?

---

[3] We generally limit the "probability of error" (i.e. the probability of rejecting a true hypothesis) to five percent.

Table 2.3 <u>Distribution of Arbitrators by Relative Caseload and Arbitration Outcomes</u>*

(Award Outcomes: N-size, row % and column % are the top, middle and bottom values, respectively)

Percent of Awards Issued per Arbitrator	Number of Arbitrators	Award Outcomes			
		Management Win	Union Win	Split Decision	Row Totals
< 1%	56	179 49.45^{a} 17.51	81 22.38 18.37	102 28.18^{c} 17.23	362 100.00 17.62^{1}
1% < 2%	10	146 49.16^{a} 14.29	74 24.92 16.78	77 25.93^{c} 13.01^{2}	297 100.00 14.45^{2}
2% < 3%	5	120 52.17^{a} 11.74	64 27.83^{3} 14.51^{3b}	46 20.00^{3c} 7.77^{3c}	230 100.00 11.19
3% < 4%	3	111 49.55^{a} 10.86	40 17.86^{4b} 9.07^{4}	73 32.59^{c} 12.33	224 100.00 10.90^{4}
4% < 5%	3	116 42.80^{5a} 11.35^{5a}	79 29.15^{5} 17.91^{b}	76 28.04^{c} 12.84^{5}	271 100.00 13.19^{5}
≥ 5%	4	350 52.16^{a} 34.25^{6a}	103 15.35^{6b} 23.36^{b}	218 32.49^{c} 36.82^{6}	671 100.00 32.65^{6}
Column Totals	81	1,022 49.73^{a} 100.00	441 21.46^{b} 100.00	592 28.81^{c} 100.00	2,055 100.00 100.00

Chi-square (10) = 41.7719, p = 0.000

* The numeric indexes 1, 2, 3, 4, 5 and 6 indicate that the percentages in row 1 and row 2, row 2 and row 3, row 3 and row 4, row 4 and row 5, row 5 and row 6, and row 6 and row 1, respectively, are statistically different at the .05 level or lower. The alphabetic indexes a, b and c indicate that the percentages in column 1 and column 2, column 2 and column 3, and column 3 and column 1, respectively, are statistically different at the .05 level or lower.

Table 2.4 Distribution of Arbitrators by Absolute Caseload and Arbitration Outcomes*

(Award Outcomes: N-size, row % and column % are the top, middle and bottom values, respectively.)

Absolute Number of Awards Issued per Arbitrator	Number of Arbitrators	Award Outcomes			
		Management Win	Union Win	Split Decision	Row Totals
< 10	40	68 52.31[a] 6.65[1]	28 21.54 6.35[1]	34 26.15[c] 5.74[1]	130 100.00 6.33[1]
10 - 19	15	105 49.53[a] 10.27[2]	46 21.70 10.43	61 28.77[c] 10.30[2]	212 100.00 10.32[2]
20 - 29	5	55 46.22[a] 5.38[3]	31 26.05 7.03[3]	33 27.73[c] 5.57[3]	119 100.00 5.79[3]
30 - 39	6	97 48.99[a] 9.49	50 25.25 11.34	51 25.76[c] 8.61	198 100.00 9.64
40 - 49	4	88 49.16[a] 8.61[5a]	54 30.17[5] 12.24[5b]	37 20.67[5c] 6.25[5]	179 100.00 8.71[5]
≥ 50	11	609 50.04[a] 59.59[6a]	232 19.06[b] 52.61[6b]	376 30.90[c] 63.51[6]	1,217 100.00 59.22[6]
Column Totals	81	1,022 49.73[a] 100.00	441 21.46[b] 100.00	592 28.81[c] 100.00	2,055 100.00 100.00

Chi-square (10) = 16.5226, p = 0.086

* The numeric indexes 1, 2, 3, 4, 5 and 6 indicate that the percentages in row 1 and row 2, row 2 and row 3, row 3 and row 4, row 4 and row 5, row 5 and row 6, and row 6 and row 1, respectively, are statistically different at the .05 level or lower. The alphabetic indexes a, b and c indicate that the percentages in column 1 and column 2, column 2 and column 3, and column 3 and column 1, respectively, are statistically different at the .05 level or lower.

To get at the answer, we reconfigured the data in Tables 2.3 and 2.4 by collapsing their top five numerical rows into one row and renumbered the tables as Table 2.3(a) and Table 2.4(a), respectively. Both tables show the distribution of award outcomes for very busy arbitrators *versus* the field of less busy arbitrators. The chi-square test in both tables support the conclusion that caseloads and outcomes are dependent, suggesting that the skewed distribution of arbitrator caseloads does affect award outcomes. Both tables show that arbitrators with heavier caseloads (i.e., ≥ 5 percent in Table 2.3(a) and ≥ 50 awards in Table 2.4(a)) were significantly less inclined to issue union win awards and significantly more inclined to issue split decisions.

Table 2.3 (a) <u>Distribution of Arbitrators by Relative Caseload and Arbitration Outcomes</u>*

(Award Outcomes: N-size, row % and column % are the top, middle and bottom values, respectively)

Percent of Awards Issued per Arbitrator	Number of Arbitrators	Award Outcomes			
		Management Win	Union Win	Split Decision	Row Totals
< 5%	77	672 48.55[a] 65.75[1a]	338 24.43[1] 76.64[1b]	374 27.02[1c] 63.18[1]	1,384 100.00 67.35[1]
≥ 5%	4	350 52.16[a] 34.25[a]	103 15.35[b] 23.36[b]	218 32.49[c] 36.82	671 100.00 32.65
Column Totals	81	1,022 49.73[a] 100.00	441 21.46[b] 100.00	592 28.81[c] 100.00	2,055 100.00 100.00

Chi-square (2) = 23.1980, p = 0.000

* The numeric index 1 indicates that the percentages in row 1 and row 2 are statistically different at the .05 level or lower. The alphabetic indexes a, b and c indicate that the percentages in column 1 and column 2, column 2 and column 3, and column 3 and column 1, respectively, are statistically different at the .05 level or lower.

Table 2.4(a) Distribution of Arbitrators by Absolute Caseload and Arbitration Outcomes*

(Award Outcomes: N-size, row % and column % are the top, middle and bottom values, respectively.)

Absolute Number of Awards Issued per Arbitrator	Number of Arbitrators	Award Outcomes			
		Management Win	Union Win	Split Decision	Row Totals
< 50	70	413 49.28[a] 40.41[1a]	209 24.94[1] 47.39[b]	216 25.78[1c] 36.49[1]	838 100.00 40.78[1]
≥ 50	11	609 50.04[a] 59.59[a]	232 19.06[b] 52.61[b]	376 30.90[c] 63.51	1,217 100.00 59.22
Column Totals	81	1,022 49.73[a] 100.00	441 21.46[b] 100.00	592 28.81[c] 100.00	2,055 100.00 100.00

Chi-square (2) = 12.5608, p = 0.002

* The numeric index 1 indicates that the percentages in row 1 and row 2 are statistically different at the .05 level or lower. The alphabetic indexes a, b and c indicate that the percentages in column 1 and column 2, column 2 and column 3, and column 3 and column 1, respectively, are statistically different at the .05 level or lower.

Do Arbitrators Who Split Awards Get More Work?

Critics of arbitration decision-making have argued that in order to increase the odds of their future selection, some arbitrators attempt partial satisfaction of both sides by finding "just cause" for discipline, but at a level below that meted out by the employer. In a classic criticism of the arbitration profession, Paul R. Hays maintained that it was a "fairly widespread" phenomenon that arbitrators issued "compromise award[s]" to maintain their acceptability for future selection by union and management representatives.[4] Similarly, Arbitrator Meyer S. Ryder asserted that arbitration advocates commonly assume that

---

[4] Paul R. Hayes, *Labor Arbitration: A Dissenting View* (New Haven, CT & London, England: Yale University Press, 1966) 59-60.

arbitrators will "split decisions in an attempt to preserve a balance of victories and losses between a given set of clients."[5]

The data in Tables 2.3(a) and 2.4(a) shed some empirical light on this proposition. Note that in both tables the inter-row difference in the share of split decisions issued by busy arbitrators *versus* less busy arbitrators is significant. For example, from the perspective of Table 2.4(a), 30.90 percent of the awards issued by busy arbitrators were split decisions, while 25.78 percent of the awards issued by our less busy arbitrators were split decisions. From this analysis, we cannot reject the theory that if split decisions result in future selections, then busier arbitrators ought to be observed issuing a larger share of split decisions. However, we must qualify this result for the reasons discussed below.

Tables 2.3(b) and 2.4(b) repeat the foregoing analysis, but here discipline (i.e., suspension and reprimand) and discharges cases are analyzed separately. Whether caseload is measured in relative or absolute terms, we see from these tables that in discipline cases the share of split awards issued by arbitrators with heavy caseloads (i.e., $\geq$ 5% or $\geq$ 50 awards issued per arbitrator) and light caseloads (i.e., < 5% or < 50 awards issued per arbitrator) is insignificantly different. However, the reverse is true for discharge cases. With reference to Table 2.4(b), for example, the proportion of split decisions issued by busy arbitrators was 31.22 percent *versus* 23.72 percent for less busy arbitrators—a difference that is statistically significant.

Based on these results, we qualify our earlier conclusion. As compared to their counterparts, in discipline cases busy arbitrators were not observed issuing relatively more split decisions. However, this result does not hold for discharge cases. To repeat, regarding discharges, busy arbitrators did issue relatively more split decisions than did less busy arbitrators. Referring again to Table 2.4(b), we should also note that busy arbitrators were, in addition, significantly more inclined to issue decisions that *fully* favored management than to issue split decisions (51.02 percent *versus* 31.22 percent.)

---

[5] Meyer S. Ryder, "The Impact of Acceptability on the Arbitrator," *Developments in American and Foreign Arbitration, Proceedings of the 21st Annual Meeting of the National Academy of* Arbitrators (Washington, D.C.: Bureau of National Affairs, Charles M. Rehmus, ed., 1968), 94, 97.

Table 2.3(b) <u>Distribution of Arbitrators by Type of Discipline, Relative Caseload and Arbitration Outcomes</u>*

(Award Outcomes: N-size, row % and column % are the top, middle and bottom values, respectively)

Percent of Awards Issued per Arbitrator	Number of Arbitrators	Award Outcomes			
		Management Win	Union Win	Split Decision	Row Totals
Discipline					
< 5%	65	180 40.09[1a] 66.42[1a]	134 29.84[1] 80.72[1]	135 30.07[c] 72.58[1]	449 100.00 72.07[1]
≥ 5%	4	91 52.30[a] 33.58[a]	32 18.39[b] 19.28	51 29.31[c] 27.42	174 100.00 27.93
Column Totals	69	271 43.50[a] 100.00	166 26.65 100.00	186 29.86[c] 100.00	623 100.00 100.00
Chi-square (2) = 10.4955, p = 0.005					
Discharge					
< 5%	70	492 52.62[a] 65.51[1a]	204 21.82[1] 74.18[1b]	239 25.56[1c] 58.87[1c]	935 100.00 65.29[1]
≥ 5%	4	259 52.11[a] 34.49[a]	71 14.29[b] 25.82[b]	167 33.60[c] 41.13[c]	497 100.00 34.71
Column Totals	74	751 52.44[a] 100.00	275 19.20[b] 100.00	406 28.35[c] 100.00	1,432 100.00 100.00
Chi-square (2) = 17.0024, p = 0.000					

* The numeric index 1 indicates that the percentages in row 1 and row 2 are statistically different at the .05 level or lower. The alphabetic indexes a, b and c indicate that the percentages in column 1 and column 2, column 2 and column 3, and column 3 and column 1, respectively, are statistically different at the .05 level or lower.

Table 2.4(b) <u>Distribution of Arbitrators by Type of Discipline, Absolute Caseload and Arbitration Outcomes</u>*

(Award Outcomes: N-size, row % and column % are the top, middle and bottom values, respectively)

Absolute Number of Awards Issued per Arbitrator	Number of Arbitrators	Award Outcomes			
		Management Win	Union Win	Split Decision	Row Totals
Discipline					
< 50	58	113 38.97[1] 41.70[1a]	91 31.38[1] 54.82	86 29.66 46.24	290 100.00 46.55
≥ 50	11	158 47.45[a] 58.30[a]	75 22.52 45.18	100 30.03[c] 53.76	333 100.00 53.45
Column Totals	69	271 43.50[a] 100.00	166 26.65 100.00	186 29.86[c] 100.00	623 100.00 100.00
Chi-square (2) = 7.1343, p = 0.028					
Discharge					
< 50	63	300 54.74[a] 39.95[1]	118 21.53 42.91[1b]	130 23.72[1c] 32.02[1c]	548 100.00 38.27[1]
≥ 50	11	451 51.02[a] 60.05	157 17.76[b] 57.09[b]	276 31.22[c] 67.98[c]	884 100.00 61.73
Column Totals	74	751 52.44[a] 100.00	275 19.20[b] 100.00	406 28.35[c] 100.00	1,432 100.00 100.00
Chi-square (2) = 10.1130, p = 0.006					

* The numeric index 1 indicates that the percentages in row 1 and row 2 are statistically different at the .05 level or lower. The alphabetic indexes a, b and c indicate that the percentages in column 1 and column 2, column 2 and column 3, and column 3 and column 1, respectively, are statistically different at the .05 level or lower.

How Does Our Distribution of Award Outcomes Compare with Other Reported Distributions?

Finally, the share of management win, union win and split decision outcomes that our 81 arbitrators issued is approximately 50 percent, 21 percent and 29 percent, respectively. (See Tables 2.3 and 2.4) Comparable distributions from three earlier studies are reported in Table 2.5.

Table 2.5 Discharge and Discipline Award Outcomes by Study
(N-size and row % are the top and bottom value, respectively)

Study	Management Win	Union Win	Split Decision	Row Totals
1986 Data Zirkel and Breslin[1]	108 46.8	43 18.6	80 34.6	231 100.00
1988-1990 Data Mesch and Dalton[2]	193 44.6	128 29.5	112 25.9	433 100.00
1987-1993 Data Mesch[3]	1,888 47.8	1,282 32.5	779 19.7	3,949 100.00
1982-2005 Data Present Study	1,022 49.73	441 21.46	592 28.81	2,055 100.00

[1] Perry A. Zirkel & Phillip H. Breslin, "Correlates of Grievance Arbitration Awards," 24(1) *Journal of Collective Negotiations* (1995), 45 (data from designated 1986 volumes of BNA, *Labor Arbitration Reports* & CCH, *Labor Arbitration Awards*).
[2] Debra J. Mesch & Dan R. Dalton, "Arbitration in Practice: Win, Lose, or Draw?" 4 *The Human Resources Professional* (Spring 1992), 37 (data from BNA, *Labor Arbitration Reports*, 1988-1990).
[3] Debra J. Mesch, "Grievance Arbitration in the Public Sector: A Conceptual Framework and Empirical Analysis of Public and Private Sector Arbitration Cases," 15 *Review of Public Personal Administration* (Fall 1995), 22 (data from BNA, *Labor Arbitration Reports*, 1987-1993).

Our study and each of these earlier studies cover different time periods and rely on samples of different sizes, and the earlier studies rely on published BNA and/or CCH discharge and discipline awards. These differences may account for some of the inter-study variance in the distribution of arbitration outcomes. Nevertheless, they do not suggest that any given study is somehow an "outlier."

Case Characteristics

Next, we describe a few key characteristics of the cases in the study's data set. During the 1982-2005 period of our survey, the number of single-grievant discharge and discipline decisions that were issued per year ranged from a low of 5 in 1982 to a high of 126 in 1990, with an annual average of 85.6 decisions. In Table 2.6, we cluster the 2,055 cases into three time periods, each eight years in duration. This table depicts a bell shaped distribution of cases with respect to time. That is, relatively few cases were decided during the early years, 1982-1989; relatively more awards were issued during the middle years, 1990-1997, when the distribution peaked; and relatively few awards were rendered during the later years, 1998-2005.

Table 2.6 Discipline and Discharge Cases by Year Clusters*
(N-size and row % are the top and bottom value, respectively)

Yearly Clusters	Row Totals
1982-1989	582 28.32[1]
1990-1997	887 43.16[2]
1998-2005	586 28.52
Column Totals	2,055 100.00

* The numeric indexes 1, 2 and 3 indicate that the percentages in row 1 and row 2, row 2 and row 3 and row 3 and row 1, respectively, are statistically different at the .05 level or lower.

Table 2.7 presents a cross-tabulation between time period clusters and award outcomes. In addition to the descriptive information imparted, this tabulation was constructed to test the assumption that case outcomes and the three time periods are independent. As the test statistic in Table 2.7 suggests, we cannot reject this assumption at the .05 level of significance. We also examined the relationship between *each* of survey's 24 years and arbitration outcomes. Again, the test statistic associated with this analysis was not significant. Apparently, arbitral outcomes did not change significantly between 1982 and 2005, inclusively, at least not with respect to the disposition of discharge and discipline cases.

Overall, about 60 percent of our cases are public sector, with the remaining 40 percent private sector. This case characteristic is further described in Table 2.8, which cross-tabulates award shares by sector and year clusters. This table's test statistic indicates there is a significant secular dependency between three time periods and the sector of the grievant's employment. Indeed, this result also holds when time is measured on a year-by-year basis (tabulation and statistical test not shown). Thus, over the 24 years covered by our survey, public sector cases accounted for an increasingly large share of awards issued. This finding is not surprising since union membership density in the public sector relative to the private sector has increased over the years covered by our survey.[6]

---

[6] Laura J. Cooper, Dennis R. Nolan, Richard A. Bales, & Stephen F. Befort *ADR in the Workplace* (St. Paul, MN: West Academic Publishing, 3d ed., 2014), 579.

Table 2.7 <u>Award Outcomes by Year Clusters</u>*
(Award Outcomes: N-size, row % and column % are the top, middle and bottom values, respectively.)

Year Clusters	Award Outcomes			
	Management Win	Union Win	Split Decision	Row Totals
1982-1989	266 45.70[1a] 26.03[1]	122 20.96[b] 27.66[1]	194 33.33[1c] 32.77[1c]	582 100.00 28.32[1]
1990-1997	458 51.63[a] 44.81[2]	192 21.65[b] 43.54[2]	237 26.72[c] 40.03[2]	887 100.00 43.16[2]
1998-2005	298 50.85[a] 29.16	127 21.67[b] 28.80	161 27.47[3c] 27.20	586 100.00 28.52
Column Totals	1,022 49.73[a] 100.00	441 21.46[b] 100.00	592 28.81[c] 100.00	2,055 100.00 100.00

Chi-square (4) = 8.6283, p = 0.071
* The numeric indexes 1, 2 and 3 indicate that the percentages in row 1 and row 2, row 2 and row 3, and row 3 and row 1, respectively, are statistically different at the .05 level or lower. The alphabetic indexes a, b and c indicate that the percentages in column 1 and column 2, column 2 and column 3, and column 3 and column 1, respectively, are statistically different at the .05 level or lower.

The final case variable we consider is "legal representation." This characteristic measures whether neither, both or only one party in our data base had attorney representation at the arbitration hearing.

Table 2.8 Case Sector by Year Clusters*
(N-size, row % and column % are the top, middle and bottom value, respectively)

Year Clusters	Public Sector	Private Sector	Row Totals
1982-1989	293 50.34[1] 24.06[1a]	289 49.66[1] 34.53[1]	582 100.00 28.32[1]
1990-1997	542 61.10[a] 44.50[2]	345 38.90 41.22[2]	887 100.00 43.16[2]
1998-2005	383 65.36[3a] 31.44[3a]	203 34.64[3] 24.25[3]	586 100.00 28.52
Column Totals	1,218 59.27 100.00	837 40.73 100.00	2,055 100.00 100.00

Chi-square (2) = 29.4449, p = 0.000
* The numeric indexes 1, 2 and 3 indicate that the percentages in row 1 and row 2, row 2 and row 3, and row 3 and row 1, respectively, are statistically different at the .05 level or lower. The alphabetic index a indicates that the percentages in column 1 and column 2 are statistically different at the .05 level or lower.

As the last column in Table 2.9 depicts, in our data neither party was represented by counsel in 22.48 percent of the cases, both had counsel in 41.90 percent of cases, and only the union or management was represented by counsel in 9.05 percent and 26.57 percent of cases, respectively. Moreover, Table 2.9's chi-square test confirms that legal representation and the awards issued by arbitrators are dependent. That is, legal representation can affect a case's outcome, but our discussion of the precise nature of this affect is reserved for Chapter 3.

Table 2.10 presents an interesting picture of how the parties' retention of legal counsel has changed over the quarter century covered by our study. Focusing on the column percentages in this table, we see the share of cases in which "only management" used legal counsel increased from about 31 percent during the 1982-1989 years to approximately 44 percent during the 1990-1997 years and then decreased to nearly 25 percent during the 1998-2005 years. Similar patterns of cyclical change were followed with respect to the share of cases in which "only union(s)," "both" parties and "neither" party used legal counsel. During the most recent cluster of years, legal counsel appeared on behalf of both parties in about 55 percent of discharge and discipline arbitration hearings. In addition, the Table 2.10 test statistic indicates that these patterns of secular change are not likely to be chance occurrences.

Table 2.9 <u>Legal Representation by Award Outcomes</u>*
(Award Outcomes: N-size, row % and column % are the top, middle and bottom value, respectively)

Legal Representation	Award Outcomes			
	Management Win	Union Win	Split Decision	Row Totals
Neither	221 47.87[a] 21.62[1]	97 21.00[b] 22.00[1]	144 31.17[c] 24.32[1]	462 100.00 22.48[1]
Both	405 47.04[a] 39.63[2]	196 22.76[b] 44.44[2]	260 30.20[c] 43.92[2]	861 100.00 41.90[2]
Only Union	83 44.62[3a] 8.12[3]	48 25.81[3] 10.88[3]	55 29.57[c] 9.29[3]	186 100.00 9.05[3]
Only Employer	313 57.33[4a] 30.63[4a]	100 18.32[b] 22.68	133 24.36[4c] 22.47[c]	546 100.00 26.57[4]
Column Totals	1,022 49.73[a] 100.00	441 21.46[b] 100.00	592 28.81[c] 100.00	2,055 100.00 100.00

Chi-square (6) = 19.0403, p = 0.004
*The numeric indexes 1, 2, 3 and 4 indicate that the percentages in row 1 and row 2, row 2 and row 3, row 3 and row 4, and row 4 and row 1, respectively, are statistically different at the .05 level or lower. The alphabetic indexes a, b and c indicate that the percentages in column 1 and column 2, column 2 and column 3, and column 3 and column 1, respectively, are statistically different at the .05 level or lower.

Table 2.10 <u>Legal Representation by Year Clusters</u>*
(Legal Representation: N-size, row % and column % are the top, middle and bottom value, respectively)

Year Clusters	Legal Representation				
	Neither	Both	Only Union	Only Management	Row Totals
1982-1989	156 26.80[a] 33.77[1a]	200 34.36[b] 23.23[1b]	56 9.62[c] 30.11[1]	170 29.21 31.14[1]	582 100.00 28.32[1]
1990-1997	222 25.03[2a] 48.05[2a]	340 38.33[2b] 39.49	83 9.36[c] 44.62[2]	242 27.28 44.32[2]	887 100.00 43.16[2]
1998-2005	84 14.33[3a] 18.18[3a]	321 54.78[3b] 37.28[3b]	47 8.02[c] 25.27	134 22.87[3d] 24.54[3d]	586 100.00 28.52
Column Totals	462 22.48a 100.00	861 41.90[b] 100.00	186 9.05[c] 100.00	546 26.57[d] 100.00	2,055 100.00 100.00

Chi-square (6) = 64.1867, p = 0.000
* The numeric indexes 1, 2 and 3 indicate that the percentages in row 1 and row 2, row 2 and row 3, and row 3 and row 1, respectively, are statistically different at the .05 level or lower. The alphabetic indexes a, b, c and d indicate that the percentages in column 1 and column 2, column 2 and column 3, column 3 and column 4, and column 4 and column 1, respectively, are statistically different at the .05 level or lower.

Grievant Characteristics

Overall, approximately three-fourths of the grievants in our data were males, as shown in Table 2.11. Moreover, this ratio has remained remarkably constant over time (i.e., across our three time period clusters). Further, the grievants in our data generally tended to be longer-term employees. Table 2.12 shows the number of years of service that grievants, by gender, were employed by their current employers. For both male (approximately 46 percent) and female (approximately 49 percent) grievants, the largest share of our cases involved grievants with from 5 to less than 20 years of service. In contrast, the smallest shares involved grievants with less than 1 year of service—male (4.46 percent) and female (2.88 percent), which is not surprising. Employees with less than 1 year of service often are in the probationary period of their employment and, by contract, their access to arbitration is limited. Also, employees with brief tenure have accrued relatively little benefit from their seniority and thus they have less reason to challenge their discharge than do their long-tenured co-workers.

Table 2.11 <u>Grievants Gender by Year Clusters</u>*
(N-size, row % and column % are the top, middle and bottom value, respectively)

Year Clusters	Male Grievant	Female Grievant	Row Totals
1982-1989	451 77.49[a] 28.74[1]	131 22.51 26.95[1]	582 100.00 28.32[1]
1990-1997	672 75.76[a] 42.83[2]	215 24.24 44.24[2]	887 100.00 43.16[2]
1998-2005	446 76.11[a] 28.43	140 23.89 28.81	586 100.00 28.52
Column Totals	1,569 76.35[a] 100.00	486 23.65 100.00	2,055 100.00 100.00

Chi-square (2) = 0.6092, p = 0.737
* The numeric indexes 1, 2 and 3 indicate that the percentages in row 1 and row 2, row 2 and row 3, and row 3 and row 1, respectively, are statistically different at the .05 level or lower. The alphabetic index a indicates that the percentages in column 1 and column 2 are statistically different at the .05 level or lower.

Table 12.13 shows the level of discipline that the employers imposed on the grievants in our data base. Nearly 70 percent of the arbitration cases we surveyed involved discharges and the remaining 30 percent involved lesser forms of discipline, which we divided into suspensions (25.11 percent) and oral or written reprimands (5.21 percent).

Table 2.12 <u>Gender of Grievant by Years of Service</u>*
(N-size, row % and column % are the top, middle and bottom value, respectively)

Years of Service	Male	Female	Row Totals
Less than 1 year	70 83.33[a] 4.46[1]	14 16.67 2.88[1]	84 100.00 4.09[1]
1 year to less than 5 years	325 72.87[a] 20.71	121 27.13 24.90[2]	446 100.00 21.70
5 years to less than 10 years	328 76.28[a] 20.91[3]	102 23.72 20.99[3]	430 100.00 20.92[3]
10 years to less than 20 years	390 74.43[a] 24.86[4]	134 25.57 27.57[4]	524 100.00 25.50[4]
20 years or more	204 82.26[a] 13.00[5]	44 17.74 9.05[5]	248 100.00 12.07[5]
Unknown	252 78.02[a] 16.06[6]	71 21.98 14.61[6]	323 100.00 15.72[6]
Column Totals	1,569 76.35[a] 100.00	486 23.65 100.00	2,055 100.00 100.00

Chi-square (5) = 11.6259, p = 0.040
* The numeric indexes 1, 2, 3, 4, 5 and 6 indicate that the percentages in row 1 and row 2, row 2 and row 3, row 3 and row 4, row 4 and row 5, row 5 and row 6, and row 6 and row 1, respectively, are statistically different at the .05 level or lower. The alphabetic index indicates that the percentages in column 1 and column 2 are statistically different at the .05 level or lower.

Table 2.13 Number and Percent of Grievants by Level of Discipline*
(N-size and row % are the top and bottom value, respectively)

Discipline Imposed by Employer	Row Totals
Discharge	1,432 69.68[1]
Suspension	516 25.11[2]
Oral or written reprimand	107 5.21[3]
Column Totals	2,055 100.00

* The numeric indexes 1, 2 and 3 indicate that the percentages in row 1 and row 2, row 2 and row 3,and row 3 and row 1, respectively, are statistically different at the .05 level or lower.

A final set of grievant characteristics is presented in Tables 2.14, 2.15 and 2.16. Table 2.14 shows the work-related offenses that our grievants are alleged to have committed, with "Insubordination" (19.35 percent) and "Violence & Aggression" (19.27 percent), the most common, followed by Dishonesty (15.55 percent), Performance Issues (15.26 percent) and Attendance/Absentee Issues (14.25 percent). A more detailed analysis of offenses appears in Chapter 4.

Table 2.15 shows whether the grievants in our data were charged with a crime based on the same behavior that resulted in their workplace discharge or discipline. Nearly five percent of grievants were charged with a crime by the justice system.

Finally, Table 2.16 shows that about eight percent of the grievants in the cases surveyed were working under the terms of "last chance agreements" at the time of their discharge or discipline. In Chapters 3 and 5 we explore how our data on "criminal activity" affects arbitration outcomes. Chapters 3 and 7 examine how last chance agreements correlate with arbitrator decisions and other aspects of the arbitration process.

Table 2.14 Offenses Grievant Allegedly Committed
(N-size and row % are the top and bottom values, respectively)

Alleged Offense Category*	Row Totals
Insubordination	469 19.35
Violence & Aggression	467 19.27
Dishonesty	377 15.55
Performance Issues	370 15.26
Attendance/Absentee Issues	352 14.52
On the Job Misconduct	175 7.22
Drugs/Alcohol	96 3.96
Off the Job Misconduct	94 3.88
Other	24 0.99
Column Totals	2,424 100.00

*Some cases implicate more than one offense category (e.g., the discipline might have been based on both poor performance and insubordination).

Table 2.15 Number and Percent of Grievants Charged with a Crime*
(N-size and row % are the top and bottom value, respectively)

Grievant Charged with Crime	Row Totals
Yes	96 4.67[1]
No	1,945 94.65[2]
Not Known	14 0.68[3]
Column Totals	2,055 100.00

*The numeric indexes 1, 2 and 3 indicate that the percentages in row 1 and row 2, row 2 and row 3, and row 3 and row 1, respectively, are statistically different at the .05 level or lower.

Table 2.16 Number and Percent of Grievants Working Under Last Chance Agreements*
(N-size and row % are the top and bottom value, respectively)

Grievants Working Under Last Chance Agreements	Row Totals
Yes, imposed by agreement	159 7.74[1]
Yes, imposed by arbitrator	6 0.29[2]
No	1,890 91.97[3]
Column Totals	2,055 100.00

*The numeric indexes 1, 2 and 3 indicate that the percentages in row 1 and row 2, row 2 and row 3, and row 3 and row 1, respectively, are statistically different at the .05 level or lower.

Summary

The empirical information about the arbitration process and arbitral decision-making imparted in this book is unique in scope and detail. To drill into the domain of disciplinary arbitration as deeply as this book does required the compilation of a large and comprehensive data base. We trust this chapter's brief review of our data base has established a foundation that supports the reliability of the empirical relationships reported in the chapters that follow.

This fleeting look at our data produced some particularly interesting results. First, relatively few arbitrators decided a proportionately larger share of awards. In this same vein, arbitrators with heavy caseloads were significantly less inclined to issue union win awards and significantly more inclined to issue split decisions. Further, arbitrators who issued split decisions in *discipline* cases did not get more work, contradicting the proposition that arbitrators who split awards will improve their odds of future selections. However, the opposite result applied in *discharge* cases.

Second, the distribution of disciplinary decisions across management win, union win and split decision categories was approximately 50 percent, 21 percent and 29 percent, respectively. In addition, we learned that this distribution has been relatively stable over the period from 1982 to 2005.

Third, over this span of years, it is not surprising to find that public sector cases have accounted for an increasingly large share of discharge and discipline awards issued. It is widely recognized that since the 1980s, public sector relative to private sector union membership density has increased.

Fourth, legal representation does matter in discharge and discipline arbitrations in the sense that representation affects the distribution of award outcomes—a subject explored in Chapter 3. However, a finding unique to this chapter is that over the period covered by this study the share of disciplinary cases that did *not* involve legal counsel increased from roughly 34 percent in 1982-1989 to about 48 percent in 1990-1997 only to fall to about 18 percent in 1998-2005.

Fifth, three-fourths of the grievants involved in disciplinary cases that made it to arbitration were males—a ratio that has remained remarkably constant over recent decades. In addition, the grievants in these cases tended to be employees with one or more years of service. That is, they tended to be largely post-probationary employees.

Finally, disciplinary cases that made it to arbitration involved mostly discharges (69.68 percent), then suspensions (25.11 percent), and, last, oral or written reprimands (5.21 percent). These cases are distributed across 43 categories of offenses—a subject examined in Chapter 4. In addition, some of these offenses resulted in criminal charges, while others involved employees who were working under the terms of last chance agreements at the time of their discharge or discipline. The relationships between these case characteristics and arbitral decisions are explored in Chapters 3, 5 and 7.

CHAPTER 3

WINS, LOSSES AND SPLIT DECISIONS IN DISCHARGE AND DISCIPLINE AWARDS

Introduction

Arbitration law, arbitral processes and the standards governing arbitral decision-making are well researched and so are the just cause standards applicable to disciplinary grievances.

However, there is a relative dearth of reliable information about the arbitration of discharge and discipline cases and, in particular, about *how* these cases are decided and *why* arbitrators reach the awards they issue. Such a paucity of information is unfortunate because these *how* and *why* questions command the attention of jurists, policy-makers, practitioners, arbitrators and academics whose target of inquiry is the arbitration award itself—the final product of the arbitration process.

The source materials needed to answer these questions begin with access to a large sample of discharge and discipline awards that must be read and coded for the decision reached and for other relevant content. As discussed in Chapter 1, we have compiled and coded 2,055 public and private sector, single grievant Minnesota-based discharge and discipline awards that were issued by 81 different arbitrators over 24 years. We classified each award's decision as: (1) *management win*, if the employer's disciplinary action was upheld by the arbitrator; (2) *union win,* if the employer's disciplinary action was reversed by the arbitrator; and (3) *split decision*, if the arbitrator reduced the employer's disciplinary action.

To elaborate on the classification regime, if the employer discharged, suspended or reprimanded an employee and the arbitrator subsequently sustained, without modification, the employer's disciplinary action, we coded the case a *management win*. On the other hand, if the arbitrator reversed the employer's action by: (a) reinstating the discharged employee with full back pay and accrued benefits; (b) overturning the suspension and ordering full back pay for the days the employee was wrongfully suspended; or (c) expunging the personnel record of the oral or written reprimand, we coded the case a *union win*. Finally, if the arbitrator modified the employer's actions by: (a) reducing the discharged employee's penalty to a suspension or reprimand, with or without back pay and accrued benefits; (b) shortening the suspended employee's length of suspension and awarding back pay or reducing it to a reprimand; or (c) converting the written reprimand to an oral reprimand and/or moderating the content of the written or oral reprimand, then we coded the case a *split decision*.

Purpose and Analytical Framework

This chapter's primary purpose is to explain *why* arbitrators reach the decisions they issue. Herein, our focus is mainly on the empirical relationship between award outcomes and a variety of prospective explanatory factors. Our secondary purpose is to present new information about *how* arbitrators decide discharge and discipline cases.

Figure 3.1 is a schematic of our explanatory model. It suggests that the awards issued in discharge and discipline cases are determined by a variety of arbitrator, grievant and case characteristic variables. The top bubble in Figure 3.1 depicts the arbitrator's decision set, as previously described. Each of the bottom three bubbles includes a list of explanatory variables that may affect the outcome awarded by the arbitrator. For example, as shown in the bottom left-hand bubble in Figure 3.1, arbitrator characteristics such as the arbitrator's gender and membership in the National Academy of Arbitrators (NAA) may affect award outcomes. So, too, may the grievant characteristics listed in the bottom middle bubble such as the grievant's gender and whether the grievant was working under the terms of a last chance agreement when discharged or disciplined. Likewise, the case characteristic variables identified in the bottom right-hand bubble such as whether the case arose out of the public or private sector and the lapse of time between the date of the employer's disciplinary action and the date of the arbitrator's decision (i.e., "delay') affects awards issued.

Each of the explanatory variables in Figure 3.1's bottom three bubbles is defined in Table 3.1. These variables were chosen either because researchers have previously shown them to affect arbitral decision-making or because hypotheses involving these variables are being considered herein for the first time. We note that many of the former variables were not based on well-defined hypotheses and, as such, we discuss their relationship to award outcomes in strictly atheoretical terms.

A concluding observation is that several of the book's subsequent chapters analyze many of the explanatory variables presented in Table 3.1. However, that work does not duplicate the analysis appearing in this chapter. Rather, it is an extensive elaboration of same. For example, Chapters 5 and 6, respectively, discuss how arbitrators assess proof (i.e., our "quantum of proof" variable) and the variable we call "Seven Tests of Just Cause." Chapter 7 analyzes remedies in discharge cases, using as covariates our "last chance agreement," "delay," "sector" and (arbitrator) "education" variables. Finally, Chapter 9 examines the proposition that a grievant's "tenure" may serve to mitigate his or her level of discipline.

Figure 3.1 Framework Explaining Arbitration Decisions

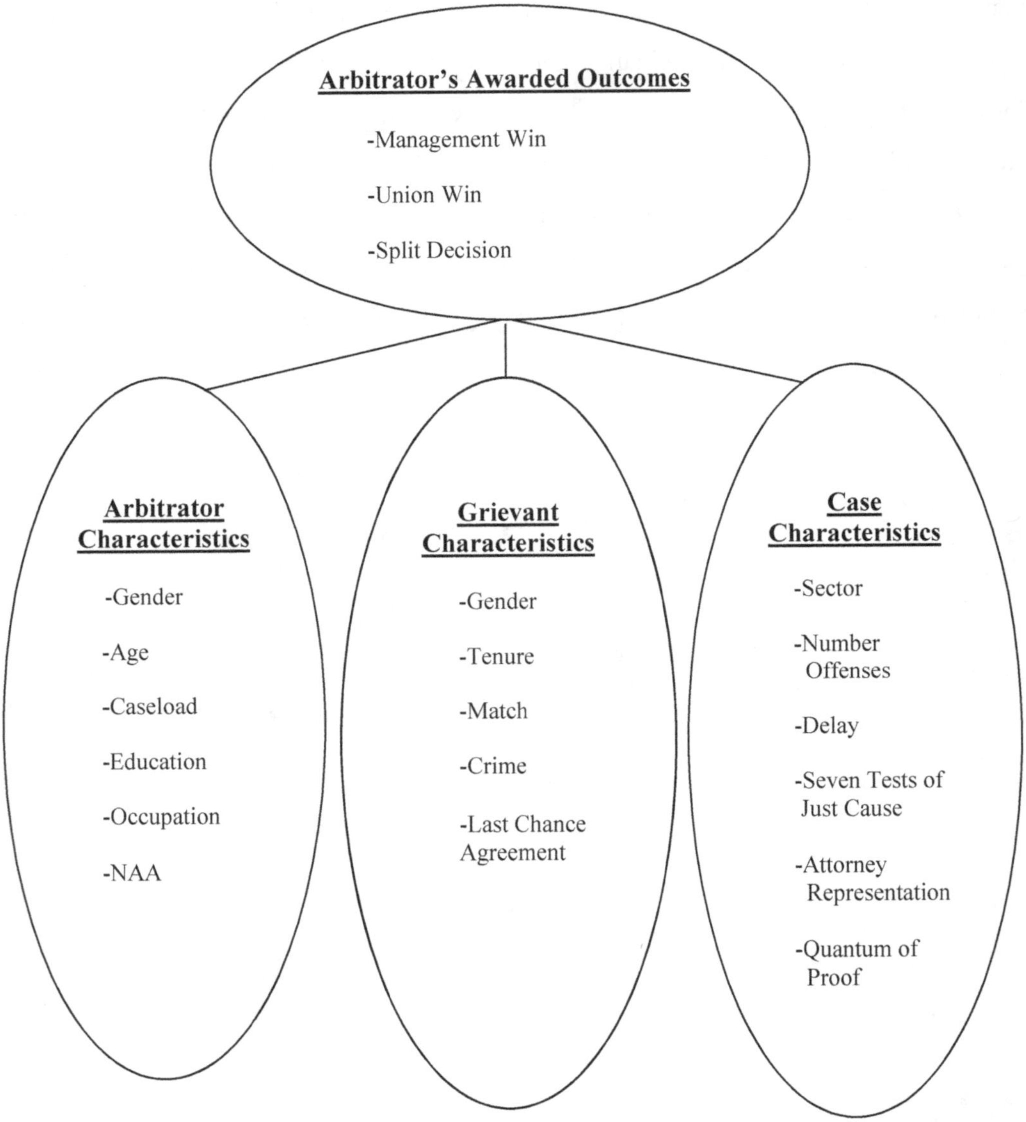

Table 3.1 Definition of Independent Variables

Arbitrator Characteristics	
Gender	Whether arbitrator is male or female.
Age	Arbitrator's age at the time the award was issued, measured as the difference between decision year and arbitrator's year of birth.
Caseload	Total number of decisions in the survey that were issued by the arbitrator: a measure of experience.
Education	Arbitrator's highest level of educational attainment—high school; bachelor's degree; master's degree; law degree; or doctorate degree.
Occupation	Arbitrator was neither an academic nor practicing attorney; academic only; practicing attorney only; or both academic and practicing attorney.
NAA	Whether arbitrator was a member of the National Academy of Arbitrators at the time the award was issued: a measure of experience.
Grievant Characteristics	
Gender	Whether grievant is male or female.
Match	Whether gender of arbitrator and gender of grievant are the same.
Tenure	Whether grievant worked ten or more years for employer.
Crime	Whether grievant was charged with a crime for the same conduct that formed the basis for employer's disciplinary action.
Last Chance Agreement	Whether grievant was working under the terms of a "last chance agreement" at the time of discipline.
Case Characteristics	
Sector	Whether grievant worked in public or private sector.
Number of Offenses	Whether grievant was charged with having committed more than one offense.
Delay	The number of lapsed days between the date of the employer's disciplinary action and the date of the arbitration decision.
Seven Tests of Just Cause	Whether one or both of the parties and/or the arbitrator invoked the Seven Tests of Just Cause.
Attorney Representation	Neither party was represented by legal counsel; both parties were represented by an attorney; the union was represented by an attorney and the employer was not; or the employer was represented by an attorney and the union was not.
Quantum of Proof	The arbitrator did not specify the quantum of proof standard used in reaching a decision; specifies "preponderance of evidence" as the standard; specifies "clear and convincing evidence" as the standard; or specified "beyond reasonable doubt" as the standard.

How Do Arbitrators Rule?

We coded the discipline imposed by employers by its level of severity: reprimand, suspension or discharge. Table 3.2 presents a cross-tabulation of award outcomes by type of discipline. The row labeled "Column Totals" shows *how* the arbitrators in our sample ruled in discharge and discipline cases. In round numbers, the percent of management win, union win and split awards is 50 percent, 21 percent and 29 percent, respectively. These percentages are significantly different.

Why Do Arbitrators Decide Cases the Way They Do?

A Fundamental Empirical Finding

The chi-square test in Table 3.2 suggests that the odds are less than 1 in 1,000 that the type of discipline imposed by the employer and award outcome are independent. That is, the employer's imposed discipline partially explains *why* arbitrators decide cases the way they do.[1] This statistical dependency exists because for each level of discipline imposed the plurality of issued awards are management win outcomes. Moreover, the largest share of management win (73.48 percent), union win (62.36 percent) and split (68.58 percent) awards involve discharge cases, and these shares are significantly different from corresponding suspension and reprimand shares.

The vast majority of disciplinary cases that were taken to arbitration involved discharges (69.68 percent). This is the first of two important results. The second is that management won a significantly larger share of discharge (52.44 percent) cases *vis a vis* suspension (43.99 percent) and reprimand (41.12 percent) cases, where the latter two percentages are not significantly different. These are original findings which suggest that researchers should analyze discharge cases separately from reprimand and suspension cases because arbitrator decision-making processes result in awards that are different based on the

[1] The type of discipline imposed variable is implicit in Figure 3.1's case characteristics bubble. As subsequently discussed, discharge cases are analyzed separately and apart from reprimand and suspension cases throughout the remainder of this chapter. In doing so, we implicitly control for this variable's affect on award outcomes.

type of discipline the employer imposed. Apparently the weight arbitrators assign to evidence and other factors that influence their decisions is different for discharge than for reprimand and suspension cases.[2]

Table 3.2 Arbitration Outcomes by Type of Discipline*
(N-size, row % and column % are the top, middle and bottom value, respectively)

Discipline Imposed	Management Win	Union Win	Split Decision	Row Totals
Reprimand	44 41.12 4.31[1a]	43 40.19[1b] 9.75[1b]	20 18.69[1c] 3.38[1]	107 100.00 5.21[1]
Suspension	227 43.99[2a] 22.21[2a]	123 23.84[2b] 27.89[2]	166 32.17[c] 28.04[2c]	516 100.00 25.11[2]
Discharge	751 52.44[3a] 73.48[3a]	275 19.20[3b] 62.36[3b]	406 28.35[3c] 68.58[3c]	1,432 100.00 69.68[3]
Column Totals	1,022 49.73[a] 100.00	441 21.46[b] 100.00	592 28.81[c] 100.00	2,055 100.00 100.00

Chi-square (4) = 35.3025, p = 0.000
* The numeric indexes 1, 2 and 3 indicate that the percentages in row 1 and row 2, row 2 and row 3, and row 3 and row 1, respectively, are statistically different at the .05 level or lower. The alphabetic indexes a, b and c indicate that the percentages in column 1 and column 2, column 2 and column 3, and column 3 and column 1, respectively, are statistically different at the .05 level or lower.

To further explore this possibility, we combine reprimand and suspension cases—henceforth, referred to as "discipline" cases—in Table 3.3. This table's chi-square shows that the discharge and our newly constructed discipline category of the employer's disciplinary action are also associated with arbitration outcomes, supporting the conclusion that discharge and discipline cases should be analyzed separately. Table 3.3 also depicts a

[2] Table 3.2 shows that: (1) nearly 50 percent of all cases involve management win awards; (2) the management win shares of suspension and reprimand outcomes are not significantly different; and (3) more than 40 percent of all suspension and reprimand cases result in management win outcomes. These combined results imply that we cannot as readily conclude that suspension and reprimand cases should also be partitioned for analytical purposes.

sharp distinction in arbitration outcomes by these discipline categories. Note that management prevailed in 52.44 percent of discharge cases, but won only 43.50 percent of discipline cases; and while the union prevailed in 26.65 percent of all discipline cases, it won only 19.20 percent of discharge cases. These differences are statistically significant, which demonstrates that the type of disciplinary action taken by management differentially affects arbitration outcomes. This conclusion holds even though the 29.86 percent of all discipline cases that resulted in split decisions is not significantly different from the 28.35 percent of all discharge cases with split decision outcomes.

Table 3.3 Arbitration Outcomes by Discipline and Discharge*
(N-size, row % and column % are the top, middle and bottom value, respectively)

Discipline Imposed	Management Win	Union Win	Split Decision	Row Totals
Discipline (suspension and reprimand cases)	271 43.50[1a] 26.52[1a]	166 26.65[1] 37.64[2b]	186 29.86[c] 31.42[3c]	623 100.00 30.32[1]
Discharge	751 52.44[a] 73.48[a]	275 19.20[b] 62.36[b]	406 28.35[c] 68.58[c]	1,432 100.00 69.68
Column Totals	1,022 49.73[a] 100.00	441 21.46[b] 100.00	592 28.81[c] 100.00	2,055 100.00 100.00

Chi-square (2) = 18.5272, p = 0.000
* The numeric index 1 indicates that the percentages in row 1 and row 2 are statistically different at the .05 level or lower. The alphabetic indexes a, b and c indicate that the percentages in column 1 and column 2, column 2 and column 3, and column 3 and column 1, respectively, are statistically different at the .05 level or lower.

To conclude, these results seem to confirm that the analysis of awards should be made conditional on the type of discipline imposed. Accordingly, in subsequent analysis, discipline cases (i.e., the sum of reprimand and suspension cases) and discharge cases are partitioned and separately analyzed.

Arbitrator Characteristics

As pictured in Figure 3.1, the arbitrator's gender, age, caseload, education, occupation and NAA membership status are shown to be prospective determinants of arbitration outcomes. Other researchers have previously studied these variables. But the literature's findings with respect to these characteristics are, at best, inconsistent.

Gender

At least three studies based on simulated or experimental data and actual or field data have found that the gender of the arbitrator and the disciplinary awards reached by the arbitrator are statistically independent.[3] Interestingly, among these studies, Scott and Shadoan found no statistical support for the null hypothesis that female arbitrators render less severe judgments than male arbitrators.[4] In contrast, Bemmels found that when the arbitrator awarded a partial reinstatement, female arbitrators, on average, awarded significantly fewer weeks of suspension than did their male counterparts.[5]

The analysis presented in Table 3.4 certainly does not clarify the gender/award outcomes relationship, if any, between arbitrator gender and arbitration awards. The top panel's chi square shows that there is no statistical relationship between arbitrator gender and award outcomes when the issue involved the suspension or reprimand of a grievant. Female arbitrators decided about 18 percent of all discipline cases and they issued about 18 percent of awards in each outcome category. Further, the respective percent of management win, union win and split decisions reached by arbitrators are roughly 44 percent, 27 percent and 30 percent, regardless of the arbitrator's gender (i.e., the vertical differences between female and male shares by outcome category are not statistically significant).

---

[3] Clyde Scott & Elizabeth Shadoan, "The Effect of Gender on Arbitration Decisions," 10 *Journal of Labor Research* 429, 431 (1989); Robert J. Thornton & Perry A. Zirkel, "The Consistency and Predictability of Arbitration Awards," 43 *Industrial and Labor Review* 294, 303 (1990); Perry A. Zirkel & Philip H. Breslin, "Correlates of Grievance Arbitration Awards," 24 *Journal of Collective Bargaining* 45, 50 (1995).

[4] Scott & Shadoan, "The Effect of Gender on Arbitration Decisions," 431.

[5] Brian Bemmels, "Arbitrator Characteristics and Arbitrator Decisions," 21 *Journal of Labor Research* 181, 187 (1990).

However, when the issue pertains to the discharge of a grievant, the arbitrator's gender and award outcomes are dependent, as the chi-square test in the bottom panel of Table 3.4 implies. The locus of significance that the chi-square test is picking up derives from the fact that female arbitrators compared to male arbitrators issued significantly more awards favoring management—60.17 percent *versus* 50.88 percent; and because male arbitrators issue relatively more split decisions than did their female counterparts—29.81 percent to 21.16 percent. The shares of union win awards that female and male arbitrators reached are statistically indistinguishable at about 19 percent.

Our arbitrator-gender results only serve to further confuse the already mixed array of findings in the literature. We uniquely find that the arbitrator's gender plays no role whatsoever in discipline cases. However, arbitrator gender does seem to affect the decisions arbitrators reach in discharge cases. Specifically, female arbitrators were more likely to favor management, and male arbitrators awards were more likely to award split decisions. An *ex post* explanation of these results is not easy to identify.

Table 3.4 Arbitration Outcomes by Type of Discipline and Arbitrator Gender*
(N-size, row % and column % are the top, middle and bottom value, respectively)

Gender	Management Win	Union Win	Split Decision	Row Totals
Discipline				
Female	44 40.37 16.24[1]	30 27.52 18.07[1]	35 32.11 18.82[1]	109 100.00 17.50[1]
Male	227 44.16[a] 83.76	136 26.46 81.93	151 29.38[c] 81.18	514 100.00 82.50
Column Totals	271 43.50[a] 100.00	166 26.65 100.00	186 29.86[c] 100.00	623 100.00 100.00
Chi-square (2) = 0.5611, p = 0.755				
Discharge				
Female	145 60.17[1a] 19.31[1]	45 18.67 16.36[2]	51 21.16[3c] 12.56[3c]	241 100.00 16.83[1]
Male	606 50.88[a] 80.69	230 19.31[b] 83.64	355 29.81[c] 87.44[c]	1,191 100.00 83.17
Column Totals	751 52.44[a] 100.00	275 19.20[b] 100.00	406 28.35[c] 100.00	1,432 100.00 100.00
Chi-square (2) = 8.6209, p = 0.013				

* The numeric index 1 indicates that the percentages in row 1 and row 2 are statistically different at the .05 level or lower. The alphabetic indexes a, b and c indicate that the percentages in column 1 and column 2, column 2 and column 3, and column 3 and column 1, respectively, are statistically different at the .05 level or lower.

Age and Caseload

The reported effects of age and caseload on arbitrator decision-making are even more varied. With respect to the arbitrator's age, two experimental (i.e., simulated) studies reported that younger arbitrators are more likely to reinstate the discharged grievant than older arbitrators,[6] while a third such study ascertained that the arbitrator's age and arbitral outcomes are wholly independent.[7] Unfortunately, field data studies do not clarify this picture. Nelson and Uddin found—at the .10 level of significance—that increases in age negatively affect the odds that the arbitrator will reinstate a discharged grievant,[8] while Bemmels reached the opposite conclusion, finding that older arbitrators are more likely to decide in the grievant's favor.[9]

Turning next to the caseload variable, two general points warrant note: first, a variety of "caseload" or "experience" measures appear in the arbitration literature; and second, most previous studies have found that their particular measure of arbitrator experience is not significantly related to arbitral outcomes. Three studies using experimental data found that arbitrators with a greater number of lifetime cases are less inclined to reinstate grievants, and that arbitrators with more years of practice are more inclined either to deny the grievance or to reinstate the grievant with full pay, as opposed to taking the middle course of reinstatement with a suspension.[10] However, at least four field studies concluded that the relationship between experience (variously measured) and arbitrator decision-making in discharge cases is not statistically significant.[11]

Table 3.5's age and caseload results do not duplicate those reported in the literature. First, consider the age variable. The "Row Totals" column shows that the mean age of

---

[6] Nels E. Nelson, "The Selection of Arbitrators," *Labor Law Journal* 703, 707 (1986); Nels E. Nelson & Earl M. Curry, Jr., "Arbitrator Characteristics and Arbitral Decisions," 20 *Industrial Relations* 312 (1981).

[7] Thornton & Zirkel, "The Consistency and Predictability of Arbitration Awards," 303.

[8] Nels E. Nelson & A.N.M. Meshquat Uddin, "The Impact of Delay on Arbitrators' Decisions in Discharge Cases," *Labor Studies Journal* (Summer 1998), 3, 15.

[9] Bemmels, "Arbitrator Characteristics and Arbitrator Decisions," 187.

[10] Brian Bemmels, "Attribution Theory and Discipline Arbitration, 44 *Industrial and Labor Relations Review* 548, 560 (1991); Nelson, "The Selection of Arbitrators," 709; Nelson & Curry, "Arbitrator Characteristics and Arbitral Decisions," 312; .

[11] Nelson & Uddin, "The Impact of Delay on Arbitrators' Decisions in Discharge Cases," 15; Allen Ponak, "Discharge Arbitration and Reinstatement in the Province of Alberta," 42 *The Arbitration Journal* 39, 46 (1987); Thornton & Zirkel, "The Consistency and Predictability of Arbitration Awards," 303; Zirkel & Breslin, "Correlates of Grievance Arbitration Awards," 50.

arbitrators in our sample was 57, regardless of type of discipline imposed.[12] Similarly, the mean age of arbitrators was about 57 for each type of discipline and award outcome cross-tabulation. Thus, with one exception, Table 3.5's upper and lower panels show that the difference in the arbitrator's mean age across award outcomes is not statistically significant. Hypothetically, even if arbitrator age was a significant determinate of award outcomes, the age differences across outcomes in Table 3.5 are too small to be of any practical consequence. Thus, unlike two of the experimental studies and both field studies discussed above, we conclude that an arbitrator's age does not materially affect discharge or discipline decisions.

[12] Arbitrator's age was computed at the time each of his/her awards was issued.

Table 3.5 Arbitration Outcomes by Type of Discipline and Arbitrator Age and Caseload*

(N-size, mean and standard deviation are the top, middle, and bottom values, respectively)

Age and Caseload	Management Win	Union Win	Split Decision	Row Totals
Discipline				
Age	271 56.91 10.15	166 58.49[b] 10.74	186 56.07 9.84	623 57.08 10.25
Caseload	271 91.77[a] 81.57	166 74.86 75.48	186 82.75 76.23	623 84.57 78.59
Discharge				
Age	751 57.04 9.74	275 58.22 9.47	406 57.05 9.62	1,432 57.27 9.66
Caseload	751 94.46 77.86	275 92.29[b] 77.54	406 110.21[c] 85.12	1,432 98.51 80.21

* The alphabetic indexes a, b and c indicate that the percentages in column 1 and column 2, column 2 and column 3, and column 3 and column 1, respectively, are statistically different at the .05 level or lower.

Next, consider the caseload results in Table 3.5. We defined this variable in Table 3.1 as the total number of decisions within our sample that were issued by each arbitrator. Although this definition is an imprecise measure of experience, we, nevertheless, examine whether the decisions of arbitrators with heavier caseloads are distinguished from those reached by arbitrators with lighter caseloads. With regard to discipline cases, Table 3.5 shows that arbitrators with the heaviest and lightest caseloads (i.e., about 92 vs. 75) were significantly most likely to issue management win and union win awards, respectively. However, in discharge cases, arbitrators with the heaviest caseloads (i.e., approximately 110) significantly reached split decision outcomes, and arbitrators with the lightest caseloads (i.e., the statistically indistinguishable 94 or 92 cases) tended to issue both management win and union win outcomes—results that only partly affirm the literature's experimental findings and that conflict with the literature's field study findings.

Education

The literature treats arbitrator education as a potential correlate with outcomes, but several recent studies found scant evidence linking the two.[13] However, with the possible exception of Nelson's experimental inquiry,[14] these studies used incomplete, truncated categorical measures of education, such as, whether the arbitrator had a law degree. Whereas, Bemmels, whose field study coded expressly the Ph.D., master's, and law degree levels of education, found that education does affect outcomes. His results indicated that arbitrators with a Ph.D. are less likely to award full reinstatement to a discharged grievant than are arbitrators with a master's degree or law degree.[15]

As shown in Table 3.1, we coded a five-part categorical variable to measure the highest level of education attained by arbitrators in our sample. Measured at this level of detail, our education-specific research contradicts the bulk of recent research. As shown in Table 3.6(a), the arbitrator's level of education and award outcomes are statistically independent with regard to discipline cases. However, there is a dependency between these two variables with reference to discharge cases, as represented in Table 3.6(b). For both types of disciplinary actions, arbitrators with law, doctorates, and master's degrees, in that order, issued the preponderance of awards. Similarly, within each outcome column, arbitrators with law degrees issued the bulk of decisions, followed by arbitrators with Ph.D. degrees and, last, by arbitrators with master's degrees.

---

[13] Clarence R. Deitsch & David A. Dilts, "An Analysis of Arbitrator Characteristics and Their Effects on Decision Making in Discharge Cases," *Labor Law Journal* 112, 114 (1989); Nelson, "The Selection of Arbitrators," 709; Nelson & Uddin, "The Impact of Delay on Arbitrators' Decisions in Discharge Cases," 15; Thornton, "The Consistency and Predictability of Arbitration Awards," 303; Zirkel, "Correlates of Grievance Arbitration Awards," 50; Zirkel & Breslin, "Correlates of Grievance Arbitration Awards," 50.

[14] Nelson, "The Selection of Arbitrators," 709.

[15] Bemmels, "Arbitrator Characteristics and Arbitrator Decisions," 198.

The discipline-related results in Table 3.6(a) show that the largest share of decisions issued by arbitrators in the three highest educational categories are management win decisions, and that arbitrators with Ph.D. degrees were not significantly more likely to favor management (51.40 percent) than were arbitrators with either law (41.31 percent) or master's (42.11 percent) degrees. Further, Ph.D.-arbitrators were significantly less likely to issue union win decisions (14.02 percent) compared to split decisions (34.58 percent). Finally, the shares of union win and split decisions issued by arbitrators with law degrees were not significantly different (29.81 percent vs. 28.87 percent). Based on this analysis it appears that while all three of the highest education group of arbitrators issued insignificantly different shares of split decisions, arbitrators with law degrees were far more likely to issue awards that favored the union over management in discipline cases, and the reverse is true for arbitrators with Ph.D. degrees.

The outcome patterns for the discharge cases appearing in Table 3.6(b) are identical to the above-discussed discipline patterns, although a somewhat nuanced difference between Tables 3.6(a) and 3.6(b) is that arbitrators in all three of the highest educational categories were more likely to issue larger shares of management win outcomes.

Table 3.6(a) Arbitration Outcomes in Discipline Cases by Arbitrator Education*

(N-size, row % and column % are the top, middle and bottom value, respectively)

Education	Management Win	Union Win	Split Decision	Row Totals
High School	14 46.67 5.17	9 30.00 5.42	7 23.33 3.76	30 100.00 4.82
Bachelor's Degree	10 45.45 3.69	4 18.18 2.41	8 36.36 4.30	22 100.00 3.53^{2}
Master's Degree	16 42.11 5.90^{3}	11 28.95 6.63^{3}	11 28.95 5.91^{3}	38 100.00 6.10^{3}
Law Degree	176 41.31^{a} 64.94^{4a}	127 29.81^{4} 76.51^{4b}	123 28.87^{c} 66.13^{4}	426 100.00 68.38^{4}
Doctorate Degree	55 51.40^{a} 20.30^{5a}	15 14.02^{5b} 9.04^{b}	37 34.58 19.89^{5}	107 100.00 17.17^{5}
Column Totals	271 43.50^{a} 100.00	166 26.65 100.00	186 29.86^{c} 100.00	623 100.00 100.00

Chi-square (8) = 12.5961, p = 0.127

* The numeric indexes 1, 2, 3, 4 and 5 indicate that the percentages in row 1 and row 2, row 2 and row 3, row 3 and row 4, row 4 and row 5, and row 5 and row 1, respectively, are statistically different at the .05 level or lower. The alphabetic indexes a, b and c indicate that the percentages in column 1 and column 2, column 2 and column 3, and column 3 and column 1, respectively, are statistically different at the .05 level or lower.

Table 3.6(b) Arbitration Outcomes in Discharge Cases by Arbitrator Education*

(N-size, row % and column % are the top, middle and bottom value, respectively)

Education	Management Win	Union Win	Split Decision	Row Totals
High School	25 53.19^{a} 3.33	11 23.40 4.00	11 23.40^{c} 2.71	47 100.00 3.28
Bachelor's Degree	25 73.53^{a} 3.33^{2}	5 14.71 1.82^{2}	4 11.76^{c} 0.99^{2c}	34 100.00 2.37^{2}
Master's Degree	86 60.56^{3a} 11.45^{3}	27 19.01 9.82^{3}	29 20.42^{3c} 7.14^{3c}	142 100.00 9.92^{3}
Law Degree	449 48.75^{4a} 59.79^{4a}	188 20.41^{b} 68.36^{4}	284 30.84^{c} 69.95^{4c}	921 100.00 64.32^{4}
Doctorate Degree	166 57.64^{a} 22.10^{5a}	44 15.28^{b} 16.00^{5}	78 27.08^{c} 19.21^{5}	288 100.00 20.11^{5}
Column Totals	751 52.44^{a} 100.00	275 19.20^{b} 100.00	406 28.35^{c} 100.00	1,432 100.00 100.00

Chi-square (8) = 21.3764, p = 0.006

* The numeric indexes 1, 2, 3, 4 and 5 indicate that the percentages in row 1 and row 2, row 2 and row 3, row 3 and row 4, row 4 and row 5, and row 5 and row 1, respectively, are statistically different at the .05 level or lower. The alphabetic indexes a, b and c indicate that the percentages in column 1 and column 2, column 2 and column 3, and column 3 and column 1, respectively, are statistically different at the .05 level or lower.

Occupation

As discussed above, the information in Tables 3.6(a) and 3.6(b) establishes that arbitrator education plays a significant role in arbitral decision-making, and that the locus of this significance is centered on the law, master's and Ph.D. degrees levels of education. In Tables 3.7(a) and 3.7(b), we carry this analysis a step further. This analysis implicitly queries whether the arbitrator who also worked as: (a) practicing attorney, (b) academic, (c) practicing attorney and academic, or (d) neither a practicing attorney nor an academic, exhibited significantly different outcome patterns. The answer to this inquiry is "yes," regardless of the type of discipline the employer imposed. Generally speaking, while this answer is consistent with the occupation/award outcome field study results that Bemmels[16] and Nelson and Uddin[17] have published, it conflicts with Zirkel and Breslin, who concluded that arbitral outcomes are not significantly related to whether the arbitrator is an academic.[18]

Consider first the discipline results in Table 3.7(a). The odds that arbitrators who practice law would issue a management win, union win or split decision were 38.98 percent, 30.35 percent and 30.67 percent, respectively. In comparison, academic arbitrators issued significantly more management win outcomes (50.42 percent) than union win outcomes (14.29 percent), and significantly more management win decisions than did attorney arbitrators (50.42 percent *versus* 38.98 percent).

The analysis of discharge cases in Table 3.7(b) exhibits very different results. Arbitrators who practiced law issued significantly different management win (48.04 percent), union win (18.58 percent) and split decision (33.38 percent) shares. Academic arbitrators and arbitrators who were neither academics nor practicing attorneys were significantly more likely than attorney arbitrators to reach management win outcomes—57.51 percent, 62.50 percent and 48.04 percent, respectively. Moreover, the largest share of union win decisions were issued by attorneys (46.55 percent), with the share of union win decisions issued by academics running a significant and distant second (22.91 percent).

---

[16] Bemmels, "Arbitrator Characteristics and Arbitrator Decisions," 189.

[17] Nelson & Uddin, "The Impact of Delay on Arbitrators' Decisions in Discharge Cases," 15.

[18] Nelson, "The Selection of Arbitrators," 709; Zirkel & Breslin, "Correlates of Grievance Arbitration Awards," 50. Nelson's experimental study also concluded that arbitrator decisions are independent of the four-part categorical variable of occupation.

Table 3.7(a) Arbitration Outcomes in Discipline Cases by Arbitrator Occupation*

(N-size, row % and column % are the top, middle and bottom value, respectively)

Occupation	Management Win	Union Win	Split Decision	Row Totals
Practicing Attorney	122 38.98[1] 45.02[1a]	95 30.35[1] 57.23[1]	96 30.67 51.61[1]	313 100.00 50.24[1]
Academic	60 50.42[a] 22.14[a]	17 14.29[2b] 10.24[2b]	42 35.29 22.58	119 100.00 19.10
Both	53 48.18[a] 19.56	31 28.18 18.67	26 23.64[c] 13.98	110 100.00 17.66[3]
Neither	36 44.44 13.28[4]	23 28.40 13.86[4]	22 27.16 11.83[4]	81 100.00 13.00[4]
Column Totals	271 43.50[a] 100.00	166 26.65 100.00	186 29.86[c] 100.00	623 100.00 100.00

Chi-square (6) = 14.8498, p = 0.021

* The numeric indexes 1, 2, 3 and 4 indicate that the percentages in row 1 and row 2, row 2 and row 3, row 3 and row 4, and row 4 and row 1, respectively, are statistically different at the .05 level or lower. The alphabetic indexes a, b and c indicate that the percentages in column 1 and column 2, column 2 and column 3, and column 3 and column 1, respectively, are statistically different at the .05 level or lower.

Table 3.7(b) Arbitration Outcomes in Discharge Cases by Arbitrator Occupation*

(N-size, row % and column % are the top, middle and bottom value, respectively)

Occupation	Management Win	Union Win	Split Decision	Row Totals
Practicing Attorney	331 48.04[1a] 44.07[1]	128 18.58[b] 46.55[1b]	230 33.38[1c] 56.65[1c]	689 100.00 48.11[1]
Academic	203 57.51[a] 27.03[2]	63 17.85[2b] 22.91	87 24.65[c] 21.43[2c]	353 100.00 24.65[2]
Both	117 50.87[3a] 15.58[a]	60 26.09[3] 21.82[3b]	53 23.04[c] 13.05	230 100.00 16.06[3]
Neither	100 62.50[4a] 13.32[4a]	24 15.00 8.73[4]	36 22.50[4c] 8.87[4c]	160 100.00 11.17[4]
Column Totals	751 52.44[a] 100.00	275 19.20[b] 100.00	406 28.35[c] 100.00	1,432 100.00 100.00

Chi-square (6) = 27.1691, p = 0.000

* The numeric indexes 1, 2, 3 and 4 indicate that the percentages in row 1 and row 2, row 2 and row 3, row 3 and row 4, and row 4 and row 1, respectively, are statistically different at the .05 level or lower. The alphabetic indexes a, b and c indicate that the percentages in column 1 and column 2, column 2 and column 3, and column 3 and column 1, respectively, are statistically different at the .05 level or lower.

NAA Membership

The last arbitrator characteristic variable considered is whether membership in the NAA affects arbitral decision-making. This variable, like "caseload," is a proxy for arbitrator "experience" that analysts often use to differentiate between experienced and inexperienced arbitrators. The experiential mechanism at work during our sampling period was that NAA applicants must have heard, decided, and issued at least fifty binding union-management awards within the previous five years.[20] While NAA membership has been used in at least four field studies, only the Stieber, Block and Corbitt study found a significant difference in the discharge outcomes reached by non-NAA and NAA members (i.e., non-NAA members issue a higher rate of awards favoring employers than do Academy members).[21] Like our "caseload" measure of experience, NAA membership has a discernable effect on arbitral outcomes.

The chi-square tests in Table 3.8 indicate that when NAA membership is used as the proxy measure for experience, we can reject the null hypothesis that arbitrators reach the same awards in disciplinary cases regardless of experience. Compared to non-NAA members, a significantly larger fraction of awards issued by Academy members favored the employer (49.00 percent vs. 38.39 percent for discipline cases, and 54.15 percent vs. 50.45 percent for discharge cases). These findings conflict with those reported by Stieber, Block and Corbitt. Additionally, non-NAA members issued a significantly larger share of union win decisions than did Academy members (31.89 percent vs. 21.00 percent for discipline cases, and 23.03 percent vs. 15.93 percent for discharge cases).

---

[20] The NAA membership guidelines were modified in 2008. See National Academy of Arbitrators, Membership Guidelines, http://www.naarb.org/member_guidelines.html.

[21] Jack Stieber, Richard N. Block & Leslie F. Corbitt, "How Representative Are Published Arbitration Decisions?" *Absenteeism, Recent Law, Panels, and Published Papers, Proceedings of the 37th Annual Meeting of the National Academy of Arbitrators* (Washington: D.C.: Bureau of National Affairs, Gerald Somers, ed., 1985), 172, 183; Bemmels, "Arbitrator Characteristics and Arbitrator Decisions," 188; Deitsch & Dilts, "An Analysis of Arbitrator Characteristics and Their Effects on Decision Making in Discharge Cases," 114; Nelson & Uddin, "The Impact of Delay on Arbitrators' Decisions in Discharge Cases," 15.

Table 3.8 Arbitration Outcomes by Type of Discipline and NAA Membership*
(N-size, row % and column % are the top, middle and bottom value, respectively)

NAA Membership Status	Management Win	Union Win	Split Decision	Row Totals
Discipline				
Member	147 49.00[1a] 54.24[a]	63 21.00[1b] 37.95[1b]	90 30.00[c] 48.39	300 100.00 48.15
Non-Member	124 38.39 45.76[a]	103 31.89 62.05[b]	96 29.72 51.61	323 100.00 51.85
Column Totals	271 43.50[a] 100.00	166 26.65 100.00	186 29.86[c] 100.00	623 100.00 100.00
Chi-square (2) = 10.9499, p = 0.004				
Discharge				
Member	418 54.15[a] 55.66[1a]	123 15.93[1b] 44.73[b]	231 29.92[c] 56.90[1]	772 100.00 53.91[1]
Non-Member	333 50.45[a] 44.34[a]	152 23.03 55.27[b]	175 26.52[c] 43.10	660 100.00 46.09
Column Totals	751 52.44[a] 100.00	275 19.20[b] 100.00	406 28.35[c] 100.00	1,432 100.00 100.00
Chi-square (2) = 11.7147, p = 0.003				

* The numeric index 1 indicates that the percentages in row 1 and row 2 are statistically different at the .05 level or lower. The alphabetic indexes a, b and c indicate that the percentages in column 1 and column 2, column 2 and column 3, and column 3 and column 1, respectively, are statistically different at the .05 level or lower.

Grievant Characteristics

A number of grievant-related variables may have an impact on the disciplinary decisions reached by arbitrators. The grievant characteristics we analyzed include the grievant's gender, gender match between the grievant and arbitrator, the grievant's length of employment ("tenure"), crime, and last chance agreement variables. While the literature reports on the outcome-related effects of the gender, match, and tenure variables, this is the first study to consider the effect on award outcomes of criminal charges having been brought against a grievant for the same conduct that led to the employer's disciplinary action, and only the second to consider the effect of a last chance agreement on award outcomes.

Gender and Gender Match

When it comes to the relationship between the grievant's gender and award outcomes, the literature is divided. Four field studies have found that the grievant's gender does not affect the decisions that arbitrators render in discharge cases.[22] In contrast, two other field studies reached the opposite conclusion. Ponak found that "male grievants were more than twice as likely as female grievants to have their discharges upheld."[23] Bemmels found that "women were twice as likely as men to have their grievances sustained and 2.7 times more likely to receive a full reinstatement, and in cases in which a suspension was imposed by an arbitrator, women received, on average, a suspension 2.1 months shorter than that for men."[24] Using experimental data, Bemmels also found that arbitrators issued more lenient penalties when the grievant was female.[25]

With respect to the gender match variable, Scott and Shadoan examined whether the arbitrator's gender and the grievant's gender interact in their affect on award outcomes. That is, if the genders "match," these analysts asked: "Are the awards female (male) arbitrators issue more favorable toward female (male) grievants than they are toward male (female) grievants?" Based on their analysis of discharge and discipline field data, the answer to this question is "no."[26]

---

[22] Richard N. Block & Jack Stieber, "The Impact of Attorneys and Arbitrators on Arbitration Awards," 40 *Industrial and Labor Relations Review* 543, 549 (1987); Nelson & Uddin, "The Impact of Delay on Arbitrators' Decisions in Discharge Cases," 15; Scott & Shadoan, "The Effect of Gender on Arbitration Decisions," 433; Stieber, "How Representative Are Published Arbitration Decisions?" 183; Zirkel & Breslin, "Correlates of Grievance Arbitration Awards," 50.

[23] Ponak, "Discharge Arbitration and Reinstatement in the Province of Alberta," 42.

[24] Brian Bemmels, "The Effect of Grievants' Gender on Arbitrators' Decisions," 41 *Industrial and Labor Relations Review* 251, 259 (1988).

[25] Bemmels, "Attribution Theory and Discipline Arbitration," 556.

[26] Scott & Shadoan, "The Effect of Gender on Arbitration Decisions," 434.

Gender

The first grievant characteristic variable considered is the grievant's gender. As shown in the top and bottom panels of Table 3.9, the grievant's gender, generally, is not a significant factor in arbitral decision-making regardless of the type of discipline imposed. However, with regard to discipline grievances, a female grievant's chances of having her suspension revoked or having her reprimand rescinded were significantly 1.36 times higher than they were for a male grievant. With regard to discharge grievances, however, female and male grievants faced equal odds of prevailing.

These results show that the grievant's gender may play a role in the arbitrator's resolution of discipline cases. This is an original finding. But our results also show that the grievant's gender does not affect arbitral decision-making in discharge cases, affirming the findings of most of the literature's field studies.

Table 3.9 Arbitration Outcomes by Discipline and Grievant's Gender*
(N-size, row % and column % are the top, middle and bottom value, respectively)

Gender	Management Win	Union Win	Split Decision	Row Totals
Discipline				
Male	217 44.65[a] 80.07[1]	120 24.69[1] 72.29[1]	149 30.66[c] 80.11[1]	486 100.00 78.01[1]
Female	54 39.42 19.93	46 33.58 27.71	37 27.01 19.89	137 100.00 21.99
Column Totals	271 43.50[a] 100.00	166 26.65 100.00	186 29.86[c] 100.00	623 100.00 100.00
Chi-square (2) = 4.3169, p = 0.116				
Discharge				
Male	573 52.91[a] 76.30[1]	201 18.56[b] 73.09[1]	309 28.53[c] 76.11[1]	1,083 100.00 75.63[1]
Female	178 51.00[a] 23.70	74 21.20 26.91	97 27.79[c] 23.89	349 100.00 24.37
Column Totals	751 52.44[a] 100.00	275 19.20[b] 100.00	406 28.35[c] 100.00	1,432 100.00 100.00
Chi-square (2) = 1.1942, p = 0.550				

* The numeric index 1 indicates that the percentages in row 1 and row 2 are statistically different at the .05 level or lower. The alphabetic indexes a, b and c indicate that the percentages in column 1 and column 2, column 2 and column 3, and column 3 and column 1, respectively, are statistically different at the .05 level or lower.

Match

The match variable measures whether the gender of the arbitrator matches the gender of the grievant. Table 3.10 examines the relationship between match and award outcomes. Our statistical examination shows that gender match does not influence the arbitrator's decisional process. This result applies to both discipline and discharge cases, in support of kindred findings by Scott and Shadoan.[27]

Table 3.10 Arbitration Outcomes by Type of Discipline and Gender Match*
(N-size, row % and column % are the top, middle and bottom value, respectively)

Gender Match	Management Win	Union Win	Split Decision	Row Totals
		Discipline		
Arbitrator & Grievant Different Genders	78 41.05[a] 28.78[1]	54 28.42 32.53[1]	58 30.53 31.18[1]	190 100.00 30.50[1]
Arbitrator & Grievant Same Gender	193 44.57[a] 71.22	112 25.87 67.47	128 29.56[c] 68.82	433 100.00 69.50
Column Totals	271 43.50[a] 100.00	166 26.65 100.00	186 29.86[c] 100.00	623 100.00 100.00
Chi-square (2) = 0.7409, p = 0.690				
		Discharge		
Arbitrator & Grievant Different Genders	245 53.96[a] 32.62[1]	91 20.04 33.09[1]	118 25.99[c] 29.06[1]	454 100.00 31.70[1]
Arbitrator & Grievant Same Gender	506 51.74[a] 67.38	184 18.81[b] 66.91	288 29.45[c] 70.94	978 100.00 68.30
Column Totals	751 52.44[a] 100.00	275 19.20[b] 100.00	406 28.35[c] 100.00	1,432 100.00 100.00
Chi-square (2) = 1.8441, p = 0.398				

* The numeric index 1 indicates that the percentages in row 1 and row 2 are statistically different at the .05 level or lower. The alphabetic indexes a, b and c indicate that the percentages in column 1 and column 2, column 2 and column 3, and column 3 and column 1, respectively, are statistically different at the .05 level or lower.

[27] Scott & Shadoan, "The Effect of Gender on Arbitration Decisions," 434.

Tenure

Arbitration literature suggests that the length of a grievant's employment (i.e., tenure) is a mitigating factor in some, but not all, just cause cases.[28] *The Common Law of the Workplace* observes that the just cause principle entitles a disciplined or discharged employee to specific mitigations, one of which is based on the "employee's seniority."[29] The rationale is that, to be fair, the employee who has been a good and loyal worker over a span of several years and, who, because of long seniority, has more to lose, warrants differential treatment compared to the employee with short tenure.[30] Refer to Chapter 9 for a continued discussion of tenure and other mitigating factors in discharge cases.

It is surprising that so few empirical studies have examined the tenure/award outcome relationship in light of the importance the arbitration literature places on it. Only Ponak, Nelson and Uddin, and Jennings and Wolters considered this variable in their studies. Ponak found a correctly signed tenure/award outcome relationship although it was not statistically significant;[31] whereas, Nelson and Uddin found that the probability that a discharged employee will be returned to work significantly increases with tenure.[32] Jennings and Wolters found that tenure affects outcomes in the expected way for the very short-term (less than 2 years) and very long-term (11 years and over) employees, but not for intermediate-term employees.[33]

The tenure (i.e., whether the grievant had worked for the employer in question for more or fewer than 10 years) and award outcome relationship is arrayed in Table 3.11. These results do not support the inference that tenure is a determinant of arbitral decision-making

---

[28] *How Arbitration Works,* 15-68 to 15-70.

[29] *The Common Law of the Workplace: The Views of Arbitrators* (Washington, D.C.: Bureau of National Affairs, Theodore J. St. Antoine, ed., 2d ed. 2005), § 6.2.

[30] As we point out in Chapter 7, one of the Seven Tests of Just Cause is the extent to which the employer's discipline was reasonably related to the employee's length of service with the employer.

[31] Ponak, "Discharge Arbitration and Reinstatement in the Province of Alberta," 42.

[32] Nelson & Uddin, "The Impact of Delay on Arbitrators' Decisions in Discharge Cases," 15.

[33] Ken Jennings & Roger Wolters, "Discharge Cases Reconsidered," *The Arbitration Journal* (September 1976) 164, 165.

in either discipline or discharge cases. The insignificant chi-square tests in Table 3.11 result from the fact that award shares for short- and long-term employees are not statistically different by outcome category, except for the case of discharged short-term employees who were significantly more likely to be reinstated (21 percent) than are discharged long-term employees (16 percent)—contradicting expectations.

In summation, it appears that long-term employees are no more likely than short-term employees to prevail either totally or partially in arbitration. This conclusion contradicts most of what has been written about this subject in the literature.

Table 3.11 Arbitration Outcomes by Type of Discipline and Grievant's Tenure*
(N-size, row % and column % are the top, middle and bottom value, respectively)

Tenure	Management Win	Union Win	Split Decision	Row Totals
Discipline				
Fewer than 10 Years	157 44.35[a] 57.93[1]	94 26.55 56.63	103 29.10[c] 55.38	354 100.00 56.82[1]
10 Years or More	114 42.38[a] 42.07	72 26.77 43.37	83 30.86[c] 44.62	269 100.00 43.18
Column Totals	271 43.50[a] 100.00	166 26.65 100.00	186 29.86[c] 100.00	623 100.00 100.00
Chi-square (2) = 0.2975, p = 0.862				
Discharge				
Fewer than 10 Years	480 51.67[a] 63.91[1]	193 20.78[1b] 70.18[1]	256 27.56[c] 63.05[1]	929 100.00 64.87[1]
10 Years or More	271 53.88[a] 36.09	82 16.30[b] 29.82	150 29.82[c] 36.95	503 100.00 35.13
Column Totals	751 52.44[a] 100.00	275 19.20[b] 100.00	406 28.35[c] 100.00	1,432 100.00 100.00
Chi-square (2) = 4.2932, p = 0.117				

* The numeric index 1 indicates that the percentages in row 1 and row 2 are statistically different at the .05 level or lower. The alphabetic indexes a, b and c indicate that the percentages in column 1 and column 2, column 2 and column 3, and column 3 and column 1, respectively, are statistically different at the .05 level or lower.

Crime

In constructing our data set we coded whether the discharged and disciplined grievant had been charged with a crime in the criminal justice system for the conduct that formed the basis of the employer's disciplinary action. In Table 3.12, we analyze the relationship between our binary measure of "crime" and award outcome, by type of discipline imposed. This is the first empirical inquiry into whether crime and award outcomes are systematically related.

The top panel in Table 3.12 indicates that our sample included only six discipline cases that involved grievants against whom criminal charges had been filed. With such a small number of observations we are unable to test reliably whether there is an association between crime and outcomes in discipline cases. However, there were enough discharge cases involving alleged employee crime to test the null hypothesis that crime and award outcomes are independent. As suggested by the bottom panel's chi-square, we cannot reject this hypothesis at the .05 level of significance. Nevertheless, it is interesting to note that when the grievant has been charged with a crime, the objective data show that the odds the arbitrator would favor management's discharge action (insignificantly) increased by approximately 5 percentage points and the odds that the arbitrator would rule in favor of the union also (insignificantly) increased by approximately 5 percentage points. This pair of results can occur only if the chances of a split decision fall by 10 percentage points, which is precisely what happened, and significantly so.

Based on these results, a likely inference is that arbitrators view crime-related discharges as presenting an "either-or" award outcome. If the alleged conduct is established, it generally will be serious enough to sustain the discipline imposed. If it is not established, no discipline is warranted. Chapter 5 examines whether arbitrators apply a higher quantum of proof in cases where employees are charged with a crime.

Table 3.12 Arbitration Outcomes by Type of Discipline and Crime*
(N-size, row % and column % are the top, middle and bottom value, respectively)

Crime	Management Win	Union Win	Split Decision	Row Totals
		Discipline		
Employee Not Charged with a Crime	268 43.44^{a} 98.89^{1}	163 26.42 98.19^{1}	186 30.15^{c} 100.00^{1}	617 100.00 99.04^{1}
Employee Charged with a Crime	3 50.00 1.11	3 50.00 1.81	0 0.00 0.00	6 100.00 0.96
Column Totals	271 43.50^{a} 100.00	166 26.65 100.00	186 29.86^{c} 100.00	623 100.00 100.00
Chi-square (2) = 3.1078, p = 0.211				
		Discharge		
Employee Not Charged with a Crime	699 52.13^{a} 93.08^{1}	253 18.87^{b} 92.00^{1b}	389 29.01^{1c} 95.81^{1}	1,341 100.00 93.65^{1}
Employee Charged with a Crime	52 57.14^{a} 6.92	22 24.18 8.00^{b}	17 18.68^{c} 4.19	91 100.00 6.35
Column Totals	751 52.44^{a} 100.00	275 19.20^{b} 100.00	406 28.35^{c} 100.00	1,432 100.00 100.00
Chi-square (2) = 4.8654, p = 0.088				

* The numeric index 1 indicates that the percentages in row 1 and row 2 are statistically different at the .05 level or lower. The alphabetic indexes a, b and c indicate that the percentages in column 1 and column 2, column 2 and column 3, and column 3 and column 1, respectively, are statistically different at the .05 level or lower.

Last Chance Agreements

A last chance agreement is a contract between the employer and the grievant and/or the grievant's union in which the employer agrees to reinstate a discharged grievant on the condition that this is the grievant's "last chance" to work up to expectations. Such an employee-specific contract expressly grants to the employer the discretion to discharge the employee for a subsequent offense and, further, the contract may state or be interpreted to state that any subsequent discipline is not arbitrable.[34] Accordingly, if an employee is subsequently discharged for violating a last chance agreement and the discharge is challenged in arbitration, the employer only needs to prove that the alleged offense occurred and that there was no reasonable basis for its occurrence. Critically, the employer need not prove "just cause," as prescribed by the collective bargaining agreement.

Based on the foregoing, it is conventionally held in labor arbitration that "an arbitrator must abide by the terms of a last-chance agreement."[35] Based on assertions like this, we hypothesize that last chance agreements and award outcomes are significantly related. More specifically, since the last chance agreement supplants the more rigorous standard of "just cause" as the decisional criterion, we anticipate that if the employer proved that the discharged grievant violated a last chance agreement then the arbitrator's award would favor a management victory. However, when the alleged breach was not proven, the award would favor the union. These combined anticipations imply that "split decisions" should be a rare occurrence in last chance cases.

The results in Table 3.13 partially support our hypotheses. First, the table's top panel shows that last chance disciplines were the issue in only 4 of the 623 cases making up our discipline data set. This finding is consistent with the foregoing description that last chance agreements are generally reached to resolve discharge cases.

Second, with respect to discharge cases, the bottom panel of Table 3.13 shows a significant association between last chance agreements and award outcomes. As hypothesized, if a grievant was working under a last chance agreement when discharged, the odds of a management victory significantly increased by approximately 22 percentage points from 49.92 percent to 72.22 percent. However, the objective data show that the chances of a union win (9.88 percent) were lower than the chances of a split decision (17.90 percent), conditional on a last chance agreement, which contradicts our expectations.[36] Interestingly,

---

[34] *Common Law of the Workplace*, § 6.3.

[35] *Id.*

[36] Namely, that split decisions should be a rare occurrence in last chance cases.

this finding implies that some arbitrators occasionally use “just cause” as opposed to “breach” standards to analyze the merits of last chance cases.[37]

[37] Even though the referenced difference between the union-win and split decision percentages is not statistically significant, this inference remains valid.

Table 3.13 Arbitration Outcomes by Type of Discipline and Last Chance Agreements*

(N-size, row % and column % are the top, middle and bottom value, respectively)

Last Chance Agreements	Management Win	Union Win	Split Decision	Row Totals
Discipline				
Employee Not Working Under Last Chance Agreement	271 43.78[a] 100.00[1]	164 26.49 98.80[1]	184 29.73[c] 98.92[1]	619 100.00 99.36[1]
Employee Working Under Last Chance Agreement	0 0.00 0.00	2 50.00 1.20	2 50.00 1.08	4 100.00 0.64
Column Totals	271 43.50[a] 100.00	166 26.65 100.00	186 29.86[c] 100.00	623 100.00 100.00
Chi-square (2) = 3.1225, p = 0.210				
Discharge				
Employee Not Working Under Last Chance Agreement	634 49.92[1a] 84.42[1a]	259 20.39[1b] 94.18[1]	377 29.69[1c] 92.86[1c]	1,270 100.00 88.69[1]
Employee Working Under Last Chance Agreement	117 72.22[a] 15.58[a]	16 9.88 5.82	29 17.90[c] 7.14[c]	162 100.00 11.31
Column Totals	751 52.44[a] 100.00	275 19.20[b] 100.00	406 28.35[c] 100.00	1,432 100.00 100.00
Chi-square (2) = 28.9366, p = 0.000				

* The numeric index 1 indicates that the percentages in row 1 and row 2 are statistically different at the .05 level or lower. The alphabetic indexes a, b and c indicate that the percentages in column 1 and column 2, column 2 and column 3, and column 3 and column 1, respectively, are statistically different at the .05 level or lower.

In Chapter 7, we further examine the relationship between award outcomes conditional on the presence or absence of a last chance agreement using *combined* discharge and discipline data, and analyze last chance award outcomes by offense categories.

Case Characteristics

With reference to Figure 3.1, we identified six variables that relate to various aspects of the grievant's case that may affect arbitration outcomes. These variables included sector, number of offenses, delay, Seven Tests of Just Cause, attorney representation and quantum of proof. Only three of these variables— sector, delay and attorney representation—have previously received the attention of empirical analysts.

Sector

With respect to the sector of case origin (public or private), Mesch argued that it should affect the distribution of arbitration awards because of inter-sector variance in legal, procedural, political and economic circumstances.[38] Her analysis of merged disciplinary (i.e., discharge, suspension and reprimand) and non-disciplinary cases suggests that the arbitration outcomes reached in the public sector are systematically different from those reached in the private sector, with public sector unions winning a larger share of their cases than private sector unions.[39] However, her analysis of the disciplinary cases only yielded insignificant public-private differences across outcome categories.[40] Similarly, the sector variable was insignificant in disciplinary studies by Ponak,[41] Zirkel and Breslin,[42] Block and Stieber,[43] and Nelson and Uddin.[44]

---

[38] Debra J. Mesch, "Grievance Arbitration in the Public Sector: A Conceptual Framework and Empirical Analysis of Public and Private Sector Cases," 15 *Review of Public Personnel Administration* 22, 22-25 (1995).

[39] *Id.* at 29.

[40] *Id.*

[41] Ponak, "Discharge Arbitration and Reinstatement in the Province of Alberta," 44.

[42] Zirkel & Breslin, "Correlates of Grievance Arbitration Awards," 50.

[43] Block & Stieber, "The Impact of Attorneys and Arbitrators on Arbitration Awards," 549.

[44] Nelson & Uddin, "The Impact of Delay on Arbitrators' Decisions in Discharge Cases," 15.

With regard to discipline cases, the top panel in Table 3.14 shows that arbitration outcomes were essentially the same, regardless of sector. However, in discharge cases, shown in the bottom panel, the distribution of arbitration outcomes reached in the public and private sectors was significantly different. Both public and private sector managers won a significantly larger percent of discharge cases than did their union counterparts (i.e., 56.17 percent vs. 16.45 percent, and 48.83 percent vs. 21.87 percent, respectively). However, within the union win category, arbitrators ruled in favor of private sector unions 57.82 percent of the time and public sector unions 42.18 percent of the time, a difference that is significant at the .05 level or lower.

Table 3.14 <u>Arbitration Outcomes by Type of Discipline and Sector</u>*
(N-size, row % and column % are the top, middle and bottom value, respectively)

Sector	Management Win	Union Win	Split Decision	Row Totals
		Discipline		
Public	223 43.47[a] 82.29[1]	136 26.51 81.93[1]	154 30.02[c] 82.80[1]	513 100.00 82.34[1]
Private	48 43.64[a] 17.71	30 27.27 18.07	32 29.09 17.20	110 100.00 17.66
Column Totals	271 43.50[a] 100.00	166 26.65 100.00	186 29.86[c] 100.00	623 100.00 100.00
Chi-square (2) = 0.0465, p = 0.977				
		Discharge		
Public	396 56.17[1a] 52.73[a]	116 16.45[1b] 42.18[1]	193 27.38[c] 47.54	705 100.00 49.23
Private	355 48.83[a] 47.27[a]	159 21.87[b] 57.82	213 29.30[c] 52.46	727 100.00 50.77
Column Totals	751 52.44[a] 100.00	275 19.20[b] 100.00	406 28.35[c] 100.00	1,432 100.00 100.00
Chi-square (2) = 9.6115, p = 0.008				

* The numeric index 1 indicates that the percentages in row 1 and row 2 are statistically different at the .05 level or lower. The alphabetic indexes a, b and c indicate that the percentages in column 1 and column 2, column 2 and column 3, and column 3 and column 1, respectively, are statistically different at the .05 level or lower.

Based on the foregoing, we conclude that while discharge outcomes differ by sector, discipline outcomes do not. In addition, with respect to discharge cases, public sector managers won a significantly larger share of discharge cases than did their private sector counterparts. Explaining these results is a subject for future research.

Number of Offenses

Whether the grievant is alleged to have committed more than one work-related offense may influence how the arbitrator decides the case. We hypothesize that the more offenses alleged, the more meritorious the employer's overall case, and the more likely that one or more of the specifically alleged offenses would be established at the arbitration hearing. It would follow, therefore, if the grievant was charged with committing more than one offense, the likelihood the arbitrator's award would favor management would increase, the likelihood the arbitrator would rule for the union would decrease, and the likelihood that the arbitrator would reach a split decision would increase. To the best of our knowledge this variable has never been considered in earlier studies of disciplinary arbitration.

The chi-square tests in Table 3.15 suggest that the number of offenses and arbitration outcomes are significantly related in the arbitration of both discipline and discharge cases. With respect to discipline cases analyzed in the top panel of Table 3.15, the probability the union would prevail in arbitration when only one offense was alleged was 28.81 percent—a value that significantly decreased to 11.54 percent when more than one offense was alleged, as hypothesized. Also, in line with our hypothesis, the corresponding probability of a split decision significantly increased from 26.24 percent to 55.13 percent. However, the probability of a management win decreased from 44.95 percent to 33.33 percent, contrary to our expectations—although this difference is not significant.

Interestingly, the latter anomaly carried over to discharge cases, as presented in the bottom panel of Table 3.15. As we change from one to more than one alleged offense, the probability of a management win increased from 51.34 percent to 57.92 percent, but this increase is insignificant. However, as predicted, the probability of a union win significantly fell from 20.64 percent to 12.08 percent, and the probability of a split decision insignificantly increased from 28.02 percent to 30.00 percent.

Table 3.15 <u>Arbitration Outcomes by Type of Discipline and Number of Offenses</u>*

(N-size, row % and column % are the top, middle and bottom value, respectively)

Number of Offenses	Management Win	Union Win	Split Decision	Row Totals
Discipline				
One	245 44.95[a] 90.41[1]	157 28.81[1] 94.58[1b]	143 26.24[1c] 76.88[1c]	545 100.00 87.48[1]
More than One	26 33.33[a] 9.59	9 11.54[b] 5.42[b]	43 55.13[c] 23.12[c]	78 100.00 12.52
Column Totals	271 43.50[a] 100.00	166 26.65 100.00	186 29.86[c] 100.00	623 100.00 100.00
Chi-square (2) = 28.8301, p = 0.000				
Discharge				
One	612 51.34[a] 81.49[1a]	246 20.64[1b] 89.45[1b]	334 28.02[c] 82.27[1]	1,192 100.00 83.24[1]
More than One	139 57.92[a] 18.51[a]	29 12.08[b] 10.55[b]	72 30.00[c] 17.73	240 100.00 16.76
Column Totals	751 52.44[a] 100.00	275 19.20[b] 100.00	406 28.35[c] 100.00	1,432 100.00 100.00
Chi-square (2) = 9.5350, p = 0.009				

* The numeric index 1 indicates that the percentages in row 1 and row 2 are statistically different at the .05 level or lower. The alphabetic indexes a, b and c indicate that the percentages in column 1 and column 2, column 2 and column 3, and column 3 and column 1, respectively, are statistically different at the .05 level or lower.

Our combined discipline and discharge results suggest that the union's prospects of totally prevailing are significantly reduced if the grievant allegedly committed more than one offense. However, since the union won a significant, albeit small, share of alleged multiple offense discipline (12 percent) and discharge (12 percent) cases, the employer is cautioned against *building* a case using evidence that cannot support its theory of multiple claims. Further, the fact that a significantly larger share of split decisions was reached in multiple claim discipline cases (55 percent) as compared to single offense discipline cases (26 percent) may suggest that employers may have combined weak and strong grounds to support their discipline cases.

Delay

We define "delay" as the time elapsed between the date of the employer's discharge decision and the date of the arbitrator's award. Our motivation for including this factor in examining *why* arbitrators reach the decisions they issue is that long delays may have consequences that could affect arbitral decision-making. A more complete examination of these consequences and their hypothesized effect on award outcomes is taken up in Chapter 7. Here, we limit analysis to Table 3.16, which displays mean numbers of lapsed days by award outcome category. The mean number of lapsed days for management win, union win and split decision outcomes was approximately 284, 268 and 264, respectively. But none of these mean differences is significant—a finding that reinforces Chapter 7's general conclusion that delay and award outcomes are independent.

Table 3.16 <u>Discharge Case Outcomes and Delay</u>

Delay	Management Win	Union Win	Split Decision	Totals
Number of Cases	751	275	406	1,432
Days elapsed from discipline to decision	283.54	267.71	263.79	274.90

Seven Tests of Just Cause

One study found that no less than 92 percent of collective bargaining agreements expressly state that the disciplinary actions taken by employers must be for "just cause" or, simply, "cause."[45] In addition, arbitrators and the courts have found this requirement to be implicit in collective bargaining agreements that do not explicitly include a just cause provision.[46] Still further, just cause provisions in union contracts generally do not explicitly define this term, leaving that task to arbitration decision-making, law, legal scholars and commentators. Although innumerable conferences, presentations at NAA and other professional meetings and books and journal articles have dealt with the meaning of just cause, no definition of just cause is more widely recognized than that first articulated by Arbitrator Carroll R. Daugherty in his 1964 *Grief Bros. Cooperage Corp.* award.[47] Daugherty designed a rule that, if violated, will signal the arbitrator that the employer's disciplinary action lacked just cause. Daugherty's rule consists of "Seven Tests," posed as seven questions, and a "no" answer to any one question "normally signifies that just and proper cause does not exist."[48] Daugherty's seven questions and further analysis of the Seven Tests can be found in Chapter 6.

On a case-by-case basis, we coded whether the arbitrator relied on the Seven Tests to determine whether the employer's disciplinary action was for just cause. We hypothesize that when the Seven Tests were used, the chances that management would succeed in proving just cause would decrease. That is, when Daugherty's tests are applied, a "no" answer to any one of his questions means, by definition, that the employer's disciplinary action *lacked* just cause. Thus, compared to cases where Daugherty's Seven Tests are not strictly applied, the odds of an employer victory should decline.

---

[45] BNA Editorial Staff, *Basic Patterns in Union Contracts*, (Washington, D.C.: Bureau of National Affairs, Inc., 14th ed., 1995), 7.

[46] See, e.g., SPIC Properties, Inc. v. International Association of Machinists & Aerospace Workers, District Lodge 94, 103 F. 3d 923 (9th Cir. 1996).

[47] Grief Bros. Cooperage Corp., 42 LA 555 (Daugherty 1964); Enterprise Wheel Co., 46 LA 359 (Daugherty 1966).

[48] Grief Bros. Cooperage Corp., 42 LA 555, 557.

The empirical results in Tables 3.17(a) and 3.17(b) test this hypothesis. Table 3.17(a) was constructed using all of our 2,055 discharge and discipline awards. Generally speaking, the chi-square tests associated with both of Table 3.17(a)'s panels suggest a significant association between the Seven Tests and arbitration outcomes. However, we see that arbitral use of the Seven Tests did not significantly affect the odds of a management win outcome in either discipline or discharge cases. That is, regarding discipline and discharge cases, respectively, the differences between 44.07 percent and 37.93 percent, and between 51.90 percent and 56.47 percent, are not significant at a .05 level or lower. Curiously, based on Table 3.17(a), we can confidently conclude that the odds the arbitrator will issue a split decision were affected by reliance on the Seven Tests for determining just cause. Use of the Seven Tests significantly increased the odds of a split decision in matters of discipline and significantly reduced the odds of a split decision in discharge cases.

Upon a closer examination of our data, we discovered that one arbitrator in our sample, whom we refer to as Arbitrator A, issued 93 discharge and discipline awards, 54.8 percent (or 51) of which relied on the Seven Tests. In total, Arbitrator A issued 22.4 percent of Table 3.17(a)'s 228 decisions in which the Seven Tests were used. To discern whether Arbitrator A's disproportionate representation in our analysis skewed Table 3.17(a)'s results, we reexamined our Seven Tests hypothesis in Table 3.17(b), after having deleted Arbitrator A's awards from the analysis. The chi-square tests in Table 3.17(b) show that after deleting Arbitrator A's awards from consideration, the arbitrator's use or non-use of the Seven Tests and arbitration outcomes were statistically independent. Otherwise, the estimated magnitudes and patterns of the results in Table 3.17(b) are indistinguishable, for all practical purposes, from those discussed in regard to Table 3.17(a).

In conclusion, the foregoing results do not support our specific hypothesis that the odds of a management win should decline in the face of the Seven Tests. In addition, the fraction of both discharge and discipline cases that relied on the Daugherty rubric for determining just cause is surprisingly low given the eminent status the Seven Tests rule enjoys in arbitration jurisprudential commentary. Table 3.17(a) shows that the Seven Tests were used in 9.31 percent of discipline cases and 11.87 percent of discharge cases. Similarly, Table 3.17(b) shows that the Seven Tests were used in 8.29 percent of discipline cases and

9.32 percent of discharge cases. Both sets of results exhibit Seven Tests use rates that are so small that we must also conclude that statements of arbitral use of Daugherty's Seven Tests as *the* definition of just cause are wildly exaggerated.

Table 3.17(a) Arbitration Outcomes by Type of Discipline and Seven Tests of Just Cause (Including Arbitrator A)*

(N-size, row % and column % are the top, middle and bottom value, respectively)

Arbitrator Invoked the Seven Tests	Management Win	Union Win	Split Decision	Row Totals
Discipline				
No	249 44.07[a] 91.88[1]	155 27.43 93.37[1b]	161 28.50[1c] 86.56[1]	565 100.00 90.69[1]
Yes	22 37.93 8.12	11 18.97[b] 6.63[b]	25 43.10 13.44	58 100.00 9.31
Column Totals	271 43.50[a] 100.00	166 26.65 100.00	186 29.86[c] 100.00	623 100.00 100.00
Chi-square (2) = 5.6310, p = 0.060				
Discharge				
No	655 51.90[a] 87.22[1]	236 18.70[b] 85.82[1b]	371 29.40[1c] 91.38[1c]	1,262 100.00 88.13[1]
Yes	96 56.47[a] 12.78	39 22.94 14.18[b]	35 20.59[c] 8.62[c]	170 100.00 11.87
Column Totals	751 52.44[a] 100.00	275 19.20[b] 100.00	406 28.35[c] 100.00	1,432 100.00 100.00
Chi-square (2) = 6.1003, p = 0.047				

* The numeric index 1 indicates that the percentages in row 1 and row 2 are statistically different at the .05 level or lower. The alphabetic indexes a, b and c indicate that the percentages in column 1 and column 2, column 2 and column 3, and column 3 and column 1, respectively, are statistically different at the .05 level or lower.

Table 3.17(b) Arbitration Outcomes by Type of Discipline and Seven Tests of Just Cause (Excluding Arbitrator A)*

(N-size, row % and column % are the top, middle and bottom value, respectively)

Arbitrator Invoked the Seven Tests	Management Win	Union Win	Split Decision	Row Totals
Discipline				
No	244 44.12[a] 93.13[1]	151 27.31 93.21[1]	158 28.57[1c] 88.27[1]	553 100.00 91.71[1]
Yes	18 36.00 6.87	11 22.00 6.79	21 42.00 11.73	50 100.00 8.29
Column Totals	262 43.45[a] 100.00	162 26.87 100.00	179 29.68[c] 100.00	603 100.00 100.00
Chi-square (2) = 3.9623, p = 0.138				
Discharge				
No	640 51.82[a] 90.01[1]	229 18.54[b] 89.45[1]	366 29.64[c] 92.66[1]	1,235 100.00 90.68[1]
Yes	71 55.91[a] 9.99	27 21.26 10.55	29 22.83[c] 7.34	127 100.00 9.32
Column Totals	711 52.20[a] 100.00	256 18.80[b] 100.00	395 29.00[c] 100.00	1,362 100.00 100.00
Chi-square (2) = 2.6569, p = 0.265				

* The numeric index 1 indicates that the percentages in row 1 and row 2 are statistically different at the .05 level or lower. The alphabetic indexes a, b and c indicate that the percentages in column 1 and column 2, column 2 and column 3, and column 3 and column 1, respectively, are statistically different at the .05 level or lower.

Legal Representation

We next inquire into the possibility that the parties use attorneys in arbitration because they believe their chances of receiving a favorable award are improved—a compelling supposition. Lawyers are schooled in preparing and presenting cases, pointing out contradictory testimony, and drafting post-hearing briefs that cast their theory and facts of the case in a most favorable light.

The relationship between attorney representation and award outcomes has been examined in earlier studies. Block and Stieber reported that awards in discharge cases are more favorable to employers when they are represented by an attorney, compared to cases when neither party uses an attorney, and they fare best when the union is not attorney-represented. In parallel fashion, awards favor unions when they are represented by an attorney compared to cases when neither party is represented by a lawyer, and unions do best when they alone are attorney-represented. Last, Block and Stieber found that awards in cases in which both sides are attorney-represented are not significantly different from awards in cases where neither side is represented by an attorney.[49] In contrast, Zirkel and Breslin found that legal representation does not significantly affect outcomes whether or not the other side is represented by legal counsel.[50] Similarly, Nelson and Uddin did not find a significant difference between employer-only represented cases and union-only represented cases *versus* cases in which neither or both parties has legal representation.[51] Tables 3.18(a) and 3.18(b) address whether legal representation affects arbitral decision-making in discipline and discharge cases, respectively. These tabulations disclose a clear divide between discipline and discharge cases with respect to legal representation. The parties' retention of legal advocates and award outcomes were not at all associated in cases involving discipline; whereas, legal representation significantly affected the decisions reached by arbitrators when the issue in dispute involved employee discharge.

---

[49] Block & Stieber, "The Impact of Attorneys and Arbitrators on Arbitration Awards," 548.

[50] Zirkel & Breslin, "Correlates of Grievance Arbitration Awards," 52.

[51] Nelson & Uddin, "The Impact of Delay on Arbitrators' Decisions in Discharge Cases," 16.

Table 3.18(a) Arbitration Outcomes in Discipline Cases by Legal Representation*

(N-size, row % and column % are the top, middle and bottom value, respectively)

Legal Representation	Management Win	Union Win	Split Decision	Row Totals
		Discipline		
Neither	78 43.82[a] 28.78	47 26.40 28.31	53 29.78[c] 28.49	178 100.00 28.57
Both	79 38.35 29.15[2]	59 28.64 35.54[2]	68 33.01 36.56[2]	206 100.00 33.07[2]
Only Union	29 48.33[a] 10.70[3]	13 21.67 7.83[3]	18 30.00 9.68[3]	60 100.00 9.63[3]
Only Employer	85 47.49[a] 31.37	47 26.26 28.31	47 26.26[c] 25.27	179 100.00 28.73
Column Totals	271 43.50[a] 100.00	166 26.65 100.00	186 29.86[c] 100.00	623 100.00 100.00

Chi-square (6) = 4.5802, p = 0.599

* The numeric indexes 1, 2, 3 and 4 indicate that the percentages in row 1 and row 2, row 2 and row 3, row 3 and row 4, and row 4 and row 1, respectively, are statistically different at the .05 level or lower. The alphabetic indexes a, b and c indicate that the percentages in column 1 and column 2, column 2 and column 3, and column 3 and column 1, respectively, are statistically different at the .05 level or lower.

The results in Table 3.18(b) indicate that awards in discharge cases were most likely to favor management when only the employer was represented by an attorney and the union was not (62.13 percent vs. 14.44 percent), and the decisions reached by arbitrators were least likely to favor management when only the union was represented by an attorney and the employer was not (42.86 percent vs. 27.78 percent). When neither or both parties were represented by legal counsel, the likelihood that management would receive a favorable award was statistically indistinguishable at about 50 percent, and the likelihood that the union would receive a favorable award was about 18 percent and 21 percent, respectively—a difference that is also insignificant.

The above-reported results show that attorney representation can affect the awards reached by arbitrators in discharge cases, but not cases of discipline. Paralleling the published results of Block and Stieber, we found the chances that the union or employer would prevail were unaffected in discharge arbitration when both or neither party used legal counsel, and the chances that the union or employer would prevail were greatest when one, but not the other, retained a lawyer advocate.

Table 3.18(b) Arbitration Outcomes in Discharge Cases by Legal Representation*

(N-size, row % and column % are the top, middle and bottom value, respectively)

Legal Representation	Management Win	Union Win	Split Decision	Row Totals
Neither	143 50.35[a] 19.04[1]	50 17.61[b] 18.18[1]	91 32.04[c] 22.41[1]	284 100.00 19.83[1]
Both	326 49.77[a] 43.41[2]	137 20.92[b] 49.82[2]	192 29.31[c] 47.29[2]	655 100.00 45.74[2]
Only Union	54 42.86[3a] 7.19[3a]	35 27.78[3] 12.73	37 29.37 9.11[3]	126 100.00 8.80[3]
Only Employer	228 62.13[4a] 30.36[4a]	53 14.44[b] 19.27	86 23.43[4c] 21.18[c]	367 100.00 25.63[4]
Column Totals	751 52.44[a] 100.00	275 19.20[b] 100.00	406 28.35[c] 100.00	1,432 100.00 100.00

Chi-square (6) = 25.1867, p = 0.000

* The numeric indexes 1, 2, 3 and 4 indicate that the percentages in row 1 and row 2, row 2 and row 3, row 3 and row 4, and row 4 and row 1, respectively, are statistically different at the .05 level or lower. The alphabetic indexes a, b and c indicate that the percentages in column 1 and column 2, column 2 and column 3, and column 3 and column 1, respectively, are statistically different at the .05 level or lower.

Quantum of Proof

A doctrine that enjoys wide acceptance among arbitrators is that in discipline and discharge cases, it is the employer who bears the burden of proving "just cause."[52] However, less well accepted is the standard or quantum of proof that is most applicable in disciplinary cases. As we discuss more fully in Chapter 5, some arbitrators apply the "preponderance of evidence" standard where the record of evidence presented by one party is, on balance, found to be more persuasive than that presented by the other party. Other arbitrators use the higher intermediate standard of "clear and convincing evidence," while still others employ the highest standard of "beyond a reasonable doubt" where one party's record evidence is utterly convincing and superior to that of the other party's.[53]

The quantum standard referenced by a single arbitrator in a specific case may not account for the decision reached by the arbitrator in that case. However, when a large number of arbitrators and discipline or discharge cases are considered, it stands to reason that when arbitrators apply higher quantum standards, the likelihood that arbitrators will reach a decision that fully supports the employers' disciplinary action will be lower. We collected data designed to test this proposition—the first published test of this hypothesis. Specifically, we coded the applicable quantum standard in each award in our data set, including awards where no specific standard was stated.

Based on casual observation and personal experience as arbitrators, we know that arbitrators do not always articulate in their awards the quantum of proof they applied. This does not mean that the arbitrator did not have in mind a specific standard to determine the issue in favor of one party over the other. Also, it does not mean that the three quantum levels discussed in the literature are somehow determinative of the issue or fact under consideration—other factors may control. For example, the individual arbitrator whose philosophy is that workers have a "right to a job," may not sustain an employer's discharge

[52] *Common Law of the Workplace*, § 6.9 Comment a; Marvin Hill, Jr. & Anthony V. Sinicropi, *Evidence in Arbitration* (Washington, D.C.: Bureau of National Affairs, 1980), 13; *How Arbitration Works*, 423; Koven & Smith, *Just Cause: The Seven Tests*, 237-241.

[53] Hill & Sinicropi, *Evidence in Arbitration*, 10-13.

decision even though the record evidence supports that level of discipline without any question or doubt.

Tables 3.19(a) and 3.19(b) show the relationship between articulated and non-articulated quantum of proof levels and award outcomes. As we show below, neither our discipline nor discharge data manifested a systematic relationship between the quantum categories and the arbitral outcome categories—a finding that will not come as a surprise to many. For years it has been argued that the entire matter of quantum of proof is "unsettled,"[54]or amounts to little more than "playing games with words"[55] or is a "distracting legalism"[56] in labor arbitration. Our results tend to support this perspective.

Perusal of Table 3.19(a) shows: (1) arbitrators did not state a specific quantum standard in 83.79 percent of discipline cases; (2) arbitration opinions that did not specify a standard of proof significantly favored management wins over both union wins and split decisions; and (3) when quantum standards were expressly stated in discipline cases, their articulation had an insignificant effect on outcomes.

---

[54] *How Arbitration Works*, 15-24.

[55] Remarks of David Feller, "Admissibility of Evidence," Arbitration 1982: Conduct of the Hearing, *Proceedings of the 35th Annual Meeting of the National Academy of Arbitrators* (Washington, D.C.: Bureau of National Affairs, James C. Stern & Barbara D. Dennis, eds., 1983), 136.

[56] *Common Law of the Workplace*, § 6.10 Comment a.

Table 3.19(a) Arbitration Outcomes in Discipline Cases by Quantum of Proof*
(N-size, row % and column % are the top, middle and bottom value, respectively)

Quantum of Proof	Management Win	Union Win	Split Decision	Row Totals
Preponderance of the Evidence	21 36.21 7.75	18 31.03 10.84	19 32.76 10.22	58 100.00 9.31[1]
Clear and Convincing Evidence	11 33.33 4.06	12 36.36 7.23[2]	10 30.30 5.38[2]	33 100.00 5.30[2]
Evidence Beyond a Reasonable Doubt	4 40.00 1.48[3]	4 40.00 2.41[3]	2 20.00 1.08[3]	10 100.00 1.61[3]
No Specific Standard Articulated	235 45.02[a] 86.72[4a]	132 25.29 79.52[4]	155 29.69[c] 83.33[4]	522 100.00 83.79[4]
Column Totals	271 43.50[a] 100.00	166 26.65 100.00	186 29.86[c] 100.00	623 100.00 100.00

Chi-square (6) = 4.9140, p = 0.555

* The numeric indexes 1, 2, 3 and 4 indicate that the percentages in row 1 and row 2, row 2 and row 3, row 3 and row 4, and row 4 and row 1, respectively, are statistically different at the .05 level or lower. The alphabetic indexes a, b and c indicate that the percentages in column 1 and column 2, column 2 and column 3, and column 3 and column 1, respectively, are statistically different at the .05 level or lower.

Table 3.19(b) Arbitration Outcomes in Discharge Cases by Quantum of Proof*
(N-size, row % and column % are the top, middle and bottom value, respectively)

Quantum of Proof	Management Win	Union Win	Split Decision	Row Totals
Preponderance of the Evidence	73 51.41[a] 9.72[a]	41 28.87 14.91[b]	28 19.72[1c] 6.90[1]	142 100.00 9.92
Clear and Convincing Evidence	71 40.80[a] 9.45[2a]	48 27.59 17.45[2]	55 31.61 13.55[2c]	174 100.00 12.15[2]
Evidence Beyond a Reasonable Doubt	12 41.38 1.60[3a]	12 41.38[3] 4.36[3b]	5 17.24 1.23[3]	29 100.00 2.03[3]
No Specific Standard Articulated	595 54.74[a] 79.23[4a]	174 16.01[4b] 63.27[4b]	318 29.25[4c] 78.33[4]	1,087 100.00 75.91[4]
Column Totals	751 52.44[a] 100.00	275 19.20[b] 100.00	406 28.35[c] 100.00	1,432 100.00 100.00

Chi-square (6) = 38.7403, p = 0.000
* The numeric indexes 1, 2, 3 and 4 indicate that the percentages in row 1 and row 2, row 2 and row 3, row 3 and row 4, and row 4 and row 1, respectively, are statistically different at the .05 level or lower. The alphabetic indexes a, b and c indicate that the percentages in column 1 and column 2, column 2 and column 3, and column 3 and column 1, respectively, are statistically different at the .05 level or lower.

As reflected in Table 3.19(b), among the discharge awards in our data base, 75.91 percent made no reference to an applicable standard of proof and, in these instances, the awards significantly favored management win outcomes over both union-win and split decision outcomes. With respect to awards that did identify a standard of proof, note that as the standard of proof increased from "preponderance of the evidence" to "clear and convincing evidence" and to proof "beyond a reasonable doubt," the percent of arbitrator awards sustaining the employer's decision to discharge decreased from 51.41 percent to 40.80 percent and to 41.38 percent, respectively, but these percentage differences are not statistically significant.

Further, note that as the articulated standard increased from "preponderance of the evidence" to "clear and convincing evidence," the share of split decisions increased significantly, but the share of management win awards remained significantly greater than the share of union win awards (40.80 percent *versus* 27.59 percent). Still further, note that as the articulated standard increased from "clear and convincing" evidence to proof "beyond a reasonable doubt," the shares of management win and union win outcomes were identical, at 41.38 percent. Like our findings in discipline cases, none of our discharge results suggest that there is any currency to the hypothesis that the odds of a management win outcome will vary inversely to the quantum level articulated in the arbitration award's opinion.

Summary

How do arbitrators rule on discharge and discipline cases? Our analysis establishes that management won the largest share of discharge and discipline cases, and that arbitrators did not shy away from issuing split decisions, which eclipsed union wins as a share of arbitration outcomes. In round numbers, management's disciplinary actions were fully sustained 50 percent of the time, followed by 29 percent of arbitral decisions that reduced the disciplinary penalty without reversing it (i.e., split decisions), and the remaining 21 percent of awards ordered management to reinstate the grievant with full back pay, accrued benefits and seniority in discharge and suspension cases and to expunge the grievant's personnel file of the oral or written warning in reprimand cases (i.e., union win).

The union's chances of fully prevailing in arbitration were greatest in reprimand cases (40.19 percent), followed by suspension cases (23.84 percent) and discharge cases (19.20 percent). Management's chances of totally winning were greatest in discharge cases (52.44 percent), followed by suspension cases (43.99 percent) and reprimand cases (41.12 percent). With respect to reprimand cases, our analysis suggests that the 40.19 percent union win rate and the 41.12 percent management win rate are not statistically different, meaning that each side stood an equal chance of prevailing in such cases. However, the differences in the management and union win rates are significantly large with respect to discharge and suspension cases, which prompted us to conclude that discharge cases ought to be analyzed separately and apart from discipline cases because it appears as though arbitrators assigned different weights to the evidence and other factors that influence the decisions they ultimately reach in these two types of cases.

Why do arbitrators reach these decisional outcomes? To answer this question, we examined the relationship between award outcomes and sets of arbitrator, grievant and case characteristics. Our findings are summarized below.

Arbitrator Characteristics

1. *Gender*: We discovered that the arbitrator's gender bore no relationship to outcomes in discipline cases. However, with regard to discharge cases, the percent of management win awards that female arbitrators issued exceeded that of male arbitrators—60.17 percent *versus* 51.88 percent; and male arbitrators issued relatively more split decisions that did their female counterparts—29.81 percent to 21.16 percent. These results are distinctive additions to the empirical literature on arbitration.

2. *Age*: The arbitrator's age was not systematically related to award outcomes, regardless of the type of discipline imposed by the employer. Previous studies suggested that *both* younger and older arbitrators are more likely to rule in the grievant's favor. However, we found whether old or young, the odds of a grievant victory in arbitration were unaffected by the arbitrator's age.

3. *Caseload*: In discipline cases, arbitrators with the heaviest caseloads tended to issue management win outcomes, and arbitrators with the lightest caseloads tended to favor unions. In discharge cases, the busiest arbitrators issue split decisions, while arbitrators with the lightest caseloads tended to issue awards that favored management and the union in statistically indistinguishable shares. These results are new additions to the arbitration literature.

4. *Education:* Generally, the arbitrator's level of educational attainment and award outcomes were not significantly related in disciplinary cases, but this relationship was significant in regard to discharge cases. Specifically, arbitrators with master's, law and doctorate degrees were significantly more likely to reach employer win decisions over union win decisions; and among these three levels of educational attainment, arbitrators with master's and Ph.D. degrees were more likely to issue employer win awards (60.56 percent and 59.64 percent, respectively) than were those with law degrees (48.75 percent).

5. *Occupation*: With regard to discipline cases, arbitrators who were academics made up the occupational group that issued the largest share of management win outcomes (50.42 percent) and the smallest share of union win outcomes (14.29 percent). Arbitrators who were academics were far more likely to favor the employer (50.42 percent) than were arbitrators who are practicing attorneys (38.98 percent). In discharge grievances, arbitrators who were neither practicing lawyers nor academics topped the management win scale with a 62.50 percent share, followed by academics (57.51 percent), and, finally, by arbitrators who were both practicing attorneys and academics who favored management in 50.87 percent of cases. Interestingly, in discharge cases, the occupational group that favored unions most often was made of arbitrators who were both practicing attorneys and academics (26.09 percent). We join Bemmels and Nelson and Uddin in concluding that the occupation variable is a significant determinant of arbitration outcomes.

6. *NAA Membership*: As a proxy measure of experience, the National Academy of Arbitrators (NAA) membership variable was significantly correlated with outcomes in both discipline and discharge cases. Experienced NAA members were more likely than inexperienced non-members to favor management over labor with probabilities of 49.00 percent *versus* 38.39 percent when the employer's disciplinary action involved a suspension or reprimand, and 54.14 percent *versus* 50.45 percent when the employer's action involved a discharge. Implicit in these probability estimates is that inexperienced arbitrators *versus* experienced arbitrators exhibited a greater tendency to fully favor the grievant (31.89 percent *versus* 21.00 percent in discipline cases; 23.03 percent versus 15.93 percent in discharge cases). With the notable exception of the Stieber, Block and Corbitt study, most others have not found the NAA measure of experience to be determinative of arbitration outcomes. Our results yield the opposite conclusion and, further, they conflict with the results of Stieber, Block and Corbitt who found that non-NAA members tend to favor management.

Grievant Characteristics

1. *Gender:* With some exceptions, most studies in the arbitration literature have found that the grievant's gender does not affect arbitrator decision-making in discharge cases. Our study affirms these results. However, with regard to discipline grievances, we found that a female grievant's chance of having her suspension revoked or having her reprimand rescinded was 1.36 times higher than for a male grievant.

2. *Match*: We established that the gender of the arbitrator and the gender of the grievant did not interact in such a way as to influence the arbitrator's decision, regardless of the type of discipline imposed by the employer. This affirms a comparable finding by Scott and Shadoan.

3. *Tenure*: Although arbitration's institutional literature suggests that the employee's length of service (i.e., fewer than 10 years of service *versus* 10 or more years of service) operates as a mitigating consideration in just cause cases, we, surprisingly, found no empirical support for this holding.

4. *Crime*: Whether the grievant was charged with a crime in the criminal justice system for the same offense that resulted in the grievant's discipline or discharge did not significantly affect the odds of an employer or union victory. However, employees not charged with a crime had a better chance of winning a split decision than did their counterparts in discharge cases. These are original results.

5. *Last Chance Agreements*: Although examining the effect of last chance agreements on arbitral decision-making seems to be an obvious undertaking, few have previously done so. With respect to the analysis of discharge awards, if a grievant was working under a last chance agreement when discharged, the odds of a full union victory fell by approximately 50 percent, and the odds of a split decision fell by about 40 percent. In contrast, the chances that management would prevail in arbitration increased from 49.92 percent to 72.22 percent.

Case Characteristics

1. *Sector*: Several analysts have considered the relevance of sector—public or private—to arbitral decision-making in disciplinary cases. Most of these studies failed to

discern any systematic differences in award outcomes by sector. While our analysis of discipline cases produced results that mirror this literature, the same cannot be said about our analysis of discharge cases. Approximately 56.17 percent of public sector and 48.83 percent of private sector discharge awards favored management. In comparison, public sector unions won 16.45 percent of discharge awards and private sector unions prevailed in 21.87 percent of discharge awards.

2. *Number of Offenses*: Grievants who were charged with having committed more than one offense were significantly less likely to prevail fully in arbitration than are grievants who were charged with only one offense, regardless of type of offense—a finding that has not previously been reported.

3. *Delay*: Our analysis suggests that delay had an insignificantly discernable effect on awards issued in discharge cases.

4. *Seven Tests of Just Cause*: Daugherty's Seven Tests are widely acclaimed to be *the* definition of just cause. Yet, our analysis showed that the Seven Tests were invoked in a surprisingly small fraction of discipline and discharge cases. Accordingly, we conclude that the high status afforded the Seven Tests is overstated. Moreover, our hypothesis that the odds of a management win would fall whenever the arbitrator used the Seven Tests was not supported by our analysis of the data.

5. *Legal Representation*: The relationship between attorney representation and arbitration outcomes has been examined by other analysts, some of whom have concluded that a relationship exists, while others have concluded that there is none. With respect to legal representation and award outcomes, we found a clear divide between discipline and discharge cases. The parties' retention of legal counsel and outcomes were not at all associated in discipline cases, whereas, in discharge cases they were. With respect to the latter, we found that when *both* or *neither* party retains legal representation the odds that either party will win are unchanged. We also found that the odds of winning were greatest when only *one* party retained a lawyer advocate. These results parallel those reported by Block and Stieber. 6. *Quantum of Proof*: The quantum of proof standard that arbitrators may use in determining award outcomes varies from the lowest standard of "preponderance of evidence," to the higher standard of "clear and convincing evidence," and to the highest

standard of evidence "beyond a reasonable doubt." This rank ordering suggests that the chances of management winning in arbitration should decrease in step with increases in the standard the arbitrator uses. We tested this hypothesis. Our test results established that the quantum of proof standard did not affect arbitration outcomes in either discipline or discharge cases. Another interesting finding is that arbitrator opinions usually made no reference whatsoever to an applicable quantum standard. This was so in 83.79 percent and 75.91 percent of our discipline and discharge cases, respectively.

CHAPTER 4

OFFENSES

Employees protected by contractual "just cause" provisions are disciplined and discharged for a variety of types of offenses. Observers of and participants in the labor arbitration process—unions, employers, arbitrators and scholars—are likely to want information about which employee offenses reach arbitration and the relationship between particular offenses and other aspects of the arbitration process. What reasons for employee discipline and discharge are most frequently challenged in arbitration? Does the frequency with which a particular offense is arbitrated differ depending on the gender of the grievant, whether the case arose in the public or private sector, or whether the employee was discharged or merely suspended or reprimanded? Have employee offenses giving rise to arbitrations changed over time? Are employers or unions more likely to prevail in cases arising from particular categories of offenses? Are some offenses more likely to produce split decisions from arbitrators? Do outcomes for specific offenses differ depending on whether the case arises in the public or private sector, or on whether the arbitrator is an attorney or a member of the National Academy of Arbitrators? Are parties more likely to be represented by counsel when arbitrating certain offenses?

Remarkably little previous empirical research on arbitration of discipline and discharge cases has addressed any of these questions. Sometimes, empirical studies of arbitrated discipline and discharge cases, while focusing on a single type of offense or on a particular decisional characteristic, have provided a passing glimpse of the distribution of offenses for which employees have been disciplined. Other studies that have looked more directly at the distribution of offenses have been limited by small numbers of cases, data bases covering only a few years, and data bases drawn only from published arbitration awards. None of the studies have focused in depth on the distribution of offenses in labor arbitration within a large data base of published and unpublished awards extending over decades or on the relationship between offenses and diverse other case characteristics. In this chapter, we do exactly that.

Previous Empirical Studies

Several previous empirical studies have briefly discussed the distribution of offenses in labor arbitration while focusing upon a different research question. Arthur Anthony Malinowski, studying the work history of reinstated employees, examined 67 published arbitration cases between 1977 and 1978 for which he was also able to obtain completed questionnaires from employers about the reinstated employee's subsequent work history.[1] In this small and obviously non-representative data base, the most common reason for discharge was "Illegal Strike, Work Stoppage, Strike Violence" (33 cases), followed by "Incompetence, Negligence, Violate Safety Rules" (29), "Absenteeism, Tardiness" (23) and "Dishonesty, Theft, Falsify Records" (23).[2] Gregory G. Dell'Omo and James E. Jones, Jr. looked only at discipline and discharge cases in which a union challenged the employer's sanction on the basis of disparate treatment.[3] These authors identified 192 disparate treatment awards published between 1963 and 1988. The largest offense category they identified was "other"[4] (23 percent), followed by attendance (17 percent) and fighting and failure to get along with co-workers (16 percent).[5] In an effort to determine the representativeness of published arbitration decisions, three Michigan researchers assembled a collection of national published awards and unpublished Michigan awards in discharge cases from various time periods.[6] They reported that the largest category of unpublished

---

[1] Arthur Anthony Malinowski, "An Empirical Analysis of Discharge Cases and the Work History of Employees Reinstated by Labor Arbitrators," 36 *Arbitration Journal* (March 1981), 31.

[2] *Id.* at 34 tbl. 1. For comparison, in our data base cataloging 2,517 offenses, there was only one case involving strike misconduct and one case alleging participation in an illegal strike.

[3] Gregory G. Dell'Omo & James E. Jones, Jr., "Disparate Treatment in Labor Arbitration: An Empirical Analysis," 41 *Labor Law Journal* 739, 740 (1990).

[4] The "other" category included horseplay, sleeping, dress codes and "other miscellaneous rules and policies." *Id.* at 741.

[5] *Id.* at 741.

[6] Jack Stieber, Richard N. Block & Leslie Corbitt, "How Representative are Published Decisions?," *Arbitration 1984: Absenteeism, Recent Law, Panels and Published Decisions, Proceedings of the 37th Annual Meeting of the National Academy of Arbitrators* (Washington, D.C.: Bureau of National Affairs, Gladys Gershenfeld, ed., 1985), 172. The collection included 759 national decisions published between 1979 and 1981, 97 unpublished Michigan decisions from the Federal

discharge awards concerned excessive absenteeism (17.5 percent), while the largest category of published awards was "miscellaneous" (32.4 percent).[7]

Three other studies focused directly on the variety of employee offenses and correlations between offenses and case outcomes. In an early effort, J. Fred Holly examined 1,055 discharge arbitration awards published in *Labor Arbitration Reports* between 1942 and 1956.[8] He classified the cases into 14 offense categories. Holly identified the largest categories of cases as "striking, instigating strike or slowdown" (15.8 percent), absenteeism (10.7 percent), and "refusal to accept job assignment or overtime work" (10.2 percent).[9] Debra J. Mesch and Dan R. Dalton studied 433 published cases on discipline and discharge arbitrated between 1988 and 1990.[10] The largest offense category they observed was use of drugs or alcohol (23.9 percent), followed by absenteeism (10.3 percent) and dishonesty (9.9 percent).[11] Ken Jennings, Barbara Sheffield and Roger Wolters collected a total of 1,724 published discharge cases from three time periods: 1942-1956, 1971-1974 and 1983-1984.[12] They classified offenses in only five categories. The largest proportion of cases (41 percent) in their study were classified as "violation of plant rules," a category that included such disparate offenses as absenteeism, altercations, dishonesty, gambling, intoxication and other specific rules.[13] They classified 20 percent of the cases as involving incompetence and

---

Mediation and Conciliation Service from 1979, and 357 unpublished Michigan decisions from the American Arbitration Association from 1979 and 1982. *Id.* at 173-174.

[7] *Id.* at 184 tbl. 2.

[8] J. Fred Holly, "The Arbitration of Discharge Cases: A Case Study," *Critical Issues in Labor Arbitration, Proceedings of the 10th Annual Meeting of the National Academy of Arbitrators* (Washington, D.C.: Bureau of National Affairs, Jean McKelvey, ed., 1957), 1.

[9] *Id.* at 2-3.

[10] Debra J. Mesch & Dan R. Dalton, "Arbitration in Practice: Win, Lose, or Draw?," 4 *The Human Resources Professional* 37, 39, 41 tbl. 3 (1992).

[11] *Id.* at 41 tbl. 3.

[12] Ken Jennings, Barbara Sheffield & Roger Wolters, "The Arbitration of Discharge Cases: A Forty-Year Perspective," 38 *Labor Law Journal* 33, 34, 35 tbl. 1 (1987). The 1942-1956 cases included in this study were drawn from the awards collected by J. Fred Holly. *Id.* at 34 n. 11. See note 8 *supra*.

[13] *Id.* at 35 tbl. 1.

inefficiency and 17 percent as involving insubordination, including refusals to accept job assignments.[14]

For a number of reasons, our research yields more reliable conclusions than these previous studies about the nature of employee offenses adjudicated in labor arbitration and the relationship between offenses and other case characteristics. First, our data base includes more cases (2,055) involving more offenses (2,517) than any of the previous studies. Second, our data base is more representative because it includes both published and unpublished awards. Third, our data base includes cases decided in more years than any of the other studies (24 years)[15] and, unlike some of the other studies that drew from arbitrary segments of years, our cases were decided in a continuous series of years (1982-2005). Fourth, while other studies classified employee offenses into 5 to 22 categories, we organized offenses into 43 different categories. The limited number of offense categories used in previous studies had resulted in a large proportion of cases classified as "other" or "miscellaneous" (e.g., 23 percent in the Dell'Omo-Jones study and 32.4 percent in the Michigan study, respectively).[16] In our study, we were able to identify a specific offense category for more than 99 percent of our cases, leaving less than 1 percent of cases in an "other" category. Finally, our study, rather than looking at a few isolated case characteristics apart from offense category, comprehensively coded dozens of case characteristics, permitting us to test relationships between specific offenses and those other characteristics.

Many of the discipline and discharge cases in our data set involve grievants who were alleged to have committed more than one offense. As offense categories assigned to an individual case are not mutually exclusive, this chapter does not generally present tests of statistical significance.

---

[14] *Id.*

[15] Although the title of the Jennings, Sheffield and Wolters article described the study as offering "A Forty-Year Perspective," note 12 *supra*, the cases reported upon were drawn from 18 selected years within that period and omitted cases from intervening time periods totaling 24 years.

[16] The Jennings, Sheffield and Wolters study that classified 41 percent of the cases as involving "violation of plant rules" offered an equivalent lack of specificity. See text accompanying note 13 *supra*.

Offense Categories and Offense Supercategories

In the discussion that follows we present some information related to each of 43 coded offense categories. In other instances, in order to provide a broader perspective, we collapsed our 43 offense categories into 9 offense "supercategories." The following table indicates how the 43 offense categories were allocated into these 9 offense supercategories.

Table 4.1 Allocation of Offense Categories to Offense Supercategories

Offense Supercategories	Offense Categories
Violence & Aggression	Verbal or Physical Abuse of Customers, or Other Members of the Public; Verbal or Physical Abuse of Students, Patients or Inmates; Abusive Language to Supervisor; Assault and Fighting Among Employees; Profane or Abusive Language; Racial/Religious Slur; Sexual Harassment; Threat or Assault of Supervisor; Threat to Co-Worker
Attendance/Absentee Issues	Absenteeism; Leaving Post; Leaving Work Early; Tardiness
Dishonesty	Property Damage; Disloyalty to Employer; Falsifying Company Records; Falsifying Employment Application; Lying; Theft from Co-worker or Customer; Theft from Employer
Drugs/Alcohol	Distribution of Drugs; Possession or Use of Alcohol; Possession or Use of Drugs; Positive Drug Test Result; or Refusal to Take Drug Test
On the Job Misconduct	Computer Misuse; Gambling; Horseplay; Misconduct During Strike; Negligence; Obscene or Immoral Conduct or Pornography With a Computer; Obscene or Immoral Conduct or Pornography Without a Computer
Off the Job Misconduct	Moonlighting; Off-Duty Misconduct
Insubordination	Insubordination; Refusal to Cross Picket Line; Refusal to Accept Job Assignment; Refusal to Accept Overtime; Failure to Follow Policy
Performance Issues	Sleeping on the Job or Loafing; Slowdown; Unsatisfactory Performance
Other	Prohibited Strike; Union Activities; Other

Distribution of Offenses

Table 4.2 identifies the conduct for which employees were discharged. Three categories each accounted for more than 10 percent of the discharge cases: Unsatisfactory performance (17.32 percent), absenteeism (15.50 percent), and contemporaneous insubordination (13.06 percent). Some categories of alleged misconduct that were commonplace in some of the earlier and smaller studies were far less common or even extremely rare in our data base. For example, unlike the Holly and Malinowski studies, we found only a single case in each of the categories of union activities, prohibited strike, and misconduct during strike. Discharge for sexual harassment, not referenced in any of the previously cited studies, was our tenth largest category, accounting for 4.61 percent of our arbitrated offenses.

Table 4.2 <u>Discharge Cases: Frequency of Alleged Offense</u>

Rank Ordered by Frequency	Alleged Offense	N	% of Discharges N=1,432
1	Unsatisfactory performance	248	17.32
2	Absenteeism	222	15.50
3	Insubordination (contemporaneous)	187	13.06
4	Theft from employer	95	6.63
5	Failure to follow other policy[1]	90	6.28
6	Falsifying company records (including time and production records)	79	5.52
7	Lying (not on company records or employment application)	73	5.10
8	Off-duty misconduct	69	4.82
9	Negligence	67	4.68
10	Sexual harassment	66	4.61
11	Verbal/physical abuse of students/patients/inmates	64	4.47
12	Possession or use of drugs, positive drug test result, or refusal to take a drug test	44	3.07
13	Possession or use of alcohol	43	3.00
14	Profane or abusive language (towards co-workers not including supervisor)	39	2.72
15	Property damage	32	2.23
16	Verbal/physical abuse of customers/members of public	32	2.23
17	Tardiness	29	2.03
18	Sleeping on job/loafing	28	1.96
19	Assault/fighting among employees	28	1.96

Table 4.2 Discharge Cases: Frequency of Alleged Offense, Cont'd.

Rank Ordered by Frequency	Alleged Offense	N	% of Discharges N=1,432
20	Threat to co-worker	27	1.89
21	Leaving post (including leaving work as a result of a dispute)	27	1.89
22	Theft from co-worker or customer	26	1.82
23	Abusive language to supervisor	22	1.54
24	Threat or assault of supervisor	20	1.40
25	Leaving work early	19	1.33
26	Falsifying employment application	15	1.05
27	Obscene or immoral conduct or pornography without a computer	13	0.91
28	Other	11	0.77
29	Disloyalty to employer (competition with employer or conflict of interest)	11	0.77
30	Computer misuse (other than obscenity/immoral conduct/ pornography)	11	0.77
31	Obscene or immoral conduct or pornography with computer	10	0.70
32	Refusal to accept job assignment	9	0.63
33	Racial/religious slur	8	0.56
34	Horseplay	7	0.49
35	Refusal to accept overtime	4	0.28
36	Moonlighting (excluding competition with employer)	4	0.28
37	Slowdown	3	0.21
38	Distribution of drugs	2	0.14
39	Union activities	1	0.07
40	Prohibited strike	1	0.07
41	Misconduct during strike	1	0.07
42	Refusal to cross picket line	0	0.00
43	Gambling	0	0.00

Table 4.2 Discharge Cases: Frequency of Alleged Offense, Cont'd.

Rank Ordered by Frequency	Alleged Offense	N	% of Discharges N=1,432
	Column Totals[2]	1,787	--

[1] This category included employee failure to follow a policy other than one identified by another specific category and excluded reasonably contemporaneous insubordination.
[2] Some cases involved more than one offense. The totals shown in the bottom row are the overall totals for each possible outcome, disregarding the multiplicity of motivating offenses.

We can compare the offenses for which employees were discharged, presented in Table 4.2, with the offenses for which employees received lesser discipline—suspensions and reprimands. Table 4.3 identifies the conduct for which employees were suspended or reprimanded.

Table 4.3 Suspension and Reprimand Cases: Frequency of Alleged Offense

Frequency Rank Order	Alleged Offense	N	% of Suspensions and Reprimands (N=623)
1	Insubordination (contemporaneous)	116	18.62
2	Unsatisfactory performance	80	12.84
3	Failure to follow other policy[1]	75	12.04
4	Negligence	56	8.99
5	Verbal/physical abuse of students/patients/inmates	45	7.22
6	Sexual harassment	42	6.74
7	Absenteeism	35	5.62
8	Profane or abusive language (towards co-workers not including supervisor)	26	4.17
9	Abusive language to supervisor	24	3.85
10	Verbal/physical abuse of customers/members of public	24	3.85

Table 4.3 Suspension and Reprimand Cases: Frequency of Alleged Offense, Cont'd.

Frequency Rank Order	Alleged Offense	N	% of Suspensions and Reprimands (N=623)
11	Lying (not on company records or employment application)	22	3.53
12	Falsifying company records (including time and production records)	22	3.53
13	Off-duty misconduct	18	2.89
14	Tardiness	15	2.41
15	Sleeping on job/loafing	13	2.09
16	Leaving post (including leaving work as a result of a dispute)	13	2.09
17	Property damage	11	1.77
18	Assault/fighting among employees	11	1.77
19	Threat to co-worker	9	1.44
20	Other	8	1.28
21	Disloyalty to employer (competition with employer or conflict of interest)	8	1.28
22	Threat or assault of supervisor	7	1.12
23	Possession or use of alcohol	7	1.12
24	Leaving work early	7	1.12
25	Union activities	4	0.64
26	Theft from employer	4	0.64
27	Racial/religious slur	4	0.64
28	Obscene or immoral conduct or pornography without a computer	4	0.64
29	Horseplay	4	0.64
30	Refusal to accept overtime	3	0.48
31	Possession or use of drugs, positive drug test result, or refusal to take a drug test	3	0.48
32	Moonlighting (excluding competition with employer)	3	0.48

Table 4.3 Suspension and Reprimand Cases: Frequency of Alleged Offense, Cont'd.

Frequency Rank Order	Alleged Offense	N	% of Suspensions and Reprimands (N=623)
33	Refusal to accept job assignment	2	0.32
34	Obscene or immoral conduct or pornography with a computer	2	0.32
35	Theft from co-worker or customer	1	0.16
36	Gambling	1	0.16
37	Falsifying employment application	1	0.16
38	Slowdown	0	0.00
39	Refusal to cross picket line	0	0.00
40	Prohibited strike	0	0.00
41	Misconduct during strike	0	0.00
42	Distribution of drugs	0	0.00
43	Computer misuse (other than obscenity/immoral conduct/ pornography)	0	0.00
	Column Totals[2]	730	--

[1] This category included employee failure to follow a policy other than one identified by another specific category and excluded reasonably contemporaneous insubordination.
[2] Some cases involved more than one offense. The totals shown in the bottom row are the overall totals for each possible outcome, disregarding the multiplicity of motivating offenses.

Comparing Tables 4.2 and 4.3, we see that insubordination and unsatisfactory performance each accounted for more than 10 percent of the offenses in both discharge cases and those in which the disciplinary sanction was a suspension or reprimand. While absenteeism was the second-ranked offense in discharge cases (15.50 percent) it was less than half as commonly arbitrated in non-discharge cases (5.62 percent). It is unsurprising that unions would manifest relatively little interest in challenging suspensions and reprimands for absenteeism because employers increasingly administer no-fault attendance programs that impose discipline based on highly objective rules that assign points for absences regardless of the legitimacy of their cause. However, if an employee is discharged for a pattern of absences, arbitrators may be more willing to consider the legitimacy of the final absence that resulted in the discharge or to address potentially mitigating factors such as an employee's length of service or work history.

Not surprisingly, the most serious kinds of employee misconduct were much more likely to be the subject of discharge arbitrations than arbitrations of a suspension or reprimand. The following offenses were more common in discharge cases than non-discharge cases: theft from employer (6.63 percent vs. 0.64 percent), drug cases (3.07 percent vs. 0.48 percent), possession or use of alcohol (3.00 percent vs. 1.12 percent), and theft from co-worker or customer (1.82 percent vs. 0.16 percent). Some conduct was more likely to be the subject of a non-discharge arbitration than a discharge arbitration. These offenses included abusive language to supervisors; verbal or physical abuse of students, patients or inmates; profane or abusive language toward co-workers; and negligence.

While Tables 4.2 and 4.3 offer detailed information about all 43 specific categories of offenses giving rise to arbitration of discharge and non-discharge discipline, respectively, Table 4.4 condenses both discipline and discharge cases in the data base into nine "supercategories" of related offenses that facilitate a broader view of the distribution of offenses in arbitration.

Table 4.4 Discipline and Discharge Cases by Alleged Offense Supercategory (Descending Order of Frequency)[1]

Alleged Offense Supercategory	N	% N=2,055
Insubordination	469	22.82
Violence & Aggression	467	22.73
Dishonesty	377	18.35
Performance Issue	370	18.00
Attendance/Absentee Issues	352	17.13
On the Job Misconduct	175	8.52
Drugs/Alcohol	96	4.67
Off the Job Misconduct	94	4.57
Other	24	1.17
Column Totals[2]	2,424	--

[1] Table 4.1 identifies which offense categories are included in each supercategory.

[2] Some cases involved more than one offense category (e.g., the discipline might have been based on both a performance issue and on insubordination). The totals shown in the bottom row are the overall totals for each possible outcome, disregarding the multiplicity of motivating offenses.

Table 4.4 shows that nearly half of all discipline and discharge arbitration cases arose from two broad offense supercategories—insubordination, and violence and aggression. Note that some of the categories of employee conduct that seem to receive the most attention in analytical arbitration literature, such as drug and alcohol cases (4.67 percent)[17] and those involving off the job misconduct (4.57 percent), account for far smaller proportions of the discipline and discharge arbitration caseload.

We also were able to assess whether there have been differences over time in the employee offenses that give rise to arbitrated grievances. Figure 4.1 presents the distribution of offenses within supercategories for the three eight-year time periods included in our study. Cases involving drugs and alcohol, insubordination, and performance have remained relatively constant over the twenty-four-year period of the study. Cases of dishonesty have been rising slightly over time. The most pronounced time effect is seen in cases involving attendance and absenteeism which have dropped in each successive eight-year period. The introduction and spreading adoption by employers of no-fault attendance plans may well have had its intended effect in reducing problems of employee absence or tardiness, or the regularity of progressive discipline under such policies may have made it less likely for unions to challenge such discipline in arbitration.

---

[17] While in our study drug and alcohol cases constituted only 4.67 percent of discipline and discharge offenses arbitrated, in the Mesch-Dalton study, based on published discipline and discharge cases, drug and alcohol cases were the largest single offense category, representing 23.9 percent of all cases. See notes 10-11 *supra* and accompanying text.

Figure 4.1 Change in Offenses over Time

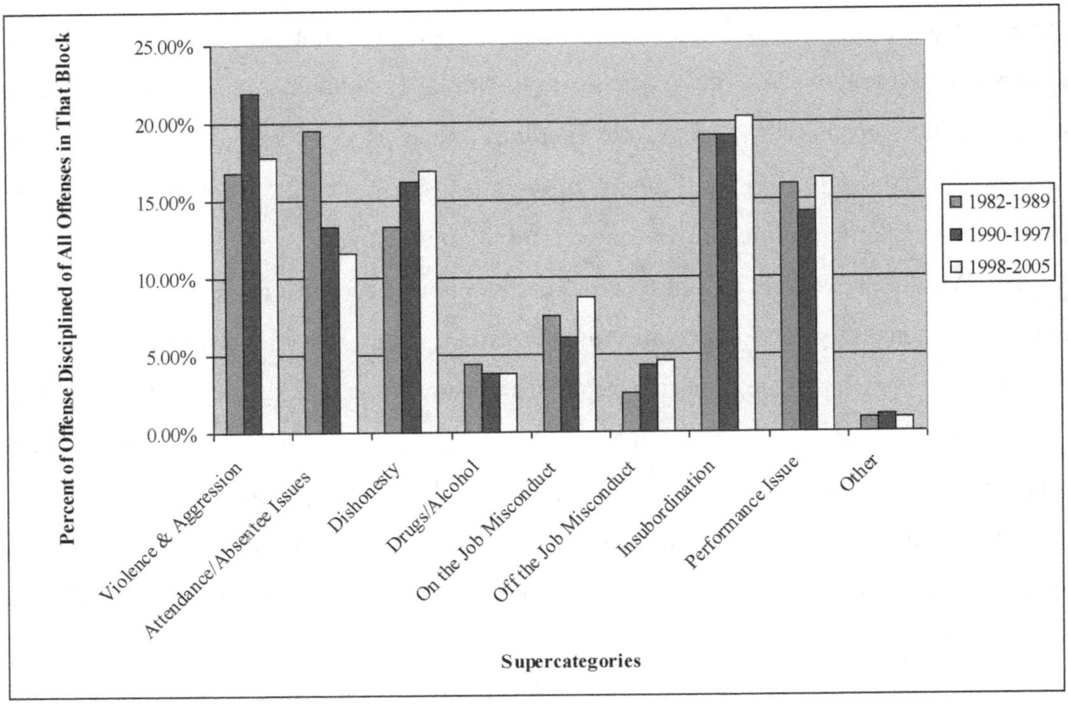

Gender and Employee Offenses

Table 4.5 displays the distribution of arbitration awards by the 43 offense categories and by gender. While male and female grievants appeared in arbitration for some offenses at comparable rates, there are some noticeable gender differences. These differences appear in two of the three largest offense categories, insubordination and unsatisfactory performance. The share of insubordination offenses arbitrated by male grievants (35.94 percent) was larger than the share arbitrated by women (14.48 percent). The share of unsatisfactory performance grievances arbitrated by women (17.64 percent) was larger than the share arbitrated by men (11.59 percent). Interestingly, women were generally comparable to men in the relative frequency with which they were arbitrating discipline or discharge for directing offensive language to supervisors and co-workers. Less than two percent of both men's and women's cases involved abusive language toward supervisors (1.88 percent of men's cases and 1.66 percent of women's cases). Profane or abusive language toward co-workers was arbitrated in 2.51 percent of the men's cases and 2.83 percent of the women's cases.

Not surprisingly, the relative share of cases alleging sexual harassment was greater, indeed more than five times greater, for men than women (5.33 percent of men's cases and 1.00 percent of women's cases). More surprising, however, is that women were more likely to be arbitrating cases involving lying (3.55 percent of men and 4.49 percent of women) and that women were more likely to be involved in theft cases (0.84 percent for men and 1.83 percent for women for theft from co-workers or customers; 3.60 percent for men and 4.99 percent for women for theft from the employer).[18] Men were more likely to be arbitrating discipline or discharge for property damage (2.09 percent of men and 0.50 percent of women). Women were more likely than men to be arbitrating cases involving verbal or physical abuse of students, patients or inmates (3.34 percent of men and 7.49 percent of women), but less likely to be arbitrating cases involving such abuse of customers or members of the public (2.45 percent for men and 1.50 percent for women). The gender differences for these two categories of abuse may simply be a reflection of the distribution of men and women in particular job categories, with women more frequently working as teachers and health care providers.[19] In Table 4.5, a superscripted letter a indicates offenses for which the difference between male and female grievants was statistically significant.

---

[18] The larger number of women arbitrating theft cases may be at least partially explained by a greater concentration of women in occupations with direct access to money. For example, the Bureau of Labor Statistics reported that, in 2009, 74.4 percent of cashiers were women, and women represented 92.2 percent of bookkeeping, accounting and auditing clerks. Bureau of Labor Statistics, Labor Force Statistics from the Current Population Survey, www.bls.gov/cps/.

[19] According to the Bureau of Labor Statistics, in 2009, women were 92.0 percent of nurses; 88.4 percent of nursing, psychiatric and home health aides; 97.8 percent of pre-school and kindergarten teachers; 81.9 percent of elementary and middle school teachers; 54.9 percent of secondary teachers; and 86.0 percent of special education teachers. *Id.*

Table 4.5 Alleged Offenses Resulting in Discharge and Discipline by Gender*

(N-size and column % are top and bottom value, respectively)

Alleged Offense	Grievant is Female	Grievant is Male	Row Totals
Absenteeism	50 8.32	207 10.81	257 100.00
Verbal/physical abuse of customers/members of public	9 1.50	47 2.45	56 100.00
Verbal/physical abuse of students/patients/inmates	45 7.49[a]	64 3.34	109 100.00
Abusive language to supervisor	10 1.66	36 1.88	46 100.00
Assault/fighting among employees	8 1.33	31 1.62	39 100.00
Computer misuse (other than obscenity/immoral conduct/pornography)	6 1.00[a]	5 0.26	11 100.00
Property damage	3 0.50[a]	40 2.09	43 100.00
Disloyalty to employer (competition with employer or conflict of interest)	5 0.83	14 0.73	19 100.00
Distribution of drugs	0 0.00	2 0.10	2 100.00
Falsifying company records (including time and production records)	24 3.99	77 4.02	101 100.00
Falsifying employment application	4 0.67	12 0.63	16 100.00
Gambling	0 0.00	1 0.05	1 100.00
Horseplay	2 0.33	9 0.47	11 100.00
Insubordination (contemporaneous)	87 14.48[a]	216 35.94	303 100.00
Leaving post (including leaving work as a result of a dispute)	5 0.83	35 5.82	40 100.00
Leaving work early	3 0.50	23 1.20	26 100.00

Table 4.5 Alleged Offenses Resulting in Discharge and Discipline by Gender, Cont'd.*
(N-size and column % are top and bottom value, respectively)

Alleged Offense	Grievant is Female	Grievant is Male	Row Totals
Lying (not on company records or employment application)	27 4.49	68 3.55	95 100.00
Misconduct during strike	0 0.00	1 0.05	1 100.00
Moonlighting (excluding competition with employer)	1 0.17	6 0.31	7 100.00
Negligence	26 4.33	96 5.01	123 100.00
Obscene or immoral conduct or pornography with computer	1 0.17	11 0.57	12 100.00
Obscene or immoral conduct or pornography without a computer	1 0.17	16 0.84	17 100.00
Off-duty misconduct	8 1.33a	79 4.13	87 100.00
Possession or use of alcohol	9 1.50	41 2.14	50 100.00
Possession or use of drugs, positive drug test result, or refusal to take a drug test	6 1.00	41 2.14	47 100.00
Profane or abusive language (towards co-workers not including supervisor)	17 2.83	48 2.51	65 100.00
Prohibited strike	0 0.00	1 0.05	1 100.00
Racial/religious slur	3 0.50	9 0.47	12 100.00
Refusal to cross picket line (usually that of other union)	0 0.00	0 0.00	0 100.00
Refusal to accept job assignment	1 0.17	10 0.52	11 100.00
Refusal to accept overtime	1 0.17	6 0.31	7 100.00
Sexual harassment	6 1.00a	102 5.33	108 100.00

Table 4.5 Alleged Offenses Resulting in Discharge and Discipline by Gender, Cont'd.*

(N-size and column % are top and bottom value, respectively)

Alleged Offense	Grievant is Female	Grievant is Male	Row Totals
Sleeping on job/loafing	6 1.00	35 1.83	41 100.00
Slowdown	0 0.00	3 0.16	3 100.00
Tardiness	11 1.83	33 1.72	44 100.00
Theft from co-worker or customer	11 1.83a	16 0.84	27 100.00
Theft from employer	30 4.99	69 3.60	99 100.00
Threat or assault of supervisor	1 0.17a	26 1.36	27 100.00
Threat to co-worker	6 1.00	30 1.57	36 100.00
Union activities	0 0.00	5 0.26	5 100.00
Unsatisfactory performance	106 17.64a	222 11.59	328 100.00
Other	5 0.83	14 0.73	19 100.00
Failure to follow other policy**	57 9.48a	108 5.64	165 100.00
Column Totals***	601 100.00	1,915 100.00	2,517 100.00

* The alphabetic index a indicates that the percentages in column 1 and column 2 are statistically different at the .05 level or lower.

** This category included employee failure to follow a policy other than one identified by another specific category and excluded reasonably contemporaneous insubordination.

*** Some cases involved more than one offense. The totals shown in the bottom row are the overall totals for each possible outcome, disregarding the multiplicity of motivating offenses.

Employee Offenses in the Public and Private Sectors

Table 4.6 compares the relative frequency of public and private sector cases by offense category. Two categories of offenses, insubordination and unsatisfactory performance, represented more than 10 percent of all offenses in both the public and private sectors. In both categories, the percentage of those cases was higher in the public sector. Insubordination cases represented 15.68 percent within the public sector and 13.38 percent in the private sector. Unsatisfactory performance cases were 18.64 percent of cases in the public sector and 12.07 percent in the private sector.

The most pronounced differences between the public and private sectors were observed in the offenses of absenteeism, sexual harassment and off-duty misconduct. Absenteeism was far more likely to be arbitrated in the private sector (19.47 of cases) than in the public sector (7.72 percent of cases). Sexual harassment was more commonly arbitrated in the public sector (7.14 percent) than in the private sector (2.51 percent). Off-duty misconduct was alleged in 6.08 percent of public sector arbitrations, but only 1.55 percent of private sector arbitrations. The greater potential for media exposure may make public sector employers more likely to discipline employees for sexual harassment, and less likely to settle sexual harassment cases, for fear of a public backlash if they are perceived as failing appropriately to discipline employees thought guilty of the offense. Public sector employers may be more likely to discipline employees for off-duty misconduct because the nature of public sector positions, such as teacher and law enforcement officer, may more likely provide a nexus with the off-duty misconduct so as to warrant discipline. We are unsurprised by the relative infrequency of the offense of verbal and physical abuse of students, patients and inmates in the private sector because public sector worksites are more likely to involve interaction with students and inmates. In Table 4.6, the superscripted letter a indicates that there was a statistically significant difference between the public and private sectors in the proportion of arbitrations arising from that offense.

Table 4.6 Alleged Offenses in Employee Discipline and Discharge by Sector*

Alleged Offense	Public Sector		Private Sector	
	N	% Public Sector Cases (N=1,218)	N	% Private Sector Cases (N=837)
Absenteeism	94	7.72[a]	163	19.47
Verbal/physical abuse of customers/members of public	43	3.53[a]	13	1.55
Verbal/physical abuse of students/patients/inmates	88	7.22[a]	21	2.51
Abusive language to supervisor	26	2.13	20	2.39
Assault/fighting among employees	12	0.99[a]	27	3.23
Computer misuse (other than obscenity/immoral conduct/pornography)	8	0.66	3	0.36
Property damage	17	1.40[a]	26	3.11
Disloyalty to employer (competition with employer or conflict of interest)	14	1.15	5	0.60
Distribution of drugs	2	0.16	0	0.00
Falsifying company records (including time and production records)	56	4.60	45	5.38
Falsifying employment application	8	0.66	8	0.96
Gambling	1	0.08	0	0.00
Horseplay	2	0.16[a]	9	1.08
Insubordination (contemporaneous)	191	15.68	112	13.38
Leaving post (including leaving work as a result of a dispute)	21	1.72	19	2.27
Leaving work early	9	0.74[a]	17	2.03
Lying (not on company records or employment application)	57	4.68	38	4.54
Misconduct during strike	0	0.00	1	0.12
Moonlighting (excluding competition with employer)	5	0.41	2	0.24
Negligence	79	6.49	44	5.26
Obscene or immoral conduct or pornography with computer	11	0.90[a]	1	0.12

Table 4.6 Alleged Offenses in Employee Discipline and Discharge by Sector, Cont'd.*

Alleged Offense	Public Sector		Private Sector	
	N	% Public Sector Cases (N=1,218)	N	% Private Sector Cases (N=837)
Obscene or immoral conduct or pornography without a computer	12	0.99	5	0.60
Off-duty misconduct	74	6.08[a]	13	1.55
Possession or use of alcohol	25	2.05	25	2.99
Possession or use of drugs, positive drug test result, or refusal to take a drug test	28	2.30	19	2.27
Profane or abusive language (towards co-workers not including supervisor)	42	3.45	23	2.75
Prohibited strike	0	0.00	1	0.12
Racial/religious slur	12	0.99[a]	0	0.00
Refusal to cross picket line (usually that of other union)	0	0.00	0	0.00
Refusal to accept job assignment	3	0.25[a]	8	0.96
Refusal to accept overtime	1	0.08[a]	6	0.72
Sexual harassment	87	7.14[a]	21	2.51
Sleeping on job/loafing	20	1.64	21	2.51
Slowdown	2	0.16	1	0.12
Tardiness	22	1.81	22	2.63
Theft from co-worker or customer	12	0.99	15	1.79
Theft from employer	51	4.19	48	5.73
Threat or assault of supervisor	14	1.15	13	1.55
Threat to co-worker	15	1.23[a]	21	2.51
Union activities	3	0.25	2	0.24
Unsatisfactory performance	227	18.64[a]	101	12.07
Other	12	0.99	7	0.84
Failure to follow other policy**	118	9.69[a]	47	5.62

Table 4.6 Alleged Offenses in Employee Discipline and Discharge by Sector, Cont'd.*

Alleged Offense	Public Sector		Private Sector	
	N	% Public Sector Cases (N=1,218)	N	% Private Sector Cases (N=837)
Column Totals***	1,524	100.00	993	100.00

* The alphabetic index a indicates that the percentages in column 2 and column 4 are statistically different at the .05 level or lower.
** This category included employee failure to follow a policy other than one identified by another specific category and excluded reasonably contemporaneous insubordination.
*** Some cases involved more than one offense. The totals shown in the bottom row are the overall totals for each possible outcome, disregarding the multiplicity of motivating offenses.

Table 4.7, comparing arbitrated offenses in the public and private sectors on the basis of offense supercategories, provides further understanding of the differences between the sectors. Offenses in the supercategories of violence and aggression, insubordination, off-duty misconduct and performance issues were more prevalent in the public sector. Offenses in the supercategories of dishonesty and absenteeism were more common in the private sector. In Table 4.7, the superscripted a indicates where such differences were statistically significant.

Table 4.7 Employee Discipline and Discharge by Offense Supercategories and Sector*

Offense Supercategory**	Public Sector		Private Sector	
	N	% Public Sector Cases (N=1,218)	N	% Private Sector Cases (N=837)
Violence & Aggression	319	26.19[a]	148	17.68
Insubordination	300	24.63[a]	169	20.19
Performance Issue	248	20.36[a]	122	14.58
Dishonesty	202	16.58[a]	175	20.91
Attendance/Absentee Issues	140	11.49[a]	212	25.33
On the Job Misconduct	112	9.20	63	7.53
Off the Job Misconduct	79	6.49[a]	15	1.79
Drugs/Alcohol	54	4.43	42	5.02
Other	14	1.15	10	1.19
Column Totals***	1,468	100.00	956	100.00

* The alphabetic index a indicates that the percentages in column 2 and column 4 are statistically different at the .05 level or lower.
** Table 4.1 identifies which offense categories are included in each supercategory.
*** Some cases involved more than one offense category (e.g., the discipline might have been based on both a performance issue and on insubordination). The totals shown in the bottom row are the overall totals for each possible outcome, disregarding the multiplicity of motivating offenses.

Alleged Offenses and Case Outcomes

Risk analysis plays an important role in deciding whether to take a case to arbitration. Both employers and unions contemplating whether to settle a particular grievance prior to arbitration are interested in the extent to which arbitration outcomes vary depending on the offense for which the employee was disciplined or discharged. Table 4.8 offers an overview of case outcomes by supercategories for discipline and discharge cases. One salient outcome measure is the likelihood that the arbitrator will completely vindicate the employer's position— the proportion of cases in which the arbitrator finds that the employer had just cause for the discipline imposed and the employee is neither returned to work nor awarded back pay. Employers were most likely to prevail fully in cases alleging drug and alcohol offenses (62.50 percent), followed closely by performance issues (61.08 percent). Apart from the small categories of offenses included within the "other" supercategory, unions were most likely to prevail in full in cases alleging off the job misconduct (28.72 percent). The odds of split decisions were greater in cases alleging on the job misconduct (40.00 percent) and insubordination (36.25 percent).

Table 4.8 Outcomes by Supercategories (Discipline and Discharge Cases)*

Offense Supercategory**	Employer Win		Split Decision		Union Win	
	N	%	N	%	N	%
Violence & Aggression	220	47.11	151	32.33	96	20.56
Insubordination	202	43.07[a]	170	36.25[b]	97	20.68
Performance Issue	226	61.08[a]	88	23.78	56	15.14[c]
Dishonesty	194	51.46	96	25.46	87	23.08
Attendance/Absentee Issues	178	50.57	103	29.26	71	20.17
On the Job Misconduct	77	44.00	70	40.00[b]	28	16.00[c]
Off the Job Misconduct	47	50.00	20	21.28[b]	27	28.72
Drugs/Alcohol	60	62.50[a]	21	21.88	15	15.63[c]
Other	7	29.17	6	25.00	11	45.83[c]
Column Totals***	1,211	49.96	725	29.91	488	20.13

* The alphabetic indexes a, b and c indicate that the percentages in column 2 and column 4, column 4 and column 6, and column 6 and column 2, respectively, are statistically different at the .05 level or lower.
** Table 4.1 identifies which offense categories are included in each supercategory.
*** Some cases involved more than one offense category (e.g., the discipline might have been based on both a performance issue and on insubordination). The totals shown in the bottom row are the overall totals for each possible outcome, disregarding the multiplicity of motivating offenses.

Table 4.9 presents in descending order the percentage of employer wins for each of the 43 offense categories. As some of the individual offense categories include only few cases, it may be helpful to identify those offense categories containing a substantial number of cases in which management win rates were particularly high or particularly low. In offense categories including at least 25 employer wins, the employer win rate was highest for drug offenses (68.09 percent), tardiness (61.36 percent), unsatisfactory performance (60.37 percent), abuse of customers and members of the public (55.36 percent), alcohol offenses (54.00 percent), falsifying company records (53.47 percent), and theft from the employer (52.53 percent). In offense categories including at least 25 employer wins, the employer win rate was lowest for abuse of students, patients or inmates (40.37 percent), sexual harassment (40.74 percent), failure to follow other policies (42.42 percent), insubordination (42.57 percent), profane or abusive language toward co-workers (43.08 percent), negligence (43.09 percent), and lying (46.32 percent).

Table 4.9 Discipline and Discharge Cases, Alleged Employee Offenses Ordered by Percentage of Employer Wins

Alleged Offense	N Management Wins	% Management Wins
Distribution of drugs	2	100.00
Gambling	1	100.00
Prohibited strike	1	100.00
Falsifying employment application	14	87.50
Racial/religious slur	9	75.00
Possession or use of drugs, positive drug test result, or refusal to take a drug test	32	68.09
Tardiness	27	61.36
Unsatisfactory performance	198	60.37
Threat or assault of supervisor	16	59.26
Threat to co-worker	21	58.33
Disloyalty to employer (competition with employer or conflict of interest)	11	57.89
Sleeping on job/loafing	23	56.10
Verbal/physical abuse of customers/members of public	31	55.36
Computer misuse (other than obscenity/immoral conduct/pornography)	6	54.55
Possession or use of alcohol	27	54.00
Falsifying company records (including time and production records)	54	53.47
Theft from employer	52	52.53
Abusive language to supervisor	24	52.17
Theft from co-worker or customer	14	51.85
Absenteeism	130	50.58
Off-duty misconduct	44	50.57
Leaving work early	13	50.00
Lying (not on company records or employment application)	44	46.32

Table 4.9 Discipline and Discharge Cases, Alleged Employee Offenses Ordered by Percentage of Employer Wins, Cont'd.

Alleged Offense	N Management Wins	% Management Wins
Horseplay	5	45.45
Property damage	19	44.19
Assault/fighting among employees	17	43.59
Negligence	53	43.09
Profane or abusive language (towards co-workers not including supervisor)	28	43.08
Moonlighting (excluding competition with employer)	3	42.86
Insubordination (contemporaneous)	129	42.57
Failure to follow other policy[1]	70	42.42
Obscene or immoral conduct or pornography with a computer	5	41.67
Obscene or immoral conduct or pornography without a computer	7	41.18
Sexual harassment	44	40.74
Verbal/physical abuse of students/patients/inmates	44	40.37
Leaving post (including leaving work as a result of a dispute)	15	37.50
Refusal to accept job assignment	4	36.36
Slowdown	1	33.33
Other	6	31.58
Refusal to accept overtime	2	28.57
Misconduct during strike	0	0.00
Refusal to cross picket line (usually that of other union)	0	0.00
Union activities	0	0.00
Column Totals[2]	1,246	49.50

[1] This category includes employee failure to follow a policy other than one identified by another specific category and excluded reasonably contemporaneous insubordination.
[2] Some cases involved more than one offense. The totals shown in the bottom row are the overall totals for each possible outcome, disregarding the multiplicity of motivating offenses.

We also examined the offense categories in which unions were most likely to prevail in full. We coded cases as a union win if the employee was awarded both reinstatement and full back pay. Table 4.10 displays the number and percent of full union victories in descending order of the percentage of cases for that offense in which the union's position was fully vindicated.

Looking only at offense categories including at least 25 union wins, unions had their highest win rates in cases in which employees were accused of theft from the employer (25.25 percent), abuse of students, patients and inmates (24.77 percent), failure to follow other policies (23.03), insubordination (19.47 percent), and absenteeism (19.46 percent). While the offense of theft may at first seem unlikely to give rise to the highest rate of union wins, theft cases can result in a finding of no just cause if the employer is unable to identify the grievant as the person responsible for the theft or if the employer had failed clearly to inform employees in advance that the item taken was not one available for employees' personal use or possession.[20]

Table 4.10 Discipline and Discharge Cases, Alleged Employee Offenses Ordered by Percent of Union Wins

Alleged Offense	N Union Wins	% Union Wins
Misconduct during strike	1	100.00
Union activities	3	60.00
Moonlighting (excluding competition with employer)	3	42.86
Refusal to accept overtime	3	42.86
Other	7	36.84
Refusal to accept job assignment	4	36.36
Slowdown	1	33.33
Leaving work early	8	30.77

[20] The assignment of the burden of persuasion to employers makes it more difficult for an employer to prevail in a theft case where evidence of the identity of the thief often may be circumstantial. Lack of notice may be an issue in theft cases if the item taken was something the business would ordinarily discard or if the employee's responsibilities included discretion whether to dispose of a particular item.

Table 4.10 Discipline and Discharge Cases, Alleged Employee Offenses Ordered by Percent of Union Wins, Cont'd.

Alleged Offense	N Union Wins	% Union Wins
Off-duty misconduct	22	25.29
Theft from employer	25	25.25
Verbal/physical abuse of students/patients/inmates	27	24.77
Possession or use of alcohol	12	24.00
Obscene or immoral conduct or pornography without a computer	4	23.53
Property damage	10	23.26
Lying (not on company records or employment application)	22	23.16
Assault/fighting among employees	9	23.08
Failure to follow other policy[1]	38	23.03
Leaving post (including leaving work as a result of a dispute)	9	22.50
Verbal/physical abuse of customers/members of public	12	21.43
Disloyalty to employer(competition with employer or conflict of interest)	4	21.05
Falsifying company records (including time and production records)	21	20.79
Negligence	24	19.51
Insubordination (contemporaneous)	59	19.47
Absenteeism	50	19.46
Sexual harassment	20	18.52
Theft from co-worker or customer	5	18.52
Profane or abusive language (towards co-workers not including supervisor)	12	18.46

Table 4.10 Discipline and Discharge Cases, Alleged Employee Offenses Ordered by Percent of Union Wins, Cont'd.

Alleged Offense	N Union Wins	% Union Wins
Unsatisfactory performance	52	15.85
Abusive language to supervisor	7	15.22
Threat to co-worker	5	13.89
Possession or use of drugs, positive drug test result, or refusal to take a drug test	5	10.64
Sleeping on job/loafing	4	9.76
Computer misuse (other than obscenity/immoral conduct/ pornography)	1	9.09
Horseplay	1	9.09
Tardiness	4	9.09
Racial/religious slur	1	8.33
Falsifying employment application	1	6.25
Threat or assault of supervisor	1	3.70
Distribution of drugs	0	0.00
Gambling	0	0.00
Obscene or immoral conduct or pornography with a computer	0	0.00
Prohibited strike	0	0.00
Refusal to cross picket line (usually that of other union)	0	0.00
Column Totals[2]	497	19.75

[1] This category included employee failure to follow a policy other than one identified by another specific category and excluded reasonably contemporaneous insubordination.

[2] Some cases involved more than one offense. The totals shown in the bottom row are the overall totals for each possible outcome, disregarding the multiplicity of motivating offenses.

Different offenses also yield different proportions of cases that result in split decisions in which the arbitrator reinstated the employee with partial or no back pay or, far more rarely, ordered that the employee be reinstated to the next available position.[21] Table 4.11 presents the offense categories in descending order of the percentage of split decisions. Looking only at those categories that included at least 25 split awards, split outcomes most likely occurred where the offense was sexual harassment (40.74 percent), insubordination (37.95 percent), negligence (37.40 percent), abuse of students, patients, and inmates (34.86 percent), and failure to follow other policies (34.55 percent). Again looking only at categories including at least 25 split awards, split decisions were least common for the offenses of unsatisfactory performance (23.78 percent), falsifying company records (25.74 percent), absenteeism (29.90 percent), and lying (30.53 percent).

Table 4.11 Alleged Employee Offenses Ordered by Percent of Split Decisions

Alleged Offense	N Split Decisions	% Split Decisions
Obscene or immoral conduct or pornography with computer	7	58.33
Horseplay	5	45.45
Sexual harassment	44	40.74
Leaving post (including leaving work as a result of a dispute)	16	40.00
Union activities	2	40.00
Profane or abusive language (towards co-workers not including supervisor)	25	38.46
Insubordination (contemporaneous)	115	37.95
Negligence	46	37.40
Threat or assault of supervisor	10	37.04
Computer misuse (other than obscenity/immoral conduct/pornography)	4	36.36
Obscene or immoral conduct or pornography without a computer	6	35.29
Verbal/physical abuse of students/patients/inmates	38	34.86

[21] See Chapter 7.

Table 4.11 Alleged Employee Offenses Ordered by Percent of Split Decisions, Cont'd.

Alleged Offense	N Split Decisions	% Split Decisions
Failure to follow other policy[1]	57	34.55
Sleeping on job/loafing	14	34.15
Assault/fighting among employees	13	33.33
Slowdown	1	33.33
Abusive language to supervisor	15	32.61
Property damage	14	32.50
Other	6	31.58
Lying (not on company records or employment application)	29	30.53
Absenteeism	77	29.90
Theft from co-worker or customer	8	29.63
Tardiness	13	29.55
Refusal to accept overtime	2	28.57
Obscene or immoral conduct or pornography with computer	7	58.33
Threat to co-worker	10	27.78
Refusal to accept job assignment	3	27.27
Falsifying company records (including time and production records)	26	25.74
Off-duty misconduct	21	24.14
Unsatisfactory performance	78	23.78
Verbal/physical abuse of customers/members of public	13	23.21
Theft from employer	22	22.22
Possession or use of alcohol	11	22.00
Possession or use of drugs, positive drug test result, or refusal to take a drug test	10	21.28
Disloyalty to employer (competition with employer or conflict of interest)	4	21.05
Leaving work early	5	19.23
Racial/religious slur	2	16.67
Moonlighting (excluding competition with employer)	1	14.29

Table 4.11 Alleged Employee Offenses Ordered by Percent of Split Decisions, Cont'd.

Alleged Offense	N Split Decisions	% Split Decisions
Falsifying employment application	1	6.25
Distribution of drugs	0	0.00
Gambling	0	0.00
Misconduct during strike	0	0.00
Prohibited strike	0	0.00
Refusal to cross picket line (usually that of other union)	0	0.00
Column Totals[2]	774	30.75

[1] This category included employee failure to follow a policy other than one identified by another specific category and excluded reasonably contemporaneous insubordination.
[2] Some cases involved more than one offense. The totals shown in the bottom row are the overall totals for each possible outcome, disregarding the multiplicity of motivating offenses.

Table 4.12 compares the extent to which case outcomes for particular offenses vary depending upon whether the discipline or discharge case arose in the public or private sector. For the most part, it does not appear that there are meaningful differences in case outcomes for particular offenses between the public and private sectors, assuming that one puts aside those offense categories in which one sector or the other, or both, had fewer than five cases.

There were nine offense categories in which there were 25 or more cases in both the public and the private sector. Comparing employer win rates for those nine offenses yields four offenses in which public sector employers had the higher win rate (absenteeism, falsifying company records, negligence, and failure to follow policy); three offense categories for which private sector employers had the higher win rate (insubordination, lying, and theft from the employer); and two categories in which the two sectors were essentially equal in employer win rates (alcohol offenses and unsatisfactory performance). In only one of these nine offense categories, negligence, was the difference in employer win rates greater than four percentage points. Public sector employers won 45.57 percent of negligence cases while private sector employers won only 38.64 percent of negligence cases.

We can also identify differences in public and private sector outcomes for various offenses that were statistically significant. In three offense categories, public and private sector outcomes were different at the .05 level of significance for all three potential outcomes. For absenteeism, arbitrators in public sector cases were more likely both to uphold in full and to reduce the employer's disciplinary sanction than in private sector cases. However, the arbitrators in private sector absenteeism cases were more likely wholly to reject the employer's disciplinary sanction and find no just cause for any discipline. For off-duty misconduct, a much more common offense in public sector arbitrations, arbitrators were significantly more likely to uphold discipline imposed by public sector than by private sector employers. The final offense category with significant differences for all three outcomes is sexual harassment. Here, arbitrators were significantly less likely fully to sustain discipline by a public sector employer than by a private sector employer. Notice also that split decisions in sexual harassment cases occurred much more often in the public sector than in the private sector.

Table 4.12 Alleged Discipline and Discharge Employee Offenses by Outcome and Sector*

(N-size and row % are top and bottom value, respectively)

Alleged Offense	Sector	Just Cause for Discipline Imposed	Just Cause for Lesser Discipline	No Just Cause for Any Discipline	Row Totals
Absenteeism	Public	49 52.13[1a]	29 30.85[1]	16 17.02[1c]	94
	Private	81 49.69[a]	46 28.22	36 22.09[c]	163
Verbal/physical abuse of customers/members of public	Public	27 62.79[1a]	10 23.26	6 13.95[c]	43
	Private	4 30.77	4 30.77	5 38.46	13
Verbal/physical abuse of students/patients/inmates	Public	39 44.32[1]	29 32.95[1]	20 22.73[c]	88
	Private	5 23.81	8 38.10	8 38.10	21
Abusive language to supervisor	Public	15 57.69[a]	6 23.08	5 19.23[c]	26
	Private	9 45.00	9 45.00[b]	2 10.00[c]	20
Assault/fighting among employees	Public	3 25.00[1]	5 41.67	4 33.33	12
	Private	15 55.56	7 25.93	5 18.52[c]	27
Computer misuse (other than obscenity/immoral conduct/ pornography)	Public	5 52.50	3 37.50	0 0.00[c]	8
	Private	1 33.33	2 66.67	0 0.00	3
Property damage	Public	10 58.82	4 23.53[1]	3 17.65[c]	17
	Private	9 34.62	10 38.46	7 26.92	26
Disloyalty to employer (competition with employer or conflict of interest)	Public	8 57.14	3 21.43	3 21.43	14
	Private	3 60.00	1 20.00	1 20.00	5

Table 4.12 <u>Alleged Discipline and Discharge Employee Offenses by Outcome and Sector, Cont'd.</u>*
(N-size and row % are top and bottom value, respectively)

Alleged Offense	Sector	Just Cause for Discipline Imposed	Just Cause for Lesser Discipline	No Just Cause for Any Discipline	Row Totals
Distribution of drugs	Public	2 100.00	0 0.00	0 0.00	2
	Private	0 0.00	0 0.00	0 0.00	0
Moonlighting (excluding competition with employer)	Public	3 60.00	1 20.00	1 20.00	5
	Private	0 0.00	0 0.00	2 100.00	2
Obscene or immoral conduct or pornography with a computer	Public	5 45.45	6 54.55[b]	0 0.00[c]	11
	Private	0 0.00	1 100.00	0 0.00	1
Obscene or immoral conduct or pornography without a computer	Public	3 25.00	5 41.67	4 33.33	12
	Private	4 80.00	1 20.00	0 0.00[c]	5
Off-duty misconduct	Public	38 51.35[1a]	16 21.62[1]	20 27.03[1c]	74
	Private	6 46.15	3 23.08	4 30.77	13
Possession or use of alcohol	Public	14 56.00	8 32.00	3 12.00[c]	25
	Private	14 56.00[a]	5 20.00	6 24.00	25
Possession or use of drugs, positive drug test result, or refusal to take a drug test	Public	20 71.43[a]	6 21.43	2 7.14[c]	28
	Private	12 63.16[a]	3 15.79	4 21.05[c]	19
Profane or abusive language (towards co-workers not including supervisor)	Public	22 52.38	11 26.19	9 21.43[c]	42
	Private	7 30.43	12 52.17[b]	4 17.39	23

Table 4.12 Alleged Discipline and Discharge Employee Offenses by Outcome and Sector, Cont'd.*
(N-size and row % are top and bottom value, respectively)

Alleged Offense	Sector	Just Cause for Discipline Imposed	Just Cause for Lesser Discipline	No Just Cause for Any Discipline	Row Totals
Prohibited strike	Public	0 0.00	0 0.00	0 0.00	0
	Private	1 100.00	0 0.00	0 0.00	1
Racial/religious slur	Public	9 75.00[1a]	2 16.67	1 8.33[c]	12
	Private	0 0.00	0 0.00	0 0.00	0
Refusal to cross picket line (usually that of other union)	Public	0 0.00	0 0.00	0 0.00	0
	Private	0 0.00	0 0.00	0 0.00	0
Refusal to accept job assignment	Public	2 66.67	1 33.33	0 0.00[1]	3
	Private	2 66.67	2 33.33	4 0.00	8
Refusal to accept overtime	Public	1 100.00	0 0.00	0 0.00[1]	1
	Private	1 16.67	2 33.33	3 50.00	6
Sleeping on job/loafing	Public	12 60.00	7 35.00[b]	1 5.00[c]	20
	Private	11 52.38	8 38.10	2 9.52[c]	21
Slowdown	Public	1 50.00	1 50.00	0 0.00	2
	Private	0 0.00	0 0.00	1 100.00	1
Tardiness	Public	12 54.55	6 27.27	4 18.18[c]	22
	Private	14 63.64	7 31.82[b]	1 4.55[c]	22

Table 4.12 Alleged Discipline and Discharge Employee Offenses by Outcome and Sector, Cont'd.*

(N-size and row % are top and bottom value, respectively)

Alleged Offense	Sector	Just Cause for Discipline Imposed	Just Cause for Lesser Discipline	No Just Cause for Any Discipline	Row Totals
Theft from co-worker or customer	Public	7 58.33	2 16.67	3 25.00	12
	Private	7 58.33	5 33.33	3 25.00	15
Theft from employer	Public	26 50.98[a]	9 17.65	16 31.37	51
	Private	26 54.17[a]	12 25.00	10 20.83[c]	48
Threat or assault of supervisor	Public	7 50.00	6 42.86	1 7.14[c]	14
	Private	9 69.23	4 30.77[b]	0 0.00[c]	13
Threat to co-worker	Public	8 53.33[1]	6 40.00	1 6.67[c]	15
	Private	13 61.90[a]	4 19.05	4 19.05[c]	21
Union activities	Public	0 0.00	2 66.67	1 33.33	3
	Private	0 0.00	0 0.00	2 100.00	2
Unsatisfactory performance	Public	140 61.67[1a]	52 22.91[1]	35 15.42[c]	227
	Private	62 61.39[a]	21 20.79	18 17.82[c]	101
Other	Public	3 25.00	4 33.33	5 41.67	12
	Private	3 42.86	1 14.29	3 42.86	7
Failure to follow other policy**	Public	52 44.07[1]	40 33.90	26 22.03[c]	118
	Private	19 40.43	17 36.17	11 23.40	47

Table 4.12 Alleged Discipline and Discharge Employee Offenses by Outcome and Sector, Cont'd.*

(N-size and row % are top and bottom value, respectively)

Alleged Offense	Sector	Just Cause for Discipline Imposed	Just Cause for Lesser Discipline	No Just Cause for Any Discipline	Row Totals
Column Totals***	Public	772 50.66	465 30.51	287 18.83	1,524
	Private	486 48.94	295 29.71	212 21.35	993

* The numeric index 1 indicates that the percentages in row 1 and row 2 within each offense category are statistically different at the .05 level or lower. The alphabetic indexes a, b and c indicate that the percentages in column 1 and column 2, column 2 and column 3, and column 3 and column 1, respectively, are statistically different at the .05 level or lower.

** This category included employee failure to follow a policy other than one identified by another specific category and excluded reasonably contemporaneous insubordination.

*** Some cases involved more than one offense. The totals shown in the bottom row are the overall totals for each possible outcome, disregarding the multiplicity of motivating offenses.

Alleged Offenses, Case Outcomes and Arbitrator Characteristics

Unions and employers selecting an arbitrator to consider a grievance concerning an employee's alleged commission of a particular offense probably are interested in whether arbitrators with particular characteristics are more likely to rule in their favor. We examine whether case outcomes for the 43 offense categories differ depending on whether the arbitrator was an attorney, as well as whether the arbitrator was a member of the National Academy of Arbitrators.

Table 4.13 compares employer win rates for each of the offenses in cases heard by arbitrators with a legal education (attorneys) and those with a non-legal educational background (non-attorneys). Here we focus on the three offense categories that include the largest number of cases: absenteeism, insubordination and unsatisfactory performance. Considering these three largest categories, there were statistically significant differences in outcomes between attorney and non-attorney arbitrators only for the categories of absenteeism and insubordination. Employers were more likely to prevail in both absenteeism and insubordination cases when their cases were heard by non-attorneys. The attorney and non-attorney difference in employer win rates was not statistically different for cases alleging unsatisfactory performance.

Table 4.13 Frequency of Employer Wins by Offense Category Correlated With Arbitrators' Attorney-Non-Attorney Status (Discipline and Discharge Cases)***

Offense	Arbitrator is an Attorney		Arbitrator is Not an Attorney	
	N***	% Employer Wins	N***	% Employer Wins
Absenteeism	167[a]	43.11	90	64.44
Verbal or physical abuse of customers or public	29	51.72	27	59.26
Verbal or physical abuse of students, patients, or inmates	65	40.00	44	40.91
Abusive language to supervisor	28	53.57	18	50.00
Assault and fighting among employees	26	50.00	13	38.46
Computer misuse (not obscenity)	7	42.86	4	75.00
Property damage	24	41.67	19	47.37
Disloyalty to employer	12	41.67	7	85.71
Distribution of drugs	1	100.00	1	100.00
Falsifying company records	60	46.67	41	63.41
Falsifying employment application	8	87.50	8	87.50
Gambling	1	100.00	0	0.00
Horseplay	4	50.00	7	42.86
Insubordination	186[a]	37.63	117	53.85
Leaving post (including leaving work as a result of a dispute)	24	20.83	16	62.50
Leaving work early	16	50.00	10	50.00
Lying (not company records or employment application)	53	43.40	42	50.00
Misconduct during strike	1	0.00	0	0.00
Lying (not company records or employment application)	53	43.40	42	50.00

Table 4.13 Frequency of Employer Wins by Offense Category Correlated With Arbitrators' Attorney-Non-Attorney Status (Discipline and Discharge Cases), Cont'd.***

Offense	Arbitrator is an Attorney		Arbitrator is Not an Attorney	
	N***	% Employer Wins	N***	% Employer Wins
Misconduct during strike	1	0.00	0	0.00
Moonlighting (excluding competition with employer)	5	40.00	2	50.00
Negligence	75	46.67	48	37.50
Obscene or immoral conduct or pornography with a computer	9	55.56	3	0.00
Obscene or immoral conduct or pornography without a computer	10	30.00	7	57.14
Off-duty misconduct	52	51.92	35	48.57
Possession or use of alcohol	25	44.00	25	68.00
Possession or use of drugs, positive drug test result, or refusal to take a drug test	27	55.56	20	85.00
Profane or abusive language	42	40.48	23	52.17
Prohibited strike	1	100.00	0	0.00
Racial/Religious slur	7	57.14	5	100.00
Refusal to cross picket line (usually that of another union)	0	0.00	0	0.00
Refusal to accept job assignment	8	25.00	3	66.67
Refusal to accept overtime	4	25.00	3	33.33
Sexual harassment	61	37.70	47	46.81
Sleeping on job or loafing	29	55.17	12	58.33
Slowdown	2	50.00	1	0.00
Tardiness	30	60.00	14	57.14
Theft from co-worker or customer	16	50.00	11	54.55

Table 4.13 Frequency of Employer Wins by Offense Category Correlated With Arbitrators' Attorney-Non-Attorney Status (Discipline and Discharge Cases), Cont'd.***

Offense	Arbitrator is an Attorney		Arbitrator is Not an Attorney	
	N***	% Employer Wins	N***	% Employer Wins
Theft from employer	52	38.46	47	68.09
Threat or assault of supervisor	21	57.14	6	66.67
Threat to co-worker	21	57.14	15	60.00
Union activities	3	0.00	2	0.00
Unsatisfactory performance (includes incompetence, poor productivity, and poor job performance)	211	62.56	117	59.83
Other	16	37.50	3	0.00
Failure to follow a policy of a type not described above	109	38.53	56	51.79
Column Totals	1,548	46.32	969	55.83

* The alphabetic index a indicates that the percentages in column 1 and column 3 are statistically different at the .05 level or lower.

** In this table, attorney/non-attorney status was determined by whether the arbitrator had a J.D. degree.

*** N = number of incidents of that offense in which the arbitrator was an attorney (or not an attorney) regardless of outcome.

In addition to the attorney or non-attorney status of arbitrators, we also examine how differences in case outcomes for various offenses correlate with whether the arbitrator was, at the time of decision, a member of the National Academy of Arbitrators (NAA). Since membership in the NAA requires a record of deciding a large number of cases over a period of years, NAA membership also signifies more experienced arbitrators.[22] Table 4.14 correlates NAA membership with offense categories and proportion of employer wins. Looking only at offense categories in which both NAA members and non-members decided at least 100 cases, the only difference that is statistically significant occurred with the offense of unsatisfactory performance where employers were fully successful in 67.90 percent of

[22] See Chapter 3.

cases before NAA-member arbitrators and only 55.42 percent of cases before non-NAA members.

Table 4.14 Frequency of Employer Wins by Offense Category Correlated With Arbitrators' NAA Status (Discipline and Discharge Cases)*

Offense	Arbitrator is NAA Member		Arbitrator is Not NAA Member	
	N Offenses**	% Employer Wins	N Offenses**	% Employer Wins
Absenteeism	151	50.99	106	50.00
Verbal or physical abuse of customers or public	32	50.00	24	62.50
Verbal or physical abuse of students, patients, or inmates	58	39.66	51	41.18
Abusive language to supervisor	24	62.50	22	40.91
Assault and fighting among employees	24	54.17	15	33.33
Computer misuse (not obscenity)	5	80.00	6	33.33
Property damage	20	60.00	23	30.43
Disloyalty to employer	10	60.00	9	55.56
Distribution of drugs	1	100.00	1	100.00
Falsifying company records	58	46.55	43	62.79
Falsifying employment application	11	90.91	5	80.00
Gambling	1	100.00	0	0.00
Horseplay	8	62.50	3	0.00
Insubordination	162	45.68	141	41.84
Leaving post	23	47.83	17	23.53
Leaving work early	11	36.36	15	60.00
Lying (not company records or employment application)	60	48.33	35	42.86

Table 4.14 Frequency of Employer Wins by Offense Category Correlated With Arbitrators' NAA Status (Discipline and Discharge Cases), Cont'd.*

Offense	Arbitrator is NAA Member		Arbitrator is Not NAA Member	
	N Offenses**	% Employer Wins	N Offenses**	% Employer Wins
Misconduct during strike	0	0.00	1	0.00
Moonlighting (excluding competition with employer)	4	50.00	3	33.33
Negligence	55	38.18	68	47.06
Obscene or immoral conduct or pornography with a computer	6	16.67	6	66.67
Obscene or immoral conduct or pornography without a computer	11	36.36	6	50.00
Lying (not company records or employment application)	60	48.33	35	42.86
Misconduct during strike	0	0.00	1	0.00
Moonlighting (excluding competition with employer)	4	50.00	3	33.33
Negligence	55	38.18	68	47.06
Obscene or immoral conduct or pornography with a computer	6	16.67	6	66.67
Obscene or immoral conduct or pornography without a computer	11	36.36	6	50.00
Off-duty misconduct	47	55.32	40	45.00
Possession or use of alcohol	32	59.38	18	50.00
Possession or use of drugs, positive drug test result, or refusal to take a drug test	19	89.47	28	53.57

Table 4.14 Frequency of Employer Wins by Offense Category Correlated With Arbitrators' NAA Status (Discipline and Discharge Cases), Cont'd.*

Offense	Arbitrator is NAA Member		Arbitrator is Not NAA Member	
	N Offenses**	% Employer Wins	N Offenses**	% Employer Wins
Profane or abusive language	34	47.06	31	41.94
Prohibited strike	0	0.00	1	100.00
Racial/Religious slur	7	57.14	5	100.00
Refusal to cross picket line (usually that of another union)	0	0.00	0	0.00
Refusal to accept job assignment	5	40.00	6	33.33
Refusal to accept overtime	3	33.33	4	25.00
Sexual harassment	65	41.54	43	41.86
Sleeping on job or loafing	22	63.64	19	47.37
Slowdown	2	50.00	1	0.00
Tardiness	19	42.11	25	72.00
Theft from co-worker or customer	9	55.56	18	50.00
Theft from employer	45	66.67	54	40.74
Threat or assault of supervisor	11	81.82	16	43.75
Threat to co-worker	26	57.69	10	60.00
Union activities	3	000	2	0.00
Unsatisfactory performance (includes incompetence, poor productivity, and poor job performance)	162a	67.90	166	55.42
Other	10	50.00	9	11.11
Failure to follow a policy of a type not described above	63	53.97	102	36.27
Column Totals	1,319	54.44	1,198	46.66

* The alphabetic index a indicates that the percentages in column 1 and column 3 are statistically different at the .05 level or lower.

** N Offenses = number of incidents of that offense in which the arbitrator was (or was not) an NAA member regardless of outcome.

Alleged Employee Offenses and Attorney Representation

Finally, we examine how the parties' use of attorney representatives in arbitration varies with the alleged employee offense giving rise to the arbitration. Table 4.15 presents union and employer attorney representation by offense categories. For offense categories with at least 25 cases, the categories in which both sides were most likely to be represented by counsel are sexual harassment (61.11 percent), drug use (55.32 percent), and off-duty misconduct (54.02 percent). Not surprisingly, these are all categories in which the issues addressed in the grievance arbitration have potentially broader implications in the legal system.[23] If we add together those cases in which the employer alone had counsel and those in which both sides were represented by counsel, we can identify three categories of offenses in which employers were represented by counsel in excess of 80 percent of the cases: threat or assault of supervisor (85.18 percent), threat to co-worker (83.33 percent), and sexual harassment (81.48 percent).

Turning to offense categories with at least 25 cases, the categories in which both sides were least likely to be represented by counsel are, with one exception, cases in which it is highly unlikely that the arbitration will address issues implicating the broader legal system. The offense categories for which parties least often had attorneys are leaving work early (46.15 percent), property damage (30.23 percent), leaving post (30.00 percent), tardiness (29.55 percent), and sleeping or loafing on the job (29.27 percent). Property damage, although it could potentially raise legal issues beyond the workplace, nevertheless is among these offenses with the least likelihood of counsel appearing for both parties.

---

[23] Off-duty conduct is likely to constitute criminal or other very serious misconduct to warrant an employer's conclusion that the off-duty activity requires workplace disciplinary consequences.

Table 4.15 Alleged Offense and Party Representation by Counsel*
(N-size and row % based on total for individual offense are top and bottom value, respectively)

Alleged Offense	N	No Counsel Used	Both Parties Used Counsel	Only Union Used Counsel	Only Employer Used Counsel
Absenteeism	257	74 28.79	82 31.91[b]	22 8.56[c]	79 30.74
Verbal/physical abuse of customers/members of public	56	10 17.86[a]	21 37.50[b]	8 14.29	17 30.36
Verbal/physical abuse of students/patients/inmates	109	32 29.36	45 41.28[b]	6 5.50[c]	26 23.85
Abusive language to supervisor	46	12 26.09	16 34.78[b]	4 8.70[c]	14 30.43
Assault/fighting among employees	39	8 20.51	14 35.90[b]	1 2.56[c]	16 41.03
Computer misuse (other than obscenity/immoral conduct/ pornography)	11	3 27.27	3 27.27	2 18.18	3 27.27
Property damage	43	13 30.23	17 39.53[b]	4 9.30	9 20.93
Disloyalty to employer (competition with employer or conflict of interest)	19	4 21.05	7 36.84	3 15.79	5 26.32
Distribution of drugs	2	1 50.00	0 0.00	0 0.00	1 50.00
Falsifying company records (including time and production records)	101	30 29.70	45 44.55[b]	7 6.93[c]	19 18.81
Falsifying employment application	16	2 12.50	8 50.00[b]	1 6.25	5 31.25
Gambling	1	0 0.00	0 0.00	0 0.00	1 100.00
Horseplay	11	1 9.09	5 45.45	1 9.09	4 36.36
Insubordination (contemporaneous)	303	58 19.14[a]	144 47.52[b]	22 7.26[c]	79 26.07
Leaving post (including leaving work as a result of a dispute)	40	12 30.00	17 42.50[b]	4 10.00	7 17.50
Leaving work early	26	12 46.15	5 19.23	3 11.54	6 23.08

Table 4.15 Alleged Offense and Party Representation by Counsel, Cont'd.*
(N-size and row % based on total for individual offense are top and bottom value, respectively)

Alleged Offense	N	No Counsel Used	Both Parties Used Counsel	Only Union Used Counsel	Only Employer Used Counsel
Lying (not on company records or employment application)	95	17 17.89[a]	46 48.42[b]	6 6.32[c]	26 27.37
Misconduct during strike	1	0 0.00	0 0.00	1 100.00	0 0.00
Moonlighting (excluding competition with employer)	7	0 0.00	3 42.86	4 57.14[c]	0 0.00
Negligence	123	27 21.95[a]	53 43.09[b]	11 8.94[c]	32 26.02
Obscene or immoral conduct or pornography with a computer	12	5 41.67	4 33.33	2 16.67	1 8.33
Obscene or immoral conduct or pornography without a computer	17	5 29.41	8 47.06[b]	1 5.88	3 17.65
Off-duty misconduct	87	18 20.69[a]	47 54.02[b]	5 5.75[c]	17 19.54
Possession or use of alcohol	50	7 14.00[a]	21 42.00[b]	7 14.00	15 30.00
Possession or use of drugs, positive drug test result, or refusal to take a drug test	47	8 17.02[b]	26 55.32[b]	3 6.38	10 21.28
Profane or abusive language (towards co-workers not including supervisor)	65	10 15.38[a]	29 44.62[b]	8 12.31[c]	18 27.69
Prohibited strike	1	0 0.00	1 100.00	0 0.00	0 0.00
Racial/religious slur	12	1 8.33	6 50.00	3 25.00	2 16.67
Refusal to cross picket line (usually that of other union)	0	0 0.00	0 0.00	0 0.00	0 0.00
Refusal to accept job assignment	11	5 45.45	3 27.27	2 18.18	1 9.09
Refusal to accept overtime	7	2 28.57	2 28.57	0 0.00	3 42.86
Sexual harassment	108	13 12.04[a]	66 61.11[b]	7 6.48[c]	22 20.37

Table 4.15 Alleged Offense and Party Representation by Counsel, Cont'd.*
(N-size and row % based on total for individual offense are top and bottom value, respectively)

Alleged Offense	N	No Counsel Used	Both Parties Used Counsel	Only Union Used Counsel	Only Employer Used Counsel
Sleeping on job/loafing	41	12 29.27	11 26.83[b]	2 4.88[c]	16 39.02
Slowdown	3	0 0.00	2 66.67	1 33.33	0 0.00
Tardiness	44	13 29.55	14 31.82	6 13.64	11 25.00
Theft from co-worker or customer	27	7 25.93	9 33.33[b]	1 3.70c	10 37.04
Theft from employer	99	18 18.18[a]	37 37.37[b]	8 8.08[c]	36 36.36[d]
Threat or assault of supervisor	27	2 7.41[a]	11 40.74[b]	2 7.41[c]	12 44.44[d]
Threat to co-worker	36	3 8.33[a]	18 50.00[b]	3 8.33[c]	12 33.33[d]
Union activities	5	1 20.00	1 20.00	1 20.00	2 40.00
Unsatisfactory performance	328	63 19.21[a]	141 42.99[b]	38 11.59[c]	86 26.22
Other	19	5 26.32	9 47.37b	1 5.26	4 21.05
Failure to follow other policy**	165	38 23.03a	64 38.79b	22 13.33c	41 24.85
Column Totals***	2,517	552 21.93	1,061 42.15	233 9.26	671 26.66

* The alphabetic indexes a, b, c and d indicate that the percentages in column 1 and column 2, column 2 and column 3, column 3 and column 4, and column 4 and column 1, respectively, are statistically different at the .05 level or lower.
** This category included employee failure to follow a policy other than one identified by another specific category and excluded reasonably contemporaneous insubordination.
*** Some cases involved more than one offense. The totals shown in the bottom row are the overall totals for each possible outcome, disregarding the multiplicity of motivating offenses.

Summary

Having coded 43 separate offense categories and multiple case characteristics of more than two thousand published and unpublished public and private sector cases, this study offers the most comprehensive understanding to date of the arbitration of alleged employee offenses and the relationship of offenses to other case characteristics. This chapter includes rich detail about the frequency of different offenses in arbitration and their relationship to union wins, employer wins and split decisions; the gender of employees; the sector of employment; the nature of discipline; the identity of arbitrators as attorneys or members of the National Academy of Arbitrators (NAA); and the representation of counsel.

The following are some of our specific findings with regard to offenses. Three categories (unsatisfactory performance, absenteeism and insubordination) individually account for more than 10 percent of all discharge offenses arbitrated and together these three categories account for more than 45 percent of all discharge offenses arbitrated. Absenteeism was much more commonly arbitrated in discharge cases than in cases where the disciplinary sanction was suspension or reprimand. The only offense category that has continued to decline in relative frequency over the 24-year period of the study is attendance and absenteeism. For alleged insubordination, property damage and sexual harassment, the grievants were more likely to be men, while women were more likely to be arbitrating discipline or discharge for unsatisfactory performance and theft. Sexual harassment and off-duty misconduct were more frequently arbitrated in the public sector, while absenteeism arbitrations were more common in the private sector. Among categories with at least 25 employer wins, employers were most successful in cases alleging drug offenses and least successful in cases alleging sexual harassment and abuse of students, patients, or inmates. In offense categories with at least 25 union wins, unions were most successful in cases alleging theft. In offense categories with at least 25 split decisions rendered, sexual harassment was most likely to yield split decisions.

Non-attorney arbitrators were more likely than attorney arbitrators to rule in favor of employers in cases in which employees were disciplined or discharged because of either insubordination or absenteeism. Members of the NAA were more likely than non-members to rule in favor of employers in cases in which employees were disciplined or discharged for unsatisfactory performance.

The offenses for which both sides were most likely to be represented by counsel are sexual harassment, drug use and off-duty misconduct. Employers were represented by attorneys in more than 80 percent of the cases involving threats and assaults of supervisors, threats to co-workers and sexual harassment.

CHAPTER 5

HOW ARBITRATORS ASSESS PROOF

Arbitrators necessarily must bring to their decision-making process some assumptions about the nature of the proof required to permit them to reach a conclusion in the face of conflicting evidence. Such assumptions must provide explicit or implicit answers to two distinct, but related, fact-finding tasks. First, which side has the burden of proof on this issue? Second, having assigned the burden of proof to a particular party, what level of proof is necessary to satisfy that party's burden?

The first question, often called the burden of persuasion, directs the arbitrator's decision when, after all the evidence has been presented, the arbitrator remains in doubt about the conclusion. The party with the burden of persuasion bears the risk of non-persuasion. For example, if the evidence on both sides is equally persuasive, the party with the burden of proof will lose.[1]

The second issue, the level, or quantum, of proof, answers the question of how much proof must be presented by the party with the burden of persuasion in order for that party to prevail. Within the legal system, depending on the context, one of three different standards for the quantum of proof is employed. In ordinary civil cases, such as those arising from an automobile collision or a claim of breach of contract, courts require the party with the burden of proof to persuade the fact-finder by a "preponderance of the evidence." This standard is satisfied if the decision-maker finds that party's evidence more convincing or, put another way, if the fact-finder concludes that the existence of a fact asserted by the party with the burden of persuasion is more probable than its nonexistence.[2] The legal system requires a level of proof higher than "preponderance of the evidence" from the party with the burden of persuasion in certain kinds of civil cases or on certain issues. For example, if a party asserts the existence of fraud, or is seeking to commit a person to a mental hospital, the judicial system will insist that the party with the burden of persuasion prove its case by "clear

---

[1] *McCormick on Evidence* (Eagan, MN: Thomson Reuters/Westlaw, Kenneth S. Broun, ed., 7th ed. 2013), Vol. 2, 645.

[2] *Id.* at 660-661.

and convincing evidence." Such a requirement is typically imposed when a deprivation of liberty apart from a criminal conviction is at stake, when the claim is thought to bear a special danger of deception, or when prior courts have concluded that the particular claim should be disfavored on policy grounds.[3] The highest quantum of proof, "beyond a reasonable doubt," is reserved in the legal system for the government's burden in criminal prosecutions. Such an elevated standard of proof is designed to minimize the risk of erroneous criminal convictions and is not used in civil cases, even when commission of a crime is contested in a civil legal proceeding.[4]

How do labor arbitrators determine which party bears the burden of persuasion in discipline and discharge cases? What quantum of proof do they require the party with the burden of persuasion to satisfy? The first question can be answered with considerable confidence. The second question is more difficult to measure and does not yield a uniform answer.

The Burden of Persuasion

In arbitration of employee discipline and discharge cases under collective bargaining agreements no one disputes that the employer bears the burden of proving that the employee was disciplined for just cause, rather than the union having to prove that there was no just cause for the discipline.[5] The placement of the burden of proof on the employer in employee discipline and discharge arbitration cases affords the employee substantially greater protection from unjust disciplinary action than in other legal contexts. In litigation alleging an employee's discharge violated statutory protections against discrimination, or claims before the National Labor Relations Board that an employee was discharged for union activity, the burden of persuasion is on the party challenging the validity of the discharge.[6]

---

[3] *Id.* at 665-668.

[4] *Id.* at 669, 674-675.

[5] *Elkouri & Elkouri, How Arbitration Works* (Arlington, VA.: Bloomberg BNA, Kenneth May, ed., 7th ed. 2012), 15-23; *The Common Law of the Workplace: The Views of Arbitrators* (Washington, D.C.: Bureau of National Affairs, Theodore J. St. Antoine, ed., 2d ed. 2005), § 6.9.

[6] 42 U.S.C. § 2000e-2(m) (2006) (employee asserting Title VII claim has burden of proving that race,

Indeed, in arbitration of other non-disciplinary issues under collective bargaining agreements the burden of persuasion is generally assigned to the party that submitted the grievance—in most cases, the union.[7]

Russell A. Smith, a past president of the National Academy of Arbitrators, listed several reasons traditionally advanced for imposing the burden of proof on employers in discipline cases, but found the propositions both over- and under-inclusive. He thought that the seriousness of the penalty did not warrant a shift in the burden of persuasion because it applied even in cases where the penalty was only a brief suspension. Smith seemed to reject as well both the analogy with criminal law and the suggested distinction that, in discipline and discharge cases, the employer bears the responsibility because it is asserting an affirmative case and the union ought not be required to prove a negative. Finally, Smith was not persuaded by the argument that the employer should have the burden because it knows why the action was taken because in most non-disciplinary cases challenging employer action the employer also has better access to information about the underlying decision, yet does not bear the burden of persuasion.[8] The National Academy of Arbitrators, in its *Common Law of the Workplace* treatise, simply concludes that the reason for reversing the burden in arbitrated discipline cases is "lost in the mists of history."[9]

---

color, religion, sex, or national origin was a motivating factor for the employer's decision); NLRB v. Transportation Management Corp., 462 U.S. 393, 398-399 (1983) (burden of persuasion on NLRB General Counsel to prove discriminatory motive for employee discharge).

[7] *Common Law of the Workplace*, § 1.92.

[8] Russell A. Smith, "The Search for Truth—The Whole Truth," *Truth, Lie Detectors, and Other Problems in Labor Arbitration, Proceedings of the 31st Annual Meeting of the National Academy of Arbitrators* (Washington, D.C.: Bureau of National Affairs, James C. Stern & Barbara D. Dennis, eds., 1979), 40, 51. For a similar analysis and critique, see Robert H. Gorske, "Burden of Proof in Grievance Arbitration," 43 *Marquette Law Review* 135, 148-153 (1959).

[9] *Common Law of the Workplace*, § 6.9 Comment a.

Quantum of Proof

Although arbitrators uniformly place the burden of persuasion in discipline cases on employers, it has been widely observed that arbitrators differ on the extent of the employer's burden, that is, whether to apply the "preponderance of the evidence," "clear and convincing evidence," or "beyond a reasonable doubt" standard.[10]

Before exploring assertions in the arbitration literature about the extent of that divergence, and our empirical testing of those assertions, some words of caution are in order. Some arbitration commentators and arbitrators reject the entire question of quantum of proof as "just playing games with words"[11] or as a "distracting legalism."[12] Marvin F. Hill and Anthony V. Sinicropi say that such evidentiary labels drawn from legal forums "are not particularly useful in labor arbitration."[13] Thus some may think this examination of the imposition of different levels of proof in employee discipline cases entirely misguided.

Even assuming one accepts the inquiry as legitimate, determining whether arbitrators employ different levels of proof in different kinds of cases is, for several reasons,

---

10 *Discipline and Discharge in Arbitration* (Arlington,VA.: BNA Books, Norman Brand & Melissa H. Biren, eds., 2008), 431; Marvin H. Hill, Jr. & Anthony V. Sinicropi, *Evidence in Arbitration* (Washington, D.C.: Bureau of National Affairs, 2d ed., 1987), 33; *How Arbitration Works*, 949; Gorske, "Burden of Proof," 162-165.

11 Remarks of David Feller, "Admissibility of Evidence," *Arbitration 1982, Conduct of the Hearing, Proceedings of the 35th Annual Meeting of the National Academy of Arbitrators* (Washington, D.C.: Bureau of National Affairs, James C. Stern & Barbara D. Dennis, eds., 1983), 136.

12 *Common Law of the Workplace*, § 6.10 Comment. A tripartite panel reporting to the National Academy of Arbitrators in 1966 concluded unanimously that "the legal concepts of burden of proof are not very relevant to an arbitrator, that he is simply going to have to make up his mind with the empathy and caution appropriate to the circumstances." "Problems of Proof in the Arbitration Process: Report of the West Coast Tripartite Committee," *Problems of Proof in Arbitration, Proceedings of the 19th Annual Meeting of the National Academy of Arbitrators* (Washington, D.C.: Bureau of National Affairs, Dallas L. Jones, ed., 1967), 196. In 1980, another West Coast tripartite panel thought that while arbitrators would apply an imprecise and undefined notion of the burden of proof in most discipline cases, "most arbitrators" would require proof beyond a reasonable doubt in discharge cases involving charges of moral turpitude. West Coast Panel Report, "Decisional Thinking," *Decisional Thinking of Arbitrators and Judges, Proceedings of the 33rd Annual Meeting of the National Academy of Arbitrators* (Washington, D.C.: Bureau of National Affairs, James C. Stern & Barbara D. Dennis, eds., 1981), 139.

13 *Evidence in Arbitration*, 38-39. See also *Fairweather's Practice and Procedure in Labor Arbitration* (Washington, D.C.: Bureau of National Affairs, Ray J. Schoonhoven, ed., 4th ed. 1999), 269-289 (overview and critique of application of burden of proof in labor arbitration).

a necessarily inexact calculation. First, an arbitrator, in an award, formally may identify by rote a legal standard to be applied, but then not actually use that, or any, standard in assessing the evidence.[14] Second, an arbitrator consciously may be applying one of the alternative legal standards, yet make no overt reference in the award to the standard applied. Third, an arbitrator not identifying any specific proof standard may nevertheless be applying a sliding scale of levels of proof, seeking a varying level of certainty appropriate to the particular issue.[15]

Despite these limitations, if one wishes to describe arbitral practice with regard to levels of proof, the best evidence is the text of arbitrators' actual awards. Such an examination forms the basis of statements from commentators about arbitral proof practices, as well as our research, but our source is a larger and more representative collection of published and unpublished awards, rather than the small samples of less representative published awards on which other commentaries rely.

Commentaries on labor arbitration practice make claims regarding the standard of proof used in most disciplinary cases as well as the standard used in cases involving allegations of crime or moral turpitude. In the *Common Law of the Workplace*, where the National Academy of Arbitrators seeks to articulate "some generally accepted approaches toward commonly encountered problems,"[16] the following assertions are made about levels

---

[14] Benjamin Aaron, "Some Procedural Problems in Arbitration," 10 *Vanderbilt Law Review* 733, 742 (1957); Kenneth W. Thornicroft, "Arbitrators and Substance Abuse Discharge Cases: An Empirical Assessment," *Labor Studies Journal* (Winter 1989), 56 ("It can be argued that the burden of proof adopted by the arbitrator is adopted *ex post* rather than *ex ante* as a mechanism for legitimating the outcome.").

[15] *Evidence in Arbitration*, 37 (quoting Edgar Jones); Theodore J. St. Antoine, "How and Why Labor Arbitrators Decide Discipline and Discharge Cases: An Empirical Examination—Comments," *Arbitration 2007: Workplace Justice for a Changing Environment, Proceedings of the 60th Annual Meeting of the National Academy of Arbitrators* (Arlington, VA: Bureau of National Affairs, Stephen F. Befort & Patrick Halter, eds., 2008), 463. Professor St. Antoine suggests that an unarticulated level of proof may represent existence of a sliding scale of proof standards. There is little evidence, however, to support his speculation because the phenomenon of awards with unarticulated standards is pervasive yet reference to a sliding scale is largely absent, not only in the awards themselves, but also in the arbitral literature that commonly addresses burdens of persuasion as a choice between fixed categories. See note 10 *supra*.

[16] *Common Law of the Workplace*, Preface to First Edition, ix.

of proof:

> (a) "For *most* arbitrators, the normal quantum of proof required in disciplinary cases is 'preponderance of the evidence.'"
>
> (b) "For a *minority*, it is 'clear and convincing evidence.'"
>
> (c) In cases involving allegations of an offense that would be "a serious breach of law or would be viewed as moral turpitude" "*most* arbitrators require a higher quantum of proof, typically expressed as 'clear and convincing evidence.'"
>
> (d) In such cases of alleged serious misconduct, "*some*" arbitrators would employ a "beyond a reasonable doubt" standard, but most conclude that such a high standard has "no place" in labor arbitration.[17]

The *Elkouri* treatise describes the distribution among arbitrators of standards of proof similarly, noting the general use of the preponderance standard, but saying that in cases of crime or stigmatizing behavior "many" arbitrators use the "clear and convincing" standard and "some" use "beyond a reasonable doubt" or "preponderance of the evidence."[18] A treatise on discipline and discharge authored by the American Bar Association, Section of Labor and Employment Law, also describes arbitrators applying a preponderance standard in most cases, but suggests the existence of a trend toward the "clear and convincing" standard in cases alleging crime or moral turpitude.[19] Marvin F. Hill and Anthony V. Sinicropi, writing in 1987, perceived a general trend toward an intermediate standard of proof in all cases, somewhat lowering the standard in cases alleging crime or moral turpitude, but raising it in other cases: "Regardless of the nature of the conduct at issue, the body of arbitral case law appears to be leaning toward a clear and convincing standard rather than proof beyond a reasonable doubt or a mere preponderance of the evidence."[20]

---

[17] *Common Law of the Workplace*, § 6.10 (emphasis added). Elsewhere in the *Common Law of the Workplace*, however, a contradictory statement is made about the nature of the standard of proof in discipline cases. "[The] burden of proof is often said to be by the preponderance of evidence in contract interpretation cases and either clear and convincing evidence or, less often, evidence beyond a reasonable doubt in discipline and discharge cases." *Id.*, § 1.93.

[18] *How Arbitration Works*, 15-25.

[19] *Discipline and Discharge in Arbitration*, 432.

[20] *Evidence in Arbitration*, 37-38 (footnote omitted).

Prior to our study, however, there had been scant empirical testing of the assertions of these commentators. The few studies previously conducted focused on whether heightened standards were used in cases alleging crimes or other matters of moral turpitude. In a survey, reported by Jeffrey Small & J. Timothy Spreche in 1984, over 1,000 arbitrators were asked what standard of proof they would apply in a hypothetical case alleging theft. Of the arbitrators responding, 34.3 percent said that they would use "clear and convincing evidence" and 22.7 percent said they would use "beyond a reasonable doubt."[21] A 1989 study by Kenneth W. Thornicroft explored the quantum of proof used in 145 published cases from 1985-1988 involving employees discharged for drug or alcohol use. He found that 35 percent of the drug cases and 47 percent of the alcohol cases employed the "clear and convincing" standard. Thornicroft said that 9 percent of the drug cases and 14 percent of the alcohol cases used "beyond a reasonable doubt."[22]

Data on Quantum of Proof

Each of the 2,055 cases in our data base was coded to identify the standard of proof applied by the arbitrator. Our results arguably support the assertion of some commentators that legal definitions of quantum of proof have no place in labor arbitration. As reported in Table 5.1, arbitrators did not state the quantum of proof they were applying in 78.30 percent of cases. In only 9.73 percent of cases did arbitrators explicitly state that they were applying the standard of "preponderance of the evidence." The finding that, in more than three-quarters of arbitration awards, arbitrators did not state the proof standard they were applying, casts uncertainty, if not doubt, on the assertion in the arbitral literature that most arbitrators are using the preponderance of the evidence standard in most discipline and discharge cases.

---

[21] Jeffrey Small & J. Timothy Spreche, "Report of American Arbitration Association Survey of Labor Arbitrators," *Daily Labor Report* (No. 234), December 5, 1984, E-14.

[22] Thornicroft, "Arbitrators and Substance Abuse," 40, 58 tbl. 1.

Table 5.1 Arbitrator Statement of Quantum of Proof*
(N-size and column % are top and bottom value, respectively)

Standard	N
Preponderance of the Evidence	200 9.73
Clear and Convincing Evidence	207 10.07[2]
Evidence Beyond a Reasonable Doubt	39 1.90[3]
No Specific Standard is Articulated by the Arbitrator	1,609 78.30[4]
Column Totals	2,055 100.00

* The numeric indexes 1, 2, 3 and 4 indicate that the percentages in row 1 and row 2, row 2 and row 3, row 3 and row 4, and row 4 and row 1, respectively, are statistically different at the .05 level or lower.

If the vast majority of arbitrators do not articulate in their arbitration awards the quantum of proof standard they applying, is there any way to know whether they are actually applying one of the three proof standards defined in the legal system, or something different than any of the three? We earlier assumed that when arbitrators did not articulate a proof standard they were necessarily applying a "preponderance of the evidence" standard.[23] Such an assumption seemed to make sense theoretically. We thought that if arbitrators did not state the standard they were using they were, without so stating, simply determining whether the employer's claim of just cause was more likely true than the union's claim of lack of just cause—the very definition of a "preponderance of the evidence" standard. We did not think that an unstated standard of proof could be equivalent to either the "beyond a reasonable doubt" or "clear and convincing evidence" standard because the arbitration literature uniformly discusses these heightened standards of quantum of proof as departures from the

---

[23] Laura J. Cooper, Mario F. Bognanno & Stephen F. Befort, "How and Why Labor Arbitrators Decide Discipline and Discharge Cases: An Empirical Examination," *Arbitration 2007: Workplace Justice for a Changing Environment, Proceedings of the 60th Annual Meeting, National Academy of Arbitrators*, (Arlington, VA: Bureau of National Affairs, Stephen F. Befort & Patrick Halter, eds., 2008), 420, 453.

norm, rather than the norm in labor arbitration. As the preponderance standard was perceived as the norm both in civil litigation[24] and in the labor arbitration literature,[25] we thought, arbitrators applying what was assumed to be the norm might feel that they did not need explicitly to articulate the standard they were applying. When we examined our data in more detail, however, we found a quite interesting phenomenon refuting our initial hypothesis.

---

[24] In civil cases litigated in courts, the "preponderance of the evidence" standard is the norm; higher standards are treated as exceptions to the norm and applicable to a limited number of special situations. *McCormick on Evidence*, Vol. 2, 487 ("While . . . the traditional measure of persuasion in civil cases is by a preponderance of evidence, there is a limited range of claims and contentions which the party is required to establish by a more exacting measure of persuasion." (footnote omitted)). See also *id.* at 488-489 (listing five categories of issues in civil cases in which the "clear and convincing" standard is typically used).

[25] *Common Law of the Workplace*, § 6.10, Comment a ("At some point in close cases, the arbitrator has to decide how much proof is 'enough.' An arbitrator satisfied with more proof on one side than on the other implicitly applies the 'preponderance of the evidence' standard.")

Table 5.2 Quantum of Proof and Outcomes*
(N-size, row % and column % are the top, middle and bottom value, respectively)

Quantum of Proof	Just Cause for Employer's Discipline	Just Cause for Lesser Discipline	No Just Cause for Any Discipline	Row Totals
Preponderance of the Evidence	94 47.00[a] 9.20	47 23.50 7.94[b]	59 29.50[c] 13.38[c]	200 100.00 9.73
Clear and Convincing Evidence	82 39.61 8.02[2a]	65 31.40 10.98[2]	60 28.99 13.61[2c]	207 100.00 10.07[2]
Beyond a Reasonable Doubt	16 41.03 1.57[3]	7 17.95 1.18[3b]	16 41.03[3] 3.63[3c]	39 100.00 1.90[3]
No Specific Standard Articulated	830 51.58[a] 81.21[4]	473 29.40[b] 79.90[4b]	306 19.02[4c] 69.39[4c]	1,609 100.00 78.30[4]
Column Totals	1,022 49.73[a] 100.00	592 28.81[b] 100.00	441 21.46[c] 100.00	2,055 100.00 100.00

Chi-square (6) = 33.4116, p = 0.000
* The numeric indexes 1, 2, 3 and 4 indicate that the percentages in row 1 and row 2, row 2 and row 3, row 3 and row 4, and row 4 and row 1, respectively, are statistically different at the .05 level or lower. The alphabetic indexes a, b and c indicate that the percentages in column 1 and column 2, column 2 and column 3, and column 3 and column 1, respectively, are statistically different at the .05 level or lower.

The middle values in Table 5.2 show case outcomes for each of the three articulated proof standards and for cases in which no proof standard was stated. Interestingly, quantum of proof was not significantly correlated with outcomes except in two instances. First, when arbitrators applied the highest burden of persuasion of "beyond a reasonable doubt," arbitrators were more likely to find no just cause for any discipline (41.03 percent) than when no standard of proof was stated (19.02 percent). Second, arbitrators were more likely to find no just cause for any discipline when applying the "preponderance of the evidence standard" (29.50 percent) than when no standard was articulated in the arbitrator's award (19.02 percent). That second finding directly calls into question our earlier assumption that an arbitrator's failure to state a burden of persuasion was equivalent to an arbitrator applying a preponderance standard. Why might an unstated proof standard be associated with the lowest rate of full union victories, even lower than when an arbitrator states reliance on the preponderance standard? We have no reason to think that this finding means that a majority of arbitrators actually have reversed the traditional placement of the burden of persuasion on employers. Instead, we speculate that arbitrators, after deciding to rule in favor of a union in a close case, choose explicitly to note reliance on the preponderance standard in the award as a means to explain the outcome to the losing employer who presented a relatively strong case.

Table 5.2 permits some additional observations, but they were not statistically significant. Unsurprisingly, unions were most likely to prevail in full when the arbitrator imposed the highest standard, of "beyond a reasonable doubt" (41.03 percent). It is, however, surprising that arbitrators who explicitly applied a preponderance standard were at least as likely as arbitrators articulating a "clear and convincing" standard to find no just cause for any discipline (29.50 percent and 28.99 percent, respectively).

Table 5.2 also permits us to draw some broader conclusions about the relationship between articulated and unarticulated arbitral quantum of proof standards and case outcomes. Most fundamentally, the overall association between proof standards and outcome is highly significant.[26] Next, although lacking in statistical significance, we observed that employers were most likely to prevail in full in cases in which arbitrators imposed the responsibility of persuasion by a preponderance of the evidence (47.00 percent) and those cases in which the standard was unstated (51.58 percent). Conversely, and unsurprisingly, employers were less likely to prevail in full when arbitrators applied one of the articulated heightened standards (39.61 percent when the "clear and convincing" standard was used and 41.03 percent when "beyond a reasonable doubt" was applied).[27] The

[26] In Chapter 3, Tables 3.19(a) and 3.19(b), we disaggregate the data with regard to the relationship between outcomes and quantum of proof between discipline cases and discharge cases. That analysis indicates that the association of quantum of proof and outcomes was not significant in either discharge or non-discharge discipline cases. Comparison of Tables 3.19(a) and 3.19(b) also shows that arbitrators are even more likely to leave unstated their standard of proof in discipline cases (83.79 percent) than in discharge cases (75.91 percent).

[27] Thornicroft also found a dependent relationship between quantum of proof and case outcomes in his drug and alcohol study. Thornicroft, "Arbitrators and Substance Abuse," 59 ("The less stringent the evidentiary burden on the employer, the more likely it is that the employer will make out its case.")

"beyond a reasonable doubt" standard was least likely to be associated with the outcome that the employee's conduct warranted just cause for lesser discipline than that imposed by the employer (17.95 percent), but note that the "beyond a reasonable doubt" standard was applied in only 39 cases. The observed infrequency of "beyond a reasonable doubt" being associated with a split decision makes sense in light of the category of cases in which the "beyond a reasonable doubt" standard is most likely to be used—those with allegations of the most serious kind of misconduct. In such cases, if the employee is found to have committed the conduct, just cause is likely to be found, but if the employee is found not to have been the perpetrator, then no discipline would be warranted. Arbitrators would be least likely to find lesser discipline appropriate if an employee actually is found to have committed a very serious offense.

As noted earlier, Marvin F. Hill and Anthony V. Sinicropi thought that a trend had become evident by 1987 that arbitrators were rejecting both the "preponderance of the evidence" standard and the "beyond a reasonable doubt" standard in favor of the standard of "clear and convincing evidence."[28] Since our awards span a period of approximately 24 years, we are able to examine whether arbitral use of heightened standards of proof have changed over time and, specifically, whether our data support the Hill and Sinicropi perception of an upward trend in use of the "clear and convincing standard" in the mid-1980s. Figure 5.1 plots the percentage of awards that employed the "clear and convincing" standard decided in each year. Figure 5.1 provides no support for the Hill and Sinicropi prediction that a trend in favor of this intermediate proof standard commenced in the 1980s. Figure 5.1 instead reveals that the "clear and convincing standard" followed a random pattern of rising and falling use over time that is closely centered on the 10 percent ordinate.

---

[28] See note 20 *supra* and accompanying text.

Figure 5.1 Change in Use of Clear and Convincing Evidence Standard Over Time

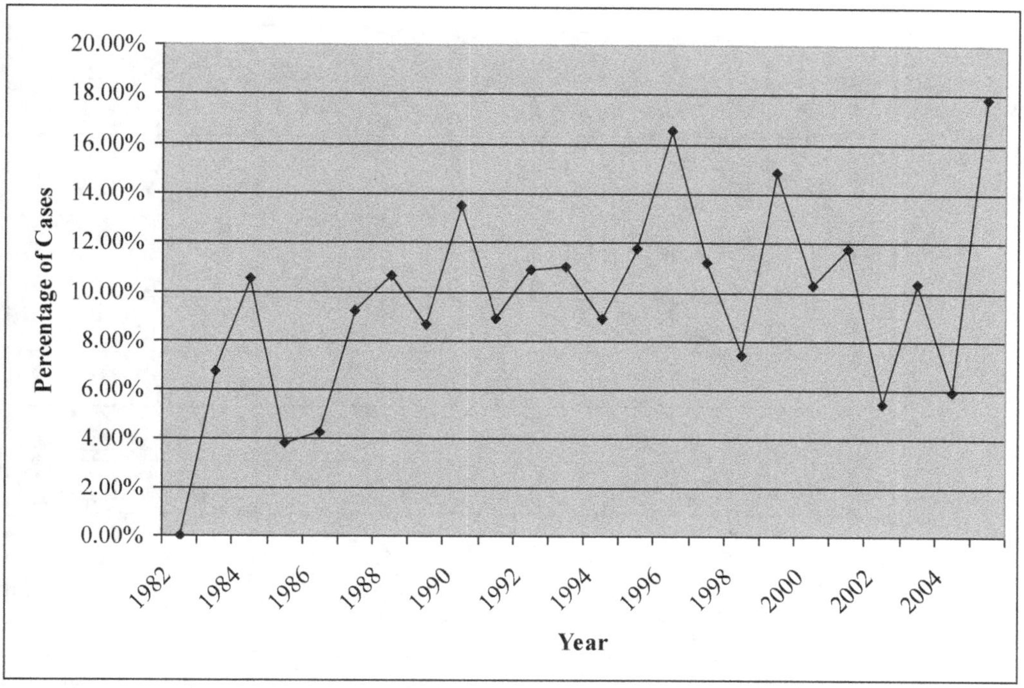

Figure 5.2 shows the "beyond a reasonable doubt" standard, although employed less frequently, peaking more than a decade earlier and declining over time with greater consistency, to the point of entirely disappearing in the most recent years included in the study.

Figure 5.2 Change in Use of Evidence Beyond a Reasonable Doubt Standard Over Time

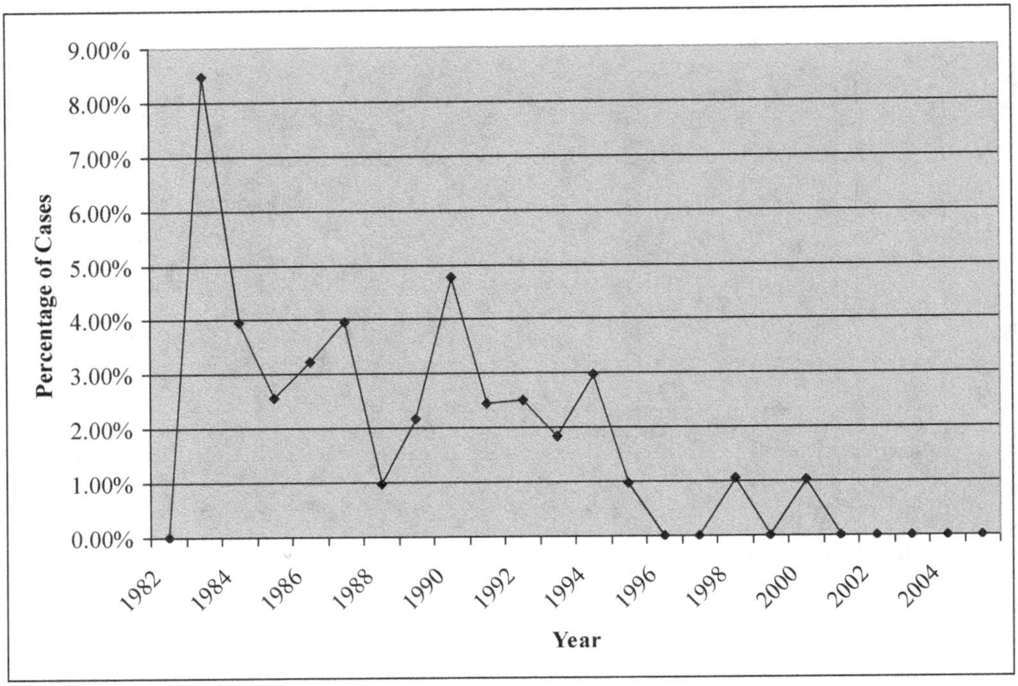

We can also test the assertion in *The Common Law of the Workplace* that in cases alleging conduct that could constitute crimes or other matters of moral turpitude[29] "most arbitrators require a higher quantum of proof, typically expressed as 'clear and convincing evidence.'"[30] The chi-square statistic reported in Table 5.3 indicates that there is a dependency relationship between the offenses considered crimes or acts of moral turpitude and the arbitrator's articulated or unarticulated proof standard. The share of awards using either the "clear and convincing" or "beyond a reasonable doubt" standard was significantly higher for offenses involving crimes or moral turpitude as compared to lesser offenses. Importantly, however, these results contradict the expectation of *The Common Law of the Workplace* that "most" arbitrators require a higher quantum of proof in cases involving

---

29 Offenses classified as "off the job misconduct" are included here as an employer would only be likely to consider disciplining an employee for misconduct away from the workplace when it was of a particularly serious nature.

30 *Common Law of the Workplace*, § 6.10(2).

crimes or moral turpitude. In fact, combining cases in which arbitrators used either the "clear and convincing" and "beyond a reasonable doubt" standards, we find that even when a crime or act of moral turpitude was alleged, in only 16.36 percent of cases did an arbitrator employ one of these heightened proof standards. Our findings do, however, support the conclusions of *The Common Law of the Workplace*, and the Thornicroft and Small-Spreche studies, that in cases alleging serious offenses, when arbitrators do apply a heightened standard of proof, they are much more likely to choose "clear and convincing" (13.01 percent), than "beyond a reasonable doubt" (3.35 percent)—a difference that is statistically significant.[31]

Table 5.3 <u>Quantum of Proof Correlated with Allegations of Crime or Moral Turpitude*</u>

(N-size, row % and column % are the top, middle and bottom value, respectively)

Alleged Offense Category**	Preponderance of the Evidence	Clear and Convincing Evidence	Beyond a Reasonable Doubt	No Specific Standard Stated	Row Totals
Cases Involving Crimes or Moral Turpitude	103 10.47 51.50^{a}	128 13.01^{1b} 61.84^{1b}	33 3.35^{1c} 84.62^{1c}	720 73.17^{1d} 44.75^{1}	984 100.00 47.88^{1}
Cases Not Involving Crimes or Moral Turpitude	97 9.06 48.50^{a}	79 7.38^{b} 38.16^{b}	6 0.56^{c} 15.38^{c}	889 83.01^{d} 55.25	1,071 100.00 52.12
Column Totals	200 9.73 100.00	207 10.07^{b} 100.00	39 1.90^{c} 100.00	1,609 78.30^{d} 100.00	2,055 100.00 100.00

Chi-square (3) = 44.6189, p = .0000

* The numeric index 1 indicates that the percentages in row 1 and row 2 are statistically different at the .05 level or lower. The alphabetic indexes a, b, c and d indicate that the percentages in column 1 and column 2, column 2 and column 3, column 3 and column 4, and column 4 and column 1, respectively, are statistically different at the .05 level or lower.

** If a case involved more than one offense category, any offense of moral turpitude is classified as a case involving crimes or moral turpitude. Offenses categorized as involving crimes or moral turpitude include dishonesty, off the job misconduct, violence & aggression, and drugs and alcohol. Offenses classified as not involving crimes or moral turpitude include on the job misconduct, insubordination, performance issues, attendance/absenteeism issues, and offenses classified as "other."

---

[31] Our results here contradict the observation of the 1980 West Coast tripartite panel described in note 12 *supra*.

Table 5.4 compares our standard of proof categories and various employee offense supercategories.[32] Disregarding the very small and heterogeneous supercategory of offenses classified as "other," we see that arbitrators were most likely to apply one of the two heightened standards of proof in cases involving allegations of dishonesty and least likely to apply one of the two heightened standards in cases involving attendance, insubordination and performance issues.[33] Arbitrators were most likely to articulate the standard of proof they were using in cases involving off the job misconduct and least likely to articulate the standard of proof they were using in cases arising from issues of attendance. The data in Table 5.4 were not the subject of a chi-square test because, as an employer may have based discipline on more than one alleged offense, the offense categories are not mutually exclusive.

---

[32] Table 4.1 in Chapter 4 identifies how the 43 offense categories were allocated among the 9 offense supercategories.

[33] In Table 5.4 we see application of heightened standards of proof in cases involving drugs and alcohol, but relatively less frequently than found in the Thornicroft study of 145 arbitration awards issued from mid-1985 through mid-1988. *Compare* Table 5.4 *with* note 22 *supra* and text accompanying. The differences between our findings and those of Thornicroft may be the result of the time periods studied. The years of his study included years when frequency of heightened proof standards was sharply rising. See Figures 5.1 and 5.2 *supra*.

Table 5.4 Quantum of Proof Correlated with Offense Supercategory*
(Arranged in descending order of likelihood of heightened quantum of proof; N-size and row % are the top and bottom value, respectively)

Cases Involving Alleged Offense Supercategory**	Preponderance of the Evidence	Clear and Convincing Evidence	Beyond a Reasonable Doubt	No Specific Standard Stated	Row Totals
Dishonesty	33 8.75[a]	52 13.79[b]	16 4.24[c]	276 73.21[d]	377 100.00
Off the Job Misconduct	13 13.83	10 10.64	5 5.32[c]	66 70.21[d]	94 100.00
Violence & Aggression	55 11.78	62 13.28[b]	8 1.71[c]	342 73.23[d]	467 100.00
Drugs/Alcohol	6 6.25	9 9.38	4 4.17[c]	77 80.21[d]	96 100.00
On the Job Misconduct	21 12.00	16 9.14[b]	2 1.14[c]	136 77.71[d]	175 100.00
Insubordination	46 9.81	38 8.10[b]	3 0.64[c]	382 81.45[d]	469 100.00
Performance Issue	42 11.35	30 8.11[b]	2 0.54[c]	296 80.00[d]	370 100.00
Attendance/ Absentee Issues	18 5.11	27 7.67[b]	2 0.57[c]	305 86.65[d]	352 100.00
Other	4 16.67	1 4.17	0 0.00[c]	19 79.17[d]	24 100.00
Column Totals	200 9.73	207 10.07[b]	39 1.90[c]	1,609 78.30[d]	2,055 100.00

* The alphabetic indexes a, b, c and d indicate that the percentages in column 1 and column 2, column 2 and column 3, column 3 and column 4, and column 4 and column 1, -respectively, are statistically different at the .05 level or lower.

** Table 4.1 identifies which offense categories are included in each supercategory. Some cases involved more than one offense category (e.g., the discipline might have been based on both a performance issue and on insubordination). If a case involved more than one offense category, any offense of moral turpitude is classified as a case involving crimes or moral turpitude.

The clearest indication that "most arbitrators" are not applying a heightened standard of proof in cases where employees are alleged to have committed the most serious kinds of misconduct comes from reviewing the cases in which arbitrators noted in their awards that the employee had been charged with a crime in the criminal justice system for the conduct for which the employee was disciplined by the employer. In Table 5.5 we observe that when arbitrators considered whether there was just cause for an employer to discipline an employee for the same conduct that had given rise to a criminal charge, arbitrators applied one of the two heightened standards of proof less than one-quarter of the time (a total of 23.71 percent). Not surprisingly though, the data do indicate that arbitrators are more likely to apply a heightened standard of proof in cases of alleged criminality than in cases in which no crime was alleged. The "clear and convincing" standard was applied in 15.46 percent of cases in which a crime was alleged, but only 9.81 percent of cases without an allegation of crime—a difference not statistically significant. There was a statistically significant difference between the application of the "beyond a reasonable doubt" standard in cases in which a crime was alleged (8.25 percent) and in non-crime cases (1.58 percent). Even in cases of alleged criminality, however, we found that arbitrators were nearly twice as likely to use the "clear and convincing" standard (15.46 percent) rather than that of proof "beyond a reasonable doubt" (8.25 percent).

Table 5.5 Quantum of Proof in Cases in Which Employees Were Charged With a Crime in the Criminal Justice System*

(N-size, row % and column % are the top, middle and bottom value, respectively)

Quantum of Proof	Employee Charged With Crime for Conduct Alleged	Employee Not Charged With Crime for Conduct Alleged	Row Totals
Preponderance of the Evidence	10 5.00[a] 10.31	190 95.00 9.70	200 100.00 9.73
Clear and Convincing Evidence	15 7.25[2a] 15.46	192 92.75[2] 9.81[2]	207 100.00 10.07[2]
Beyond a Reasonable Doubt	8 20.51[3a] 8.25[3a]	31 79.49[3] 1.58[3]	39 100.00 1.90[3]
No Specific Standard Articulated	64 3.98[a] 65.98[4a]	1,545 96.02 78.91[4]	1,609 100.00 78.30[4]
Column Totals	97 4.72[a] 100.00	1,958 95.28 100.00	2,055 100.00 100.00

Chi-square (3) = 26.5726, p = 0.000

* The numeric indexes 1, 2, 3 and 4 indicate that the percentages in row 1 and row 2, row 2 and row 3, row 3 and row 4, and row 4 and row 1, respectively, are statistically different at the .05 level or lower. The alphabetic index a indicates that the percentages in column 1 and column 2 are statistically different at the .05 level or lower.

Table 5.6 examines whether practices with regard to articulation and application of proof standards differ between the more experienced arbitrators who were members of the National Academy of Arbitrators (NAA) at the time of issuance of their awards and the generally less experienced arbitrators who were not members of the Academy. Table 5.6 shows no statistically significant difference in the extent to which the awards of NAA and non-NAA arbitrators omit reference to any standard of proof (78.92 percent and 77.62 percent, respectively). Among arbitration awards that referenced a proof standard, "clear and convincing evidence" was most frequently mentioned in the awards of NAA arbitrators and "preponderance of the evidence" was most frequently cited in the awards of non-NAA arbitrators. NAA arbitrators relied on "preponderance of the evidence" in 7.65 percent of cases, "clear and convincing evidence" in 12.41 percent of cases and "beyond a reasonable doubt" in 1.03 percent of cases—differences that are significant. The comparable percentages for non-NAA arbitrators were 12.00 percent, 7.53 percent and 2.85 percent, respectively, values that are significantly different and also significantly different from those for NAA arbitrators.

Table 5.6 Arbitrator's Quantum of Proof Correlated with the Arbitrator's NAA Status*

(N-size, row % and column % are top, middle and bottom value, respectively)

Quantum of Proof Articulated by Arbitrator	Arbitrator is NAA Member	Arbitrator is Not NAA Member	Row Totals
Preponderance of the Evidence	82 41.00[1a] 7.65[1a]	118 59.00[1] 12.00[1]	200 100.00 9.73[1]
Clear and Convincing Evidence	133 64.25[2a] 12.41[2a]	74 35.75[2] 7.53[2]	207 100.00 10.07[2]
Evidence Beyond a Reasonable Doubt	11 28.21[3a] 1.03[3a]	28 71.79[3] 2.85[3]	39 100.00 1.90[3]
No Specific Standard Articulated	846 52.58[4a] 78.92[4]	763 47.42[4] 77.62[4]	1,609 100.00 78.30[4]
Column Totals	1,072 52.17[a] 100.00	983 47.83 100.00	2,055 100.00 100.00

Chi-square (3) = 31.1922, p = 0.000

* The numeric indexes 1, 2, 3 and 4 indicate that the percentages in row 1 and row 2, row 2 and row 3, row 3 and row 4, and row 4 and row 1, respectively, are statistically different at the .05 level or lower. The alphabetic index a indicates that the percentages in column 1 and column 2 are statistically different at the .05 level or lower.

Finally, Table 5.7 examines whether arbitrators with a legal education address the issue of quantum of proof differently than non-attorney arbitrators. One would expect that attorney arbitrators, by virtue of their legal education and, often also, their work practicing law, would, as arbitrators, draw on their experience with the legal system in which differentiated proof standards are pervasively articulated. We indeed found that attorney arbitrators were more likely than non-attorneys to state a proof standard explicitly. Table

5.7 shows that fewer attorney awards stated no standard (76.04 percent) than non-attorney awards (81.93 percent), a statistically significant difference. Attorney awards were significantly more likely than non-attorney awards to rely explicitly on the standard of "preponderance of the evidence" (11.74 percent versus 6.49 percent). There were no statistically significant differences between the awards of attorneys and those of non-attorneys with regard to the frequency of use of the "clear and convincing" and "beyond a reasonable doubt" standards. Among attorney arbitrators who stated a standard of proof, the one most frequently cited was "preponderance of the evidence." Among non-attorney arbitrators who referenced a standard, the one most frequently stated was "clear and convincing evidence."

Table 5.7 <u>Arbitrator's Quantum of Proof Correlated with Attorney-Non-Attorney Status of Arbitrator</u>*

(N-size, row % and column % are top, middle and bottom value, respectively)

Quantum of Proof Articulated by Arbitrator	Arbitrator is an Attorney	Arbitrator is Not an Attorney	Row Totals
Preponderance of the Evidence	149 74.50[1a] 11.74[1a]	51 25.50[1] 6.49	200 100.00 9.73
Clear and Convincing Evidence	135 65.22[a] 10.64[2]	72 34.78 9.16[2]	207 100.00 10.07[2]
Evidence Beyond a Reasonable Doubt	20 51.28 1.58[3]	19 48.72 2.42[3]	39 100.00 1.90[3]
No Specific Standard Articulated	965 59.98[4a] 76.04[4a]	644 40.02[4] 81.93[4]	1,609 100.00 78.30[4]
Column Totals	1,269 61.75 100.00	786 38.25 100.00	2,055 100.00 100.00

Chi-square (3) = 18.7745, p = 0.000

* The numeric indexes 1, 2, 3 and 4 indicate that the percentages in row 1 and row 2, row 2 and row 3, row 3 and row 4, and row 4 and row 1, respectively, are statistically different at the .05 level or lower. The alphabetic index a indicates that the percentages in column 1 and column 2 are statistically different at the .05 level or lower.

Summary

In summary, in the vast majority of awards arbitrators did not explicitly state the quantum of proof they applied. Arbitrators not specifying any standard of proof were less likely than arbitrators applying any one of the specific standards (preponderance of the evidence, clear and convincing evidence, or beyond a reasonable doubt) to render an award wholly exonerating the employee. Heightened standards, requiring proof that is "clear and convincing" or "beyond a reasonable doubt," were rarely used. Contrary to much of the arbitral literature that assumes application of heightened standards in cases in which discipline arises from allegations of crime or moral turpitude, we found heightened standards of proof rarely applied even in such cases. Analyzing the use of heightened proof standards over time, we found no consistent pattern in the use of the "clear and convincing" standard, but a decline, to the point of disappearance, in the most recent years of our study, in the use of the "beyond a reasonable doubt" standard.

Awards of attorney arbitrators were more likely than those of non-attorneys explicitly to include mention of a quantum of proof standard. Among attorney arbitrators who identified a proof standard, the one most frequently cited was "preponderance of the evidence." For non-attorneys referencing a standard, the most common was "clear and convincing evidence." There was no statistically significant difference in the proportion of awards written by arbitrators who were members of the National Academy of Arbitrators (NAA) and those who were non-members with regard to omission of mention of a specific quantum of proof standard. Among arbitrators citing a specific standard of proof, awards of NAA arbitrators most frequently cited the "clear and convincing" standard and non-NAA arbitrator awards most often relied on the "preponderance of the evidence" standard.

CHAPTER 6

THE SEVEN TESTS OF JUST CAUSE

Arbitrators adjudicating employee discipline cases are asked to determine, in the language of the parties' collective bargaining agreements, whether the employee has been discharged or disciplined for "just cause."[1] Because contracts typically do not further specify the meaning of "just cause," advocates for employers or unions necessarily must present their evidence and arguments, and arbitrators their analysis, within a more defined understanding of the concept. Of all the countless attempts in articles, books and conference presentations more precisely to define "just cause," no single statement has gained the salience of "The Seven Tests of Just Cause," first articulated by Arbitrator Carroll R. Daugherty in the 1960s.[2]

The arbitration literature includes many assertions about the significance of the Seven Tests.[3] One commentator described it as "the single most definitive statement of just cause."[4] Another said that it was an "incisive codification" that "sets the standard for

---

[1] One survey found the requirement of "just cause" or "cause" for employee discipline included in 92 percent of collective bargaining agreements. *Basic Patterns in Union Contracts* (Washington, D.C.: Bureau of National Affairs, 14th ed. 1995), 7. Arbitrators and courts have found the requirement implicit in contracts without an explicit "just cause" provision. See, for example, SFIC Properties, Inc. v. Machinists, District Lodge 94, 103 F.3d 923 (9th Cir. 1996) (just cause implicit "in all modern day collective bargaining agreements").

[2] The seven tests were first listed in Grief Bros. Cooperage Corp., 42 LA 555 (Daugherty 1964), and further explained in Enterprise Wire Co., 46 LA 359 (Daugherty 1966).

[3] A notable omission from this list of sources remarking on the significance of the Seven Tests is the classic arbitration treatise, *Elkouri & Elkouri*, which does not even include a citation to either of Daugherty's decisions in *Grief Bros.* and *Enterprise Wire*, nor any discussion of the Seven Tests. *Elkouri & Elkouri, How Arbitration Works* (Arlington, VA.: Bloomberg BNA, Kenneth May, ed., 7th ed. 2012). An alternative thoughtful formulation of the meaning of just cause, articulated in Roger I. Abrams & Dennis R. Nolan, "Toward a Theory of 'Just Cause' in Employee Discipline Cases," 85 *Duke Law Journal* 594 (1985), has never received attention comparable to the Seven Tests.

[4] Christine D. Ver Ploeg, "Investigatory Due Process and Arbitration," *Arbitration 1992: Improving Arbitral and Advocacy Skills, Proceedings of the 45th Annual Meeting of the National Academy of Arbitrators* (Washington, D.C.: Bureau of National Affairs, Gladys W. Gruenberg, ed., 1993), 220, 223-224.

exploring the relationship between disciplinary due process and just cause."[5] The National Academy of Arbitrator's *Common Law of the Workplace* describes the Seven Tests as "undeniably influential."[6] Another book, a 560-page treatise on just cause, now in its third edition, is entirely structured around application of the Seven Tests.[7] Since the 1960s, the Seven Tests have been widely used in materials designed for the training of arbitrators and labor arbitration advocates, including those of the American Arbitration Association and American Bar Association.[8]

The Seven Tests

The Seven Tests are posed in the form of questions. In this articulation, a "no" answer to any one of the questions "normally signifies that just and proper cause did not exist."[9] The questions are:

> 1. Did the company give to the employee forewarning or foreknowledge of the possible or probable disciplinary consequences of the employee's conduct?
>
> 2. Was the company's rule or managerial order reasonably related to (a) the orderly, efficient, and safe operation of the company's business and (b) the performance that the company might properly expect of the employee?
>
> 3. Did the company, before administering discipline to an employee, make an effort to discover whether the employee did in fact violate or disobey a rule or order of management?

---

5 Donald S. McPherson, "The Evolving Concept of Just Cause: Carroll R. Daugherty and the Requirement of Disciplinary Due Process," 38 *Labor Law Journal* 387, 387 (1987).

6 *The Common Law of the Workplace: The Views of Arbitrators* (Washington, D.C.: Bureau of National Affairs, Theodore J. St. Antoine, ed., 2d ed. 2005), § 6.12 Comment.

7 Adolph M. Koven & Susan L. Smith, *Just Cause: The Seven Tests* (Washington. D.C.: Bureau of National Affairs, Kenneth May, rev. 3d ed., 2006). Although the first edition of the book was intended to advocate use of the Seven Tests, the current edition presents the tests "in a dispassionate manner, rather than as a volume advocating their unwavering application." *Id.* at 2.

8 John E. Dunsford, "Arbitral Discretion: The Tests of Just Cause," *Arbitration 1989, The Arbitrator's Discretion During and After the Hearing, Proceedings of the 42nd Annual Meeting of the National Academy of Arbitrators* (Washington, D.C.: Bureau of National Affairs, Gladys W. Gruenberg, ed., 1990), 23, 33. It was even the subject of a training film, "Arbitration: The Seven Tests of Just Cause." McPherson, "The Evolving Concept," at 389-390.

9 Grief Bros. Cooperage Corp., 42 LA 555, 557 (Daugherty 1964).

4. Was the company's investigation conducted fairly and objectively?

5. At the investigation, did the "judge" obtain substantial evidence or proof that the employee was guilty as charged?

6. Has the company applied its rules, orders, and penalties evenhandedly and without discrimination to all employees?

7. Was the degree of discipline administered by the company in a particular case reasonably related to (a) the seriousness of the employee's proven offense and (b) the record of the employee in his service with the company?

When Daugherty first announced these tests, he described them as a statement of the "common law" derived from the innumerable discipline decisions of arbitrators over the years.[10] Commentators, however, have criticized the formulation first, as a matter of theory, and second, as a matter of descriptive accuracy.

The theoretical criticism has been principally directed at three concerns: (1) that the tests excessively limit the arbitrator's exercise of discretion;[11] (2) that the tests suggest that the arbitrator is not determining just cause *de novo* but rather deferentially reviewing an employer's disciplinary decision;[12] and (3) that the tests inappropriately require an arbitrator to overturn a disciplinary action because of an employer's procedural defect, regardless of the seriousness of the employee's offense or the extent to which the defect prejudiced the employee.[13]

---

[10] *Id.*

[11] Dunsford, "Arbitral Discretion," 37-40; Richard Mittenthal & M. David Vaughn, "Working at the Margins of 'Just Cause': The Never-Ending Dispute Over Arbitral Discretion on the Discharge Penalty," *Arbitration 2006: Taking Stock in a New Century, Proceedings of the 59th Annual Meeting of the National Academy of Arbitrators* (Washington, D.C.: Bureau of National Affairs, Paul F. Gerhart & Stephen F. Befort, eds., 2007), 32, 44-45.

[12] Dunsford, "Arbitral Discretion," 23, 32-33; Ver Ploeg, "Investigatory Due Process," 233.

[13] Jack Clarke, "To What Extent Do and Should the Seven Tests Guide Arbitrators or the Parties?," *Arbitration 2002, Workplace Arbitration: A Process in Evolution, Proceedings of the 55th Annual Meeting of the National Academy of Arbitrators* (Washington, D.C.: Bureau of National Affairs, Charles J. Coleman, ed., 2003), 51; Ver Ploeg, "Investigatory Due Process," 229-231.

Although the Seven Tests were initially offered as a description of what arbitrators actually do, several commentators have expressed doubt about whether the Seven Tests are an accurate description of arbitral practice.[14] We are aware of no previous empirical study that sought to determine the proportion of arbitration awards that rely upon the Seven Tests.[15]

Measuring Arbitral Use of the Seven Tests

As we test the influence of the Seven Tests, we should be clear about what we are measuring and what we are not. We are not assessing here whether some of the inquiries posed by the Seven Tests are, individually, relevant to the arguments of the parties and the decisions of arbitrators, as indeed they surely are. For example, Table 9.4 in Chapter 9 notes that arbitrators sometimes do mitigate penalties because an employee's discipline appears disproportionate to the offense or because of the length of the employee's employment with that employer. Rather, we are examining here, to the extent possible, whether the rubric of the Seven Tests, as a unified defining formulation of the meaning of just cause, explicitly manifests itself in the arguments of parties and the awards of arbitrators.

In our study, we coded the answer to the question: "Does the arbitrator draw on Daugherty's Seven Tests in reaching the arbitrator's 'guilt' and/or 'just cause' determinations?" As seen in Table 6.1, we found that 91.44 percent of disciplinary decisions did *not* express reliance on the Seven Tests; and significantly, only 8.56 percent of decisions explicitly used that structure for analysis of just cause.

---

[14] *Discipline and Discharge in Arbitration* (Arlington, VA.: BNA Books, Norman Brand & Melissa H. Biren, eds., 2008), 33, 34 (The Seven Tests are a "good preliminary tool for . . . discussion of just cause," but enthusiasm for their use is "far from universal."); Dunsford, "Arbitral Discretion," 9.

[15] The closest to an empirical examination was Professor Ver Ploeg's reading of ten years of published arbitral decisions from which she concluded that there was no consensus among arbitrators on the question of whether an employer's investigatory procedural irregularities should invalidate the employer's discipline. Ver Ploeg, "Investigatory Due Process," 228. Professor Ver Ploeg, however, provided no tally of the cases taking alternative perspectives. Despite the title of the article by Jack Clarke cited in note 13 *supra* ("To What Extent Do and Should the Seven Tests Guide Arbitrators or the Parties?"), the article makes no attempt to measure arbitrators' use of the Seven Tests.

Table 6.1 Use of the Seven Tests by Advocates and Arbitrators (All Cases)*
(N-size, row % and column % are the top, middle and bottom value, respectively)

	Arbitrator Used Seven Tests	Arbitrator Did Not Use Seven Tests	Row Totals
One or Both Parties Invoked Seven Tests	28 35.00[1a] 15.91[1a]	52 65.00[1] 2.77[1]	80 100.00 3.89[1]
Neither Party Invoked Seven Tests	148 7.49[a] 84.09[a]	1,827 92.51 97.23	1,975 100.00 96.11
Column Totals	176 8.56[a] 100.00	1,879 91.44 100.00	2,055 100.00 100.00

Chi-square (1) = 74.2839, p = 0.000
* The numeric index 1 indicates that the percentages in row 1 and row 2 are statistically different at the .05 level or lower. The alphabetic index a indicates that the percentages in column 1 and column 2 are statistically different at the .05 level or lower.

In the course of examining our data with regard to this question, however, we discovered a surprising fact. A single arbitrator accounted for 27.7 percent of all cases in which the Seven Tests were used. This one arbitrator, whom we will call Arbitrator A, both decided a lot of discipline and discharge cases (90 awards), and used the Seven Tests in a high proportion of them (48 cases or 53.33 percent of awards issued by Arbitrator A). To prevent the decisions of Arbitrator A from distorting our report of the general use of the Seven Tests, we have removed all of Arbitrator A's decisions from the reported findings in many of the tables that follow. Table 6.2 replicates Table 6.1 with Arbitrator A's awards omitted. Excluding Arbitrator A's awards, only 6.51 percent of the decisions employed the Seven Tests. Thus, in 93.49 percent of awards the arbitrator did not rely on the Seven Tests.

Table 6.2 Use of the Seven Tests by Advocates and Arbitrators (Arbitrator A's Decisions Omitted)*

(N-size, row % and column % are the top, middle and bottom value, respectively)

	Arbitrator Used Seven Tests	Arbitrator Did Not Use Seven Tests	Row Totals
One or Both Parties Invoked Seven Tests	23 31.94[1a] 17.97[1a]	49 68.06[1a] 2.67[1]	72 100.00 3.66[1]
Neither Party Invoked Seven Tests	105 5.55[a] 82.03[a]	1,788 94.45 97.33	1,893 100.00 96.34
Column Totals	128 6.51[a] 100.00	1,837 93.49 100.00	1,965 100.00 100.00

Chi-square (1) = 79.3704, p = 0.000

* The numeric index 1 indicates that the percentages in row 1 and row 2 are statistically different at the .05 level or lower. The alphabetic index a indicates that the percentages in column 1 and column 2 are statistically different at the .05 level or lower.

We also sought to assess the extent to which party advocacy was based on the Seven Tests, and the extent to which such advocacy affected arbitrators' reliance on that standard. As arbitrators' awards typically summarize the parties' arguments, we measured party reliance by whether there was any mention in the arbitrator's award of either the employer or the union invoking the Seven Tests.[16] Using that measure, Tables 6.1 and 6.2 show that, regardless of inclusion of Arbitrator A's awards, in slightly more than 96 percent of all cases neither the union nor the employer advocates referenced the Seven Tests. Both Tables 6.1 and 6.2 show that arbitrators were much more likely to employ the Seven Tests in cases in which advocates invoked it. Table 6.2 (with Arbitrator A excluded) shows that arbitrators were nearly six times more likely to rely on the Seven Tests in cases where advocates had done so than where they had not. That suggests that when arbitrators rely on the Seven Tests they often do so to accommodate the perspective of the advocates rather than because the

[16] Arbitration awards and advocate arguments were coded as relying upon the Seven Tests if that label was explicitly used or if the specific questions that comprise the Seven Tests were noted in the award, respectively, as part of the arbitrator's analysis or the arbitrator's description of the parties' arguments. As we did not have available the parties' briefs or oral arguments, our measure of the extent to which parties invoked the Seven Tests and our measure of the extent to which arbitrators declined to follow a party's advocacy of use of the Seven Tests are likely both understated.

arbitrators independently believed that the Seven Tests was the appropriate method of analysis. On the other hand, arbitrators frequently rejected the parties' reliance on the Seven Tests in writing their awards. Table 6.2 also indicates that in cases in which the arbitrator's award noted that one or both advocates relied on the Seven Tests, arbitrators were more than twice as likely *not* to use the Seven Tests in reaching their conclusions (68.06 percent of the time) as to adopt the advocate's approach (31.94 percent of the time). These findings suggest that arbitrators largely decide whether to employ the Seven Tests as a matter of personal philosophy and not because of party advocacy or particular case characteristics. In our study, some arbitrators employed the Seven Tests with relatively great frequency, while two-thirds of arbitrators never did. Of the 81 arbitrators who issued awards in the data base, only 27 arbitrators (33.33 percent) ever employed the Seven Tests. Recall also that a single arbitrator, Arbitrator A, alone decided 27.27 percent of all cases in the data base in which the Seven Tests were used.

In Table 6.3 we cross-tabulate the attorney representation and Seven Tests variables separately for unions and employers. The chi-square tests in the table's top and bottom panels are not statistically significant, indicating that these variables are not dependent.[17] In addition, though, the table shows us that union advocates referenced the Seven Tests more frequently (2.73 percent of the time) than employer advocates (1.75 percent of the time). This finding may be explained by the fact that the Seven Tests direct an arbitrator to overturn employee discipline, even if the arbitrator finds the employee engaged in the alleged misconduct, if the employer made a procedural error. Another interesting finding here concerns a difference between attorney-represented unions and employers in their invocation of the Seven Tests. Whether the union's advocate is an attorney does not appear to affect the advocate's reliance on the Seven Tests. For employers, however, attorney advocates are approximately twice as likely as non-attorney advocates to invoke the Seven Tests—a significant difference.

[17] In Table 6.3 we are reporting on all cases, rather than excluding the decisions of Arbitrator A, both because the percentages are not that different and because reporting on a larger number of cases provides us with a more accurate picture of advocate behavior generally.

Table 6.3 Attorney Representation and Invocation of the Seven Tests (All Cases)*

(N-size, row % and column % are the top, middle and bottom value, respectively)

Attorney Representation	Advocate Invoked Seven Tests	Advocate Did Not Invoke Seven Tests	Row Totals
Union – Attorney	30 2.87[a] 53.57	1,017 97.13 50.88	1,047 100.00 50.95
Union – No Attorney	26 2.58[a] 46.43	982 97.42 49.12	1,008 100.00 49.05
Column Totals	56 2.73[a] 100.00	1,999 97.27 100.00	2,055 100.00 100.00
Chi-square (1) = .1584, p = .691			
Employer – Attorney	24 1.71[a] 66.67	1,383 98.29 68.50[1]	1,407 100.00 68.47[1]
Employer – No Attorney	12 1.85[a] 33.33	636 98.15 31.50	648 100.00 31.53
Column Totals	36 1.75[a] 100.00	2,019 98.25 100.00	2,055 100.00 100.00
Chi-square (1) = .055, p = .815			

* The numeric index 1 indicates that the percentages in row 1 and row 2 are statistically different at the .05 level or lower. The alphabetic index a indicates that the percentages in column 1 and column 2 are statistically different at the .05 level or lower.

Moreover, although Table 6.3 shows that union advocates, both attorneys and non-attorneys, were more likely than employer advocates to invoke the Seven Tests, Table 6.4 shows that when arbitrators did rely on the Seven Tests there was no statistically significant improvement in the union's likelihood of prevailing. The most controversial aspect of the Seven Tests is its directive to an arbitrator to impose no discipline, despite a finding that an employee committed an act otherwise appropriate for discipline, if the employer failed to follow fair investigatory procedures. If arbitrators invoking the Seven Tests were actually following that directive we would expect to see such arbitrators finding just cause for discipline less frequently than arbitrators not using the Seven Tests. As Table 6.4 shows, there was no such effect.[18] Arbitrators using the Seven Tests found just cause for discipline in 50.78 percent of cases while arbitrators not using the Seven Tests found just cause in 49.43 percent of the cases, a difference not significant at the .05 level or less.

Table 6.4 Arbitrators' Use of the Seven Tests and Outcome (Arbitrator A's Decisions Omitted)*

(N-size, row % and column % are the top, middle and bottom value, respectively)

Arbitrator Used Seven Tests	Found Just Cause for Discipline	Found No Just Cause for Any Discipline	Found Just Cause for Lesser Discipline	Row Totals
Yes	65 50.78[a] 6.68[1]	28 21.88 6.70[1]	35 27.34[c] 6.10[1]	128 100.00 6.51[1]
No	908 49.43[a] 93.32	390 21.23[b] 93.30	539 29.34[c] 93.30	1,837 100.00 93.49
Column Totals	973 49.52[a] 100.00	418 21.27[b] 100.00	574 29.21[c] 100.00	1,965 100.00 100.00

Chi-square (2) = 0.2311, p = 0.891

* The numeric index 1 indicates that the percentages in row 1 and row 2 are statistically different at the .05 level or lower. The alphabetic indexes a, b and c indicate that the percentages in column 1 and column 2, column 2 and column 3, and column 3 and column 1, respectively, are statistically different at the .05 level or lower.

While arbitrators employing the Seven Tests were not significantly more likely wholly to exonerate employees because of the employer's procedural failings, they were more likely to use a procedural defect as a reason for reducing (rather than overturning in full) the discipline imposed. In cases in which the arbitrator reduced discipline we coded the

[18] When all cases were considered, including those of Arbitrator A, there was also no significant increase in the percentage of cases finding no cause for any discipline when arbitrators employed the Seven Tests. See also, Table 3.17(a) in Chapter 3, which compares arbitral use of the Seven Tests and outcomes separately for discipline cases and for discharge cases. Table 3.17(b) also shows that arbitral use of the Seven Tests and outcomes are statistically independent.

reasons the arbitrators gave for the reduction. Arbitrators who cited the Seven Tests in their awards were significantly more likely to list a procedural defect as one of the reasons for the reduction in penalty. Table 6.5 (which omits the decisions of Arbitrator A) shows that arbitrators relying on the Seven Tests listed procedural defects as part of the rationale for reduction in discipline in 16.41 percent of their cases, while arbitrators not citing the Seven Tests relied on a procedural defect in only 8.87 percent of their cases.[19]

Table 6.5 Arbitrators' Use of the Seven Tests and Reliance on a Procedural Fault for Reduction in Discipline (Arbitrator A's Decisions Omitted)*

(N-size, row % and column % are the top, middle and bottom value, respectively)

Arbitrator Used Seven Tests	No Reliance on Procedural Fault	Reliance on Procedural Fault	Row Totals
Yes	107 83.59[1a] 6.01[1a]	21 16.41[1] 11.41[1]	128 100.00 6.51[1]
No	1,674 91.13[a] 93.99[a]	163 8.87 88.59	1,837 100.00 93.49
Column Totals	1,781 90.64[a] 100.00	184 9.36 100.00	1,965 100.00 100.00

Chi-square (1) = 8.0010, p = 0.005

* The numeric index 1 indicates that the percentages in row 1 and row 2 are statistically different at the .05 level or lower. The alphabetic index a indicates that the percentages in column 1 and column 2 are statistically different at the .05 level or lower.

While our results show that, generally among all arbitrators, use of the Seven Tests is rare, we also found that more experienced and more prolific arbitrators used the Seven Tests even less. Here we use membership in the National Academy of Arbitrators (NAA) as a proxy for identifying more experienced arbitrators because the NAA requires as a minimum condition for membership that arbitrators have decided at least 50 cases. We were able to determine for each arbitrator the initial date of NAA membership, if any, and thus to identify whether an arbitrator was, in the year of an award's issuance, a member of the NAA.

[19] Considering all cases, including those of Arbitrator A, the percentage of arbitrators relying on the Seven Tests reducing discipline for a procedural reason was 14.20 percent, while 8.94 percent of arbitrators not relying on the Seven Tests relied on procedural reasons for reducing discipline.

Table 6.6 indicates that cases decided by less experienced, non-members of the NAA were nearly three times more likely than cases decided by NAA members to rely upon the Seven Tests. Or expressed differently, disregarding the decisions of Arbitrator A, non-NAA members used the Seven Tests in 9.99 percent of their cases, while NAA members used the Seven Tests in only 3.25 percent of their cases—a difference that is significant.

Table 6.6 NAA Membership and Use of the Seven Tests (Arbitrator A's Decisions Omitted)*

(N-size, row % and column % are the top, middle and bottom value, respectively)

Arbitrator Used Seven Tests	Arbitrator is NAA Member	Arbitrator is Not NAA Member	Row Totals
Yes	33 25.78[1a] 3.25[1a]	95 74.22[1] 9.99[1]	128 100.00 6.51[1]
No	981 53.40[a] 96.75[a]	856 46.60 90.01	1,837 100.00 93.49
Column Totals	1,014 51.60[a] 100.00	951 48.40 100.00	1,965 100.00 100.00

Chi-square (1) = 36.5547, p = 0.000

* The numeric index 1 indicates that the percentages in row 1 and row 2 are statistically different at the .05 level or lower. The alphabetic index a indicates that the percentages in column 1 and column 2 are statistically different at the .05 level or lower.

We also found that less prolific arbitrators were more likely to employ the Seven Tests. Table 6.7 correlates use of the Seven Tests with the number of awards from an arbitrator that were found within our data base. Table 6.7 shows that those arbitrators who issued the fewest awards were significantly more likely to employ the Seven Tests. Arbitrators who rendered fewer than 50 awards were more than three times more likely to use the Seven Tests (10.62 percent of cases) than arbitrators who had issued 50 or more awards (3.46 percent of cases).

Table 6.7 Arbitrators' Number of Awards Issued and Use of the Seven Tests (Arbitrator A's Decisions Omitted)*

(N-size, row % and column % are the top, middle and bottom value, respectively)

Arbitrator Used Seven Tests	Fewer Than 50 Awards	50 or More Awards	Row Totals
Yes	89 69.53[1a] 10.62[1a]	39 30.47[1] 3.46[1]	128 100.00 6.51[1]
No	749 40.77[a] 89.38[a]	1,088 59.23 96.54	1,837 100.00 93.49
Column Totals	838 42.65[a] 100.00	1,127 57.35 100.00	1,965 100.00 100.00

Chi-square (1) = 40.4612, p = 0.000

* The numeric index 1 indicates that the percentages in row 1 and row 2 are statistically different at the .05 level or lower. The alphabetic index a indicates that the percentages in column 1 and column 2 are statistically different at the .05 level or lower.

Although nonuse of the Seven Tests is significantly associated with an arbitrator's NAA membership and large caseload, an arbitrator's status as an attorney or non-attorney was not related to use of the Seven Tests. The chi-square test in Table 6.8 shows that attorney and non-attorney arbitrators were not significantly different in the extent to which they employed the Seven Tests as a decision-making rubric.

Table 6.8 Arbitrators' Attorney Status and Use of the Seven Tests (Arbitrator A's Decisions Omitted)*

(N-size, row % and column % are top, middle and bottom value, respectively)

Arbitrator Used Seven Tests	Arbitrator is an Attorney	Arbitrator is Not an Attorney	Row Totals
Yes	82 64.06[a] 6.46[1]	46 35.94 6.61[1]	128 100.00 6.51[1]
No	1,187 64.62[a] 93.54	650 35.38 93.39	1,837 100.00 93.49
Column Totals	1,269 64.58[a] 100.00	696 35.42 100.00	1,965 100.00 100.00

Chi-square (1) = 0.0160, p = 0.899

* The numeric index 1 indicates that the percentages in row 1 and row 2 are statistically different at the .05 level or lower. The alphabetic index a indicates that the percentages in column 1 and column 2 are statistically different at the .05 level or lower.

Finally, we explored the relative frequency of reliance on the Seven Tests in the public and private sectors. As shown in Table 6.9, there was no statistically significant difference between the frequency that a public sector union advocate (3.52 percent of public sector cases) and a private sector union advocate (2.59 percent of private sector cases) relied upon the Seven Tests. Nor was there a statistically significant difference between the frequency that a public sector management advocate (1.42 percent of public sector cases) and a private sector management advocate (1.81 percent of private sector cases) cited the Seven Tests. Despite this absence of a difference in party advocacy between the public and private sectors, there was nevertheless a significant difference in arbitrators' reliance on the Seven Tests in the public and private sectors. As shown in Table 6.10, arbitrators were significantly more likely to rely on the Seven Tests in private sector cases (8.55 percent) than in public sector cases (5.20 percent).

Table 6.9 Reliance on Seven Tests by Sector (Arbitrator A's Decisions Omitted)*
(N-size, row % and column % are the top, middle and bottom value, respectively)

Party Invoked Seven Tests	Public Sector	Private Sector	Row Totals
Union – Yes	42 67.74[a] 3.52[1]	20 32.26 2.59[1]	62 100.00 3.16[1]
Union – No	1,151 60.48[a] 96.48	752 39.52 97.41	1,903 100.00 96.84
Column Totals	1,193 60.71[a] 100.00	772 39.29 100.00	1,965 100.00 100.00
Chi-square(1) = 1.3263, p = 0.249			
Management – Yes	17 54.84 1.42[1]	14 45.16 1.81[1]	31 100.00 1.58[1]
Management – No	1,176 60.81[a] 98.58	758 39.19 98.19	1,934 100.00 98.42
Column Totals	1,193 60.71[a] 100.00	772 39.29 100.00	1,965 100.00 100.00
Chi-square (1) = 0.4556, p = 0.500			

* The numeric index 1 indicates that the percentages in row 1 and row 2 are statistically different at the .05 level or lower. The alphabetic index a indicates that the percentages in column 1 and column 2 are statistically different at the .05 level or lower.

Table 6.10 Arbitrator Application of Seven Tests as Percentage of Cases within Sector (Arbitrator A's Decisions Omitted)*

(N-size, row % and column % are top, middle, and bottom value, respectively)

Seven Tests Invoked by Arbitrator	Public Sector	Private Sector	Row Totals
Yes	62 48.44[1] 5.20[1a]	66 51.56[1] 8.55[1]	128 100.00 6.51[1]
No	1,131 61.57[a] 94.80[a]	706 38.43 91.45	1,837 100.00 93.49
Column Totals	1,193 60.71[a] 100.00	772 39.29 100.00	1,965 100.00 100.00

Chi-square (1) = 8.6491, p = 0.003

* The numeric index 1 indicates that the percentages in row 1 and row 2 are statistically different at the .05 level or lower. The alphabetic index a indicates that the percentages in column 1 and column 2 are statistically different at the .05 level or lower.

Summary

In summary, we find the Seven Tests argued by advocates and utilized by arbitrators much less frequently than most of the arbitration literature would suggest. We found no mention of an advocate's reliance on the Seven Tests in more than 95 percent of cases. Union advocates were more likely than employer advocates to rely on the Seven Tests. Although one would expect reliance on the Seven Tests to increase the likelihood of an arbitrator finding no just cause for any discipline, it did not have that effect. It did, however, increase the likelihood of an arbitrator citing an employer's procedural failing as the reason for reducing employer-imposed discipline.

More than 90 percent of the time arbitrators did not rely upon the Seven Tests. Of the arbitrators in our data base, two-thirds never used the Seven Tests. More experienced arbitrators (as shown by membership in the National Academy of Arbitrators) and more prolific arbitrators were least likely to rely upon the Seven Tests in crafting their awards. Arbitrators were more likely to rely on the Seven Tests in private sector cases than in public sector cases.

CHAPTER 7

REMEDIES IN DISCHARGE CASES

Arbitral Remedial Authority

An arbitrator's analysis in a discharge or discipline case typically involves two distinct steps. The first step concerns whether the employer has submitted sufficient proof that the employee actually engaged in the alleged misconduct or other behavior warranting discipline. The second question concerns whether the level of discipline imposed by the employer is appropriate in light of the relevant facts and circumstances. Put another way, if an arbitrator determines that just cause does not support the employer's disciplinary sanction, the arbitrator must determine the appropriate remedy to rectify that misstep. This chapter reviews our findings with regard to remedies imposed in discharge cases, while Chapter 8 focuses on remedies in other types of disciplinary cases.

Although some early arbitration decisions took the position that arbitrators should defer to the disciplinary sanctions imposed by employers unless arbitrary or capricious,[1] the majority view is that arbitrators have broad authority to assess the reasonableness of management penalties and to modify them in like fashion.[2] This authority is inherent and exists even where the collective bargaining agreement is silent, although the parties have the ability to limit such authority through more restrictive contract language.[3]

The Supreme Court appears to have endorsed the majority view in its 1960 *Enterprise Wheel* decision. In that case, the Court described a labor arbitrator's remedial power in the following language:

---

[1] Stockham Pipe Fittings Co., 1 LA 160, 162 (McCoy 1945) (stating that an arbitrator should not "substitute his judgment and discretion for those honestly exercised by management" and should disturb a penalty imposed by management only where there has been an abuse of discretion).

[2] *Discipline and Discharge in the Workplace* (Washington, D.C.: Bureau of National Affairs, Norman Brand & Melissa H. Biren, eds., 2nd ed. 2008), 462, 486-488.

[3] *The Common Law of the Workplace: The Views of Arbitrators* (Washington, D.C.: Bureau of National Affairs, Theodore J. St. Antoine, ed., 2d ed. 2005) § 10.2; Marvin F. Hill, Jr. & Anthony V. Sinicropi, *Remedies in Arbitration* (Washington, D.C.: Bureau of National Affairs, 2d ed., 1991), 267-271.

> When an arbitrator is commissioned to interpret and apply the collective bargaining agreement, he is to bring his informed judgment to bear in order to reach a fair solution of a problem. This is especially true when it comes to formulating remedies. There the need is for flexibility in meeting a wide variety of situations. The draftsmen may never have thought of what specific remedy should be awarded to meet a particular contingency. Nevertheless, an arbitrator is confined to interpretation and application of the collective bargaining agreement; he does not sit to dispense his own brand of industrial justice. He may of course look for guidance from many sources, yet his award is legitimate only so long as it draws its essence from the collective bargaining agreement.[4]

Thus, it is generally agreed that an arbitrator is empowered to craft an appropriate remedy so long as it is consistent with the parties' contract and effectuates the contract's intent and purposes.[5]

Our study provides empirical support for the majority view. As indicated in Table 7.1, arbitrators in nearly 29 percent of our cases reduced the level of discipline imposed by the employer. Moreover, our raw data show that 62 of the 81 arbitrators who heard our discipline and discharge cases reduced management-imposed discipline to a lesser penalty in at least one decision. This represents more than 76 percent of the arbitrators in our study. This percentage increases to 100 percent when only those arbitrators who have issued 25 or more decisions are examined.[6]

The remedies ordered by arbitrators generally vary with the equities of the case and fall into three categories. The first category consists of those cases in which the arbitrator concludes that the employer's discipline was a reasonable response to employee conduct. Here, the arbitrator will sustain the employer's sanction and no remedy is warranted.

In a second category of cases, the arbitrator finds that the employer's discipline is unsupported by just cause and sustains the Union's grievance. The typical remedies ordered

---

[4] Steelworkers v. Enterprise Wheel & Car Corp., 363 U.S. 593, 597 (1960).

[5] *Elkouri & Elkouri, How Arbitration Works* (Washington, D.C.: Bureau of National Affairs, Kenneth May, ed., 7th ed. 2012), 18-8.

[6] All 23 of the arbitrators who issued 25 or more decisions reduced a management penalty to a less severe sanction in at least one decision.

in this context are reinstatement and back pay.[7] The guiding principle here is to make the employee whole for the employer's wrongful discharge decision. Accordingly, arbitrators generally award full back pay to compensate for all lost earnings, although this amount may be reduced by other earnings received by the grievant or other earnings that the grievant would have received through reasonable mitigation efforts.[8]

The third category of cases involves those outcomes in which an arbitrator finds that the employee engaged in inappropriate conduct, but also concludes that the employer's discipline was excessive. In these "split' decisions, arbitrators generally will order reinstatement, but accompanied by a reduced amount of back pay. The arbitrator may employ either of two methods to accomplish this reduction. One method is to reduce the severity of the disciplinary sanction. As an example, an arbitrator may reduce a discharge to a suspension of 10 days. In this instance, the amount of the back pay deduction coincides with the length of the resulting period of unpaid suspension.[9] The other method frequently used by arbitrators in discharge cases is to reinstate the grievant without any back pay award. Under this approach, the amount of pay denied to the grievant is determined by the length of time between the employer's discharge decision and implementation of the arbitrator's reinstatement award. Our study also identified a third, seldom used split outcome–an order entitling the grievant to a future vacancy.

Discharge Remedies in General

Discharge cases accounted for 1,432 decisions or approximately two-thirds of our aggregate data set. As depicted in Table 7.1, the overall relationship between arbitration outcomes and type of discipline is statistically significant. Specifically, arbitrators were significantly more likely to rule for employers in discharge cases than in other types of disciplinary matters.

---

[7] *How Arbitration Works*, 18-46.

[8] *Discipline and Discharge in the Workplace*, 468-485. Labor arbitrators generally lack the authority to award compensatory, consequential, or punitive damages. *Id.* at 472-473.

[9] *How Arbitration Works*, 18-47.

Table 7.1 Arbitration Outcomes by Types of Discipline*
(N-size, row % and column % are the top, middle and bottom value, respectively)

Arbitration Outcomes	Discharge Cases	Non-Discharge Cases	Row Totals
Arbitrator Found Just Cause for Discipline (Management Win)	751 73.48[1a] 52.44[1a]	271 26.52[1] 43.50[1]	1,022 100.00 49.73[1]
Arbitrator Found No Just Cause for Any Discipline (Union Win)	275 62.36[2a] 19.20[2a]	166 37.64[2] 26.65	441 100.00 21.46[2]
Arbitrator Found Just Cause for Lesser Discipline than that Imposed by Employer (Split Decision)	406 68.58[3a] 28.35[3]	186 31.42[3] 29.86[3]	592 100.00 28.81[3]
Column Totals	1,432 69.68[a] 100.00	623 30.32 100.00	2,055 100.00 100.00

Chi-square (2) = 18.5272, p = 0.000
* The numeric indexes 1, 2 and 3 indicate that the percentages in row 1 and row 2, row 2 and row 3, and row 3 and row 1, respectively, are statistically different at the .05 level or lower. The alphabetic index a indicates that the percentages in column 1 and column 2 are statistically different at the .05 level or lower.

Other Studies

Three prior studies have examined specific remedial outcomes in discharge cases. The findings of these studies are summarized in Table 7.2. In general, these studies found that arbitrators rule fully for employers in approximately half of all discharge cases, while fully ruling for unions in approximately 20 percent of all cases. They also generally showed that reinstatement without back pay constituted about two-thirds of all split discharge decisions with reduction to a suspension comprising the remaining one-third of decisions. In another study, Arthur Malinowski analyzed 153 cases in which arbitrators ordered reinstatement. He found that arbitrators ordered reinstatement without back pay three times more often than reinstatement with partial back pay.[10]

---

10 Arthur Anthony Malinowski, "An Empirical Analysis of Discharge Cases and the Work History of Employees Reinstated by Labor Arbitrators," 36 *Arbitration Journal* (March 1981), 31.

Table 7.2 Studies of Remedy Outcomes
(in percent)

Discharge Study	Uphold the Discharge	Reinstate - Full Back Pay	Reinstate - Partial Back Pay	Reinstate - No Back Pay
Jones (1963-1968)[1]	46.2	15.6	12.3	25.9
Jennings & Wolters (1971-1974)[2]	46.0	22.0	12.0	20.0
Shearer (1982-1986)[3]	51.0	20.0	8.0	21.0

[1] Dallas L. Jones, "Ramifications of Back-Pay Awards in Suspension and Discharge Cases," *Arbitration and Social Change, Proceedings of the 22nd Annual Meeting of the National Academy of Arbitrators* (Washington, D.C.: Bureau of National Affairs, Gerald Somers, ed. 1970), 163 (analyzing 665 discharge cases reported in Labor Arbitration Reports for 1963-1968).
[2] Ken Jennings & Roger Wolters, "Discharge Cases Reconsidered," 31 *Arbitration Journal* (September 1976), 164 (reporting on 220 discharge cases appearing in Labor Arbitration Reports between 1971 and 1974).
[3] John C. Shearer, "Reinstatement Without Back Pay—An Appropriate Remedy?" 42 *Arbitration Journal* (December 1987), 47 (examining 539 discharge cases reported in Labor Arbitration Reports for 1982-1986).

Our Study

Table 7.3 presents the distribution of remedial outcomes for discharge cases in our study. The percent of employer wins (52.44 percent) and union wins (19.76 percent) generally fell within the range found in the prior studies. Indeed, our findings with respect to those outcomes are virtually identical to the most recent study reported by Shearer. That similarity diminishes, however, once we turn to split outcomes. With respect to split decisions, two outlier findings are manifest. First, our overall share of split outcomes—28.35 percent—is below the 29 to 38 percent range found in other studies.[11] Second, reinstatement without back pay constitutes a smaller proportion of our split decisions than found in previous studies, namely 60.3 percent versus percentages that range from a low of 62.5 percent to a high, in Malinowski's study, of about 75 percent. Our lower incidence of reinstatement without back pay outcomes ultimately accounts for both of these outlier findings.

---

[11] Here again, our findings most nearly resemble those of the more recent Shearer study which reports a prevalence of split decisions that is only 1.21 percent higher than in our study.

Table 7.3 Reinstatement Outcomes in Discharge Cases*
(N-size and column % are the top and bottom value, respectively)

Reinstatement Outcomes	Row Totals
Uphold the Discharge	751 52.44[1]
Reinstate – Full Back Pay	283 19.76[2]
Reinstate – Partial Back Pay	149 10.41[3]
Reinstate – Without Back Pay	240 16.76[4]
Entitlement to Future Vacancy	9 0.63[5]
Column Totals	1,432 100.00

* The numeric indexes 1, 2, 3, 4 and 5 indicate that the percentages in row 1 and row 2, row 2 and row 3, row 3 and row 4, row 4 and row 5, and row 5 and row 1, respectively, are statistically different at the .05 level or lower.

The large size of our data set also enables a uniquely meaningful look at how remedy outcomes correlate with offense types. The results set out in Table 7.4 reveal several interesting findings. First, employers were most likely to prevail in discharge cases involving drug/alcohol issues (65.12 percent) and performance issues (64.62 percent). Second, employer win outcomes fell below 50 percent with respect to three other offense categories: on-the-job misconduct, off-the-job misconduct, and insubordination. For on-the-job misconduct cases, employer losses most often took the form of union victories which entail reinstatement with full back pay. The latter two categories, plus the attendance category, in contrast, had the highest incidence (>30 percent) of split decisions. The attendance and insubordination categories showed the highest frequency (>20 percent) of outcomes in which arbitrators direct reinstatement without back pay.

Recognizing that the results of our study are based on a much larger sample of cases that also encompass a longer time frame (1982-2005) than earlier studies, it is nonetheless instructive to draw comparisons to prior studies in terms of outcomes by offense categories. In this regard, the comparative record is mixed. We found that arbitrators were more likely to deny performance-based discharge grievances (64.62 percent), a finding that is consistent with Fred Holly's 1951-1956 study,[12] but contradicts his earlier 1942-1951 study[13] as well as Jennings and Wolters' 1971-1974 study.[14] We also found that employers won 65.12 percent of discharge grievances alleging drug/alcohol issues, which is approximately 13 percent higher than Kenneth Thornicroft's findings in a 1985-1988 analysis of 145 alcohol and drug-based discharge decisions.[15] On the other hand, our finding that discharges premised on insubordination resulted in fewer employer wins and a greater frequency of orders calling for reinstatement without back pay are wholly consistent with a number of prior studies.[16] Jennings, Sheffield, and Wolters suggest that this latter result occurs due to the frequent occurrence of mitigating factors in insubordination cases,[17] an assertion that we scrutinize in Chapter 9. Because the offense categories in Table 7.4 are not mutually exclusive, (*i.e.*, an employer may have based discipline on more than one type of offense in a case), the resulting cross-tabulation was not the subject of a chi-square test.

---

[12] J. Fred Holly, "The Arbitration of Discharge Cases: A Case Study," *Critical Issues in Labor Arbitration, Proceedings of the 10th Annual Meeting of the National Academy of Arbitrators* (Washington, D.C.: Bureau of National Affairs, Jean McKelvey, ed., 1957), 1, 7 tbl. 2 (showing 53 percent employer wins).

[13] *Id.* at 7 tbl. 2 (showing 42 percent employer wins).

[14] Jennings & Wolter, "Discharge Cases Reconsidered," 169 tbl. 1 (showing 35 percent employer wins).

[15] Kenneth W. Thornicroft, "Arbitrators and Substance Abuse Discharge Grievances: An Empirical Assessment," 14 *Labor Studies Journal* (1989), 40, 58 tbl. 1 (showing 52.4 percent employer wins).

[16] Ken Jennings, Barbara Sheffield, & Roger Wolters, "The Arbitration of Discharge Cases: A Forty-Year Perspective," 38 *Labor Law Journal* 33, 35 tbl.1 (1987); Holly, "The Arbitration of Discharge Cases," 12 tbl. 3; Jennings & Wolters, "Discharge Cases Reconsidered," 169 tbl. 1.

[17] Jennings, Sheffield, & Wolters, "A Forty-Year Perspective," 36-37.

Table 7.4 Reinstatement Outcomes by Offense Categories*
(N-size and row % are the top and bottom value, respectively)

Offense Category	Uphold the Discharge	Reinstate Full Back Pay	Reinstate Partial Back Pay	Reinstate Without Back Pay	Entitlement to Future Vacancy	Row Totals
Violence and Aggression	144 50.88[a]	53 18.73	34 12.01	48 16.96[d]	4 1.41[e]	283 100.00
Attendance/ Absentee Issues	153 54.06[a]	44 15.55[b]	25 8.83[c]	61 21.55[d]	0 0.00[e]	283 100.00
Dishonesty	165 53.23[a]	73 23.55[b]	30 9.68	40 12.90[d]	2 0.65[e]	310 100.00
On the Job Misconduct	49 45.37[a]	22 20.37	16 14.81	19 17.59[d]	2 1.85[e]	108 100.00
Off the Job Misconduct	36 49.32[a]	20 27.40[b]	5 6.85	12 16.44[d]	0 0.00[e]	73 100.00
Drugs/Alcohol	56 65.12[a]	9 10.47	7 8.14	13 15.12[d]	1 1.16[e]	86 100.00
Insubordination	124 44.29[a]	55 19.64	44 15.71	56 20.00[d]	1 0.36[e]	280 100.00
Performance Issue	179 64.62[a]	44 15.88[b]	24 8.66	27 9.75[d]	3 1.08[e]	277 100.00
Other	5 38.46	6 46.15	1 7.69	1 7.69	0 0.00[e]	13 100.00
Column Totals**	751 52.44[a]	283 19.76[b]	149 10.41[c]	240 16.76[d]	9 0.63[e]	1,432 100.00

* The alphabetic indexes a, b, c, d and e indicate that the percentages in column 1 and column 2, column 2 and column 3, column 3 and column 4, column 4 and column 5, and column 5 and column 1, respectively, are statistically different at the .05 level or lower.
** Multiple offenses may apply per case. Therefore, row totals may exceed the number of case observations.

Last Chance Agreements

Another remedial issue concerns last chance agreements. A last chance agreement "provide[s] for the conditional reinstatement of an employee who otherwise faces discharge in exchange for an agreement that any future violation will result in termination."[18] Such

[18] Donald S. McPherson & Burt R. Metzger, "'Last Chance' Discharges at Arbitration: Emergent Standards of Judicial Review," *Industrial Relations Research Association Series: Proceedings of the 46th Annual Meeting* (Madison, WI: Industrial Relations Research Association, 1994), 315.

agreements displace the usual just cause standard for discipline for a specified period, typically in the range of six months to one year.[19] A last chance provision usually is the result of a union-management grievance settlement, although such an arrangement also may be imposed by an arbitrator as a condition of reinstatement.

A last chance agreement may impact arbitral remedies in two ways. First, an employer may contend in arbitration that a discharge is warranted because the employee in question allegedly violated the terms of the last chance agreement by engaging in conduct proscribed by the agreement. Second, an arbitrator may order the reinstatement of a discharged employee conditioned upon future compliance with the terms of a last chance agreement.

As to the former context, *The Common Law of the Workplace* states that "*Generally*, arbitrators will enforce last-chance agreements."[20] We can directly test the validity of this assertion. We coded answers to the questions, "What was the outcome of the award?" and "Was the employee, at the time of the discipline, working under a 'last chance' condition?" A total of 162 employees in our study were working under the terms of a last-chance agreement at the time of their discharge. As shown in Table 7.5, employers won 72.21 percent of such cases, a rate approximately 20 percentage points higher than in discharge cases generally. Correspondingly, the prevalence of "union win" and "split decision" outcomes each fell by about 10 percentage points when the discharged employee was working under a last chance agreement.

---

[19] Donald J. Peterson, "Last Chance Agreement," 52 *Dispute Resolution Journal* (Summer 1997), 36, 38.

[20] *Common Law of the Workplace*, § 6.29 Comment (emphasis added).

Table 7.5 Arbitrator's Award in Discharge Cases by Last-Chance Agreement*
(N-size, row % and column % are the top, middle and bottom value, respectively)

Arbitration Outcome	Last-Chance	No Last-Chance	Row Totals
Arbitrator Found Just Cause for Discipline (Management Win)	117 15.58[1a] 72.22[1a]	634 84.42[1] 49.22[1]	751 100.00 52.44[1]
Arbitrator Found No Just Cause for Any Discipline (Union Win)	16 5.82[a] 9.88[a]	259 94.18 20.39[2]	275 100.00 19.20[2]
Arbitrator Found Just Cause for Lesser Discipline than that Imposed by Employer (Split Decision)	29 7.14[3a] 17.90[3a]	377 92.86[3] 29.69[3]	406 100.00 28.35[3]
Column Totals	162 11.31a 100.00	1,270 88.69 100.00	1,432 100.00 100.00

Chi-square (2) = 32.5155, p = 0.000
* The numeric indexes 1, 2 and 3 indicate that the percentages in row 1 and row 2, row 2 and row 3, and row 3 and row 1, respectively, are statistically different at the .05 level or lower. The alphabetic index a indicates that the percentages in column 1 and column 2 are statistically different at the .05 level or lower.

These results provide compelling statistical support for the *Common Law of the Workplace* assertion that arbitrators "will enforce last chance agreements." This is not surprising since it is widely accepted that an employer does not have to establish just cause in order to justify discharge in such circumstances, but only need show that the employee committed the type of misconduct forbidden by the terms of the agreement.[21] Indeed, several courts of appeal have held that arbitrators exceed their authority if they substitute a just cause analysis for the more restrictive determination of whether the employee engaged in the "triggering" misconduct prohibited by the last chance agreement.[22]

---

[21] McPherson & Metzger, "'Last Chance' Discharges at Arbitration," 315; Peterson, "Last Chance Agreement," 37.

[22] See, e.g., Tootsie Roll Industries v. Local Union No. 1, Bakery Workers, 832 F.2d 81 (7th Cir. 1987).; Bakers Union Local 326 v. ITT Continental Baking Co., Inc., 749 F.2d 350 (6th Cir. 1984).

Our findings generally are consistent with those of a prior study published by Donald McPherson and Burt Metzger in 1994. They reviewed 45 published decisions involving the discharge of an employee subject to the terms of a last chance agreement and found that employers prevailed in 35 or 77.8 percent of those decisions. Unions obtained reinstatement in the remaining 10 decisions, representing 22.2 percent of the sample.[23]

Although the McPherson and Metzger article does not detail the back pay status of the examined reinstatement awards, one would expect very few split decisions if arbitrators utilize the "triggering event" test as opposed to traditional just cause analysis. If an arbitrator's sole task is to ascertain whether the alleged triggering event actually occurred, the expected outcome would be an employer win for a "yes" determination and a union win for a "no" determination. As noted in *The Common Law of the Workplace* treatise, "[a]rbitrators have generally ruled that last-chance agreements . . . are binding on the parties and an arbitrator has no authority to modify a penalty once a violation of the last-chance agreement is found."[24] Table 7.5 supports this hypothesis, showing that only about 18 percent of last chance cases resulted in a split sward as compared to approximately 30 percent of discharge cases not subject to a last chance agreement, a difference that is statistically significant. Nonetheless, the fact that even 18 percent of last change discharge arbitrations resulted in a split outcome suggests that some arbitrators may be applying a just cause mode of analysis in spite of the presence of a last chance arrangement.

As noted in Table 7.6, arbitrators in our study most frequently issued split decisions in cases subject to a last change agreement in discharges involving insubordination (26.09 percent) and attendance (23.64 percent) issues. The relatively small number of observations in numerous tabular cells, however, preclude us from reaching definitive conclusions as to these correlations.

---

23 McPherson & Metzger, "'Last Chance' Discharges at Arbitration," 318. The authors state the arbitrators in their studied cases employed the triggering event standard in 73.3 percent of those cases, while improperly using just cause analysis in the remainder of the cases. *Id.*

24 *Common Law of the Workplace,* § 10.24.

Table 7.6 Last Chance Outcomes by Offense Categories*
(N-size and row % are the top and bottom value, respectively)

Offense Category***	Uphold the Discharge	Reinstate Full Back Pay	Reinstate Partial Back Pay	Reinstate Without Back Pay	Row Totals
Violence and Aggression	18 75.00[a]	4 16.67	1 4.17	1 4.17[d]	24 100.00
Attendance/ Absentee Issues	38 69.09[a]	4 7.27	0 0.00[c]	13 23.64[d]	55 100.00
Dishonesty	8 66.67[a]	2 16.67	0 0.00	2 16.67[d]	12 100.00
On the Job Misconduct	3 42.86	3 42.86	1 14.29	0 0.00	7 100.00
Off the Job Misconduct	5 83.33[a]	1 16.67	0 0.00	0 0.00[d]	6 100.00
Drugs/Alcohol	19 82.61[a]	1 4.35	0 0.00	3 13.04[d]	23 100.00
Insubordination	16 69.57[a]	1 4.35	2 8.70	4 17.39[d]	23 100.00
Performance Issue	25 73.53[a]	3 8.82	4 11.76	2 5.88[d]	34 100.00
Column Totals**	117 72.22[a]	16 9.88	7 4.32	22 13.58[d]	162 100.00

* The alphabetic indexes a, b, c and d indicate that the percentages in column 1 and column 2, column 2 and column 3, column 3 and column 4, and column 4 and column 1, respectively, are statistically different at the .05 level or lower.
** Multiple offenses may apply per case. The totals shown in the bottom row are the overall totals for each possible outcome, disregarding the multiplicity of motivating offenses.
*** This data set contains no offenses categorized as "Other" and no cases resulting in an Entitlement to Future Vacancy.

In terms of the second context in which last chance agreements may impact remedial outcomes, arbitrators in our study conditioned reinstatement on future employee compliance with a last chance provision in 12.2 percent of all discharge cases awarding reinstatement (82 occurrences). Arbitrator-imposed last chance agreements were most prevalent when paired with an arbitral order for reinstatement without back pay. These two directives coincided in 70.7 percent of all decisions in which an arbitrator ordered a last chance arrangement. As a prior study conjectured,[25] our data show that last change arrangements are most commonly used in cases involving drug/alcohol and attendance issues.

A Closer Look at Split Decisions

Reinstatement Without Back Pay

As shown in Table 7.3, reinstatement without back pay was the most frequently occurring type of split decision, accounting for 16.76 percent of all discharge cases in our study. This outcome constitutes 35.7 percent of all cases in which reinstatement was ordered. Reinstatement without back pay was most often ordered (> 20 percent) in cases involving attendance or insubordination issues and least often ordered (< 13 percent) in cases involving dishonesty or performance issues.

Reinstatement without back pay is the most controversial of the four principal remedial outcomes. A number of commentators have criticized the reinstatement without back pay option as imposing a remedy that does not replicate employer disciplinary practices.[26] A commonly voiced notion of arbitral jurisprudence is that an arbitrator's remedy should mirror that which an employer would have imposed if the employer had properly assessed the facts and circumstances of the case.[27] But, most employer disciplinary policies only employ disciplinary suspensions up to a maximum of a few weeks.[28] In contrast, a reinstatement without back pay order typically has the effect of an unpaid

---

[25] Kenneth Grinstead, "The Arbitration of Last Chance Agreements," 48 *Arbitration Journal* (March 1993), 71, 72.

[26] Arnold M. Zack, *Arbitrating Discipline and Discharge Cases* (Horsham, PA: LRP Publications, 2000), 148; Philip K. Kienast, "Reinstatement Without Back Pay and Back Pay Without Reinstatement: A Question of Appropriateness," 16 *LERC Monograph Series* (Eugene, OR: Labor Education and Research Center, 2000), 117, 118, 123; Shearer, "Reinstatement Without Back Pay," 48-49; John W. Teele, "'But No Back Pay is Awarded,'" 19 *Arbitration Journal* (June 1964), 103, 107-112.

[27] Kienast, "Reinstatement Without Back Pay and Back Pay Without Reinstatement," 118; Shearer, "Reinstatement Without Back Pay," 48-49.

[28] Kienast, "Reinstatement Without Back Pay and Back Pay Without Reinstatement," 118, 123.

suspension of several months. Employers and unions alike look with suspicion on this "compromise" outcome. As summarized by John Teele in a 1964 article:

> The former is inclined to feel that if the man was guilty enough to be deprived of several months' back pay, then he should not have been returned to the payroll at all. The latter may be heard to argue that if the man was not guilty as charged, he should have been made whole.[29]

Our findings support the underlying factual assertions made by these critics. Of the 516 cases in which employers themselves imposed a disciplinary suspension, 47.5 percent of those cases resulted in a suspension of less than one week in duration and 52.5 percent resulted in a suspension of more than one week. While we did not code the precise length of employer-imposed suspensions, these results suggest that the median length of employer-imposed disciplinary suspensions is approximately one week or five work days. In contrast, of the 240 cases in our study in which an arbitrator reinstated a discharged employee without back pay, the mean period of lost pay equaled 8.67 months or about 37 weeks, which translates into a suspension of about 175 work days (assuming the suspended employee would work 20 days per month). As displayed in Figure 1, these outcomes ranged from a high mean of 14.08 months for off-the-job misconduct cases to a low mean of 6.62 months for drug/alcohol cases. Thus, our data suggest that that the typical arbitrator-imposed order for reinstatement without back pay resulted in a period of denied pay that is 35 times longer than that which the typical employer would have imposed, assuming the employer properly had evaluated the circumstances resulting in discipline.

---

[29] Teele, "'But No Back Pay is Awarded,'" 104.

Figure 1. Mean Length of No Back Pay Period by Offense Categories

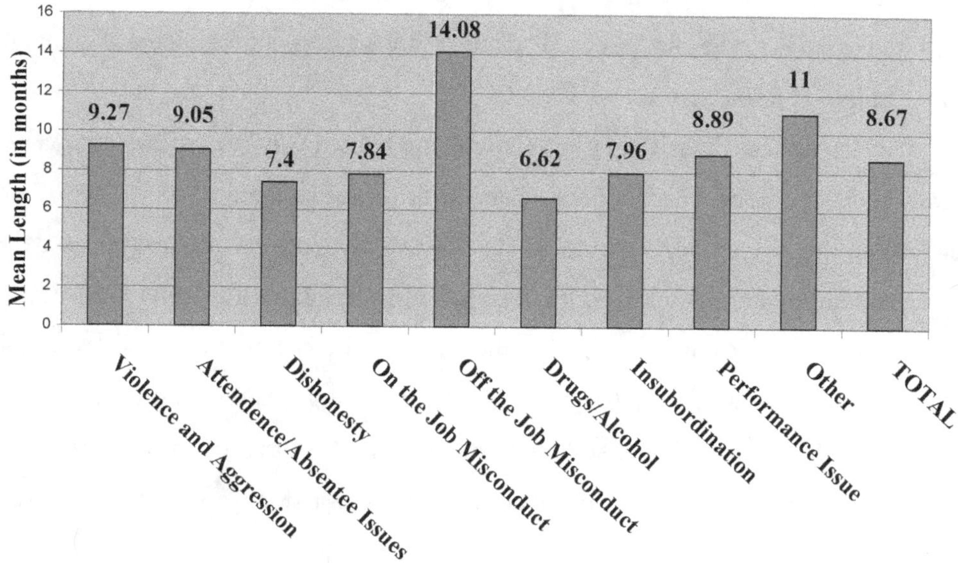

We also examined the impact of delay on reinstatement outcomes. As discussed in Chapter 3, we define "delay" as the length of time between the date of the employer's discharge decision and the date of the corresponding arbitration award. The literature suggests two possible and somewhat contradictory effects in this regard. Saxton, Miller and Fallon have theorized that arbitrators may use the reinstatement without back pay option more frequently in cases as the length of time between the date of discharge and the date of the arbitrator's award increases.[30] The underlying notion, apparently, is that arbitrators are increasingly reluctant to saddle employers with the cost of back pay as that sum grows over time. In contrast, Nelson and Uddin have suggested that arbitrators may be reluctant to order reinstatement in any form as the length of time between the date of discharge and date of award expands. They contend that delay often leads to a "new status quo" resulting from the employer's hire of a permanent replacement for the discharged employee and the

---

[30] See, e.g., William M. Saxton, Bruce A. Miller, & William J. Fallon, "The Discipline and Discharge Case: Two Devil's Advocates on What Arbitrators are Doing Wrong," *Arbitration of Subcontracting and Wage Incentive Disputes: Proceedings of the 32nd Annual Meeting of the National Academy of Arbitrators* (Washington, D.C.: Bureau of National Affairs, James L. Stern & Barbara D. Dennis, eds., 1980), 63, 84-85.

discharged employee's acceptance of alternative employment.[31] Nelson and Uddin tested this hypothesis in an empirical study which found that the likelihood that a grievant would be reinstated in a discharge case generally declined by 8.6 percent for each additional month of delay leading up to the arbitral decision.[32]

We tested these theories in two separate, but related ways. First, we compared case outcomes and the amount of delay associated with those outcomes. As Table 7.7 shows, longer delays, those averaging about 284 days, were associated with arbitration decisions that favor the employer, whereas shorter delays, those averaging from 268 to 264 days, were associated with outcomes that favor either the union or the prospect of a split award. These differences, however, are not statistically significant. These results contradict the Saxton, Miller, and Fallon hypothesis that longer delays should correlate positively with split decisions, while providing modest but inconclusive support for Nelson and Uddin's "new status quo" theory.

Table 7.7 <u>Outcomes and Delay in Discharge Cases</u>*

Delay	Management Win	Union Win	Split Decision	Row Totals
Case Outcomes	751	275	406	1,432
Days elapsed from discipline to decision	283.54	267.71	263.79	274.90

As a second method of comparison, we tracked outcomes though seven time-specific periods measuring the length of delay between discharge and arbitration award. Table 7.8 shows for each delay category (1) the share of all discharge cases that were upheld, (2) the share that resulted in the grievant's reinstatement without back pay, and (3) the share that resulted in the grievant's reinstatement under any condition (i.e., with full, partial, or no back

---

[31] Nelson & Uddin, "The Impact of Delay on Arbitrators' Decisions in Discharge Cases," 3, 6-7.

[32] *Id.* at 12.

pay). These results are graphically depicted in Figure 2 and illustrate two findings. First, the bottom graph in Figure 2 is "flat," which again is dismissive of the Saxton, Miller and Fallon hypothesis that delay and reinstatement without back pay outcomes are positively related. Second, the top graph in Figure 2 illustrates that cases decided following eighteen months or more of delay correlate positively with the discharge decision being upheld.[33] This finding also lends some mild support for the Nelson and Uddin hypothesis that delay and reinstatement are inversely related, but only in the context of cases that are atypical in duration.

---

[33] The issuance of a reinstatement award was 29 percent less likely in those cases in which the award followed the discharge by more than two years as compared to those awards issued following a span of only ten to twelve months. On the other hand, the number of awards ordering reinstatement without back pay fell by an even larger proportion (37 percent) over that same span. These findings suggest that arbitrators in delayed proceedings are more greatly influenced by a reluctance to reinstate long-departed employees than they are by a motivation to spare employers the rising cost of a back pay award.

Table 7.8 Delay and Reinstatement Outcomes*

(N-size, row % and column % are the top, middle and bottom value, respectively)

Delay (in months)	Discharge Upheld	Reinstate – No Back Pay	All Reinstatements	Row Totals
0-3	26 40.00[1] 3.47[1]	13 20.00 5.44[1]	39 60.00[1] 5.80[1]	65 100.00 4.57
4-6	236 54.13 31.47	79 18.12 33.05	200 45.87 29.76	436 100.00 30.66
7-9	224 51.73 29.87[3]	64 14.78 26.78[3]	209 48.27 31.10[3]	433 100.00 30.45
10-12	120 51.50 16.00[4]	43 18.45 17.99[4]	113 48.50 16.82[4]	233 100.00 16.39
13-17	76 53.90 10.13[5]	23 16.31 9.62	65 46.10 9.67[5]	141 100.00 9.92
18-23	41 56.16 5.47	12 16.44 5.02	32 43.84 4.76[6]	73 100.00 5.13
24+	27 65.85[7] 3.60	5 12.20 2.09	14 34.15[7] 2.08[7]	41 100.00 2.88
Column Totals**	750 52.74 100.00	239 16.81 100.00	672 47.26 100.00	1,422 100.00 100.00

* The numeric indexes 1, 2, 3, 4, 5, 6 and 7 indicate that the percentages in row 1 and row 2, row 2 and row 3, row 3 and row 4, row 4 and row 5, row 5 and row 6, row 6 and row 7, and row 7 and row 1, respectively, are statistically different at the .05 level or lower.

Figure 2. Outcomes per Variation in Length of Time from Discharge to Date of Award

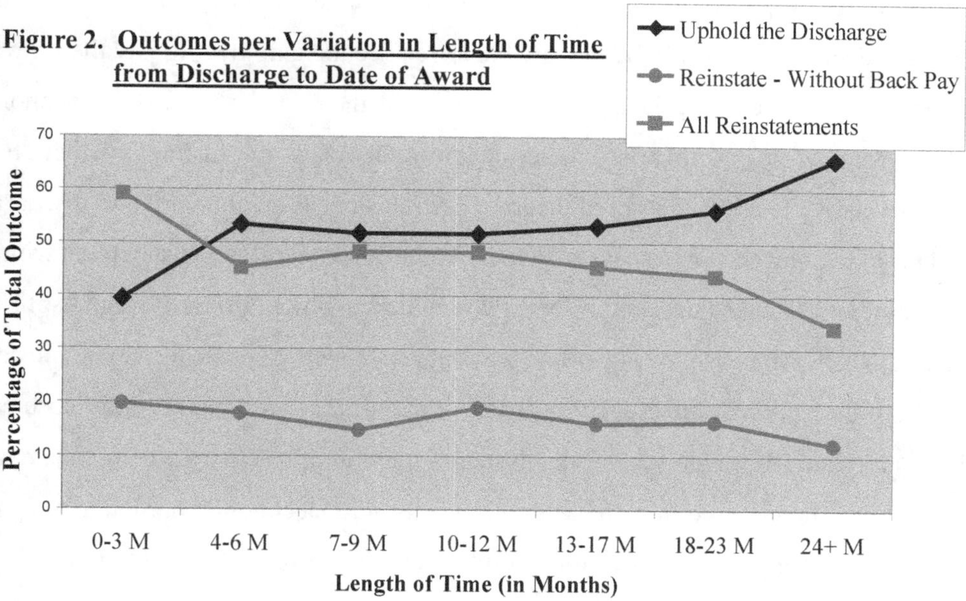

A fundamental question remains concerning why arbitrators so frequently utilize reinstatement without back pay as a remedy. Some commentators suggest that arbitrators use reinstatement without back pay as a means to provide partial satisfaction to both parties.[34] Two prior studies, on the other hand, reviewed published cases and found that the most frequently-noted reason for arbitrators choosing the reinstatement without back pay option was a belief that discharge would be too severe a penalty under the specific circumstances of the case.[35] This finding suggests that these arbitrators use reinstatement without back pay primarily as a means to mitigate an employer's termination decision that is viewed as too harsh under the circumstances.

We individually reviewed all 240 cases ordering a reinstatement without back pay remedy in our sample in an attempt to determine the arbitrator's rationale for choosing that option. In contrast to the earlier studies, by far the most frequent explanation used to justify

---

[34] See Laura J. Cooper, Dennis R. Nolan, Richard A. Bales & Stephen F. Befort, *ADR in the Workplace* (St. Paul, MN: West Academic Publishing, 3rd ed., 2014), 386.

[35] Kienast, "Reinstatement Without Back Pay and Back Pay Without Reinstatement," 117, n.1; Shearer, "Reinstatement Without Back Pay," 51.

this choice of remedy was that the grievant's serious conduct warranted a denial of back pay. Slightly more than 50 percent of our sample decisions invoked that explanation. As stated in one typical decision, "it would be inequitable to require the employer to pay the grievant for time not worked when the grievant's misconduct was the primary cause of his economic loss." This seems to suggest that the Minnesota arbitrators view reinstatement without back pay as an alternative to a lesser form of discipline rather than as an alternative to discharge.

This viewpoint arguably sheds new light on the purpose of the reinstatement without back pay remedy. Rather than simply being a device by which arbitrators can "split the baby," perhaps arbitrators use reinstatement without back pay to allocate the economic costs resulting from the administrative delay inherent in the arbitration process. In a close case requiring significant discipline but not the ultimate sanction of discharge, the reinstatement without back pay directive permits the arbitrator to assign the economic burden to the party whose misconduct triggered the need for discipline in the first place—the employee. From this vantage point, accordingly, it is perhaps mistaken to compare reinstatement without back pay periods with the length of a typical employer-imposed suspension because that is not the underlying objective of the reinstatement without back pay remedy.

Another matter warranting closer inspection is the lower prevalence of reinstatement without back pay outcomes in our data. As noted in Table 7.2 above, earlier studies generally showed that reinstatement without back pay outcomes comprised between 20 and 26 percent of all discharge cases. Our findings, in contrast, exhibit a much lower 16.76 percent frequency.

One possible explanation for this difference is that published awards contain more reinstatement without back pay outcomes than awards in general because publishers think that those borderline cases will be more interesting to their readership. Another possible explanation is that the incidence of reinstatement without back pay outcomes may be declining in response to the persistent drumbeat of scholarly criticism. If that were the case, one would expect to see a decline in the proportion of reinstatement without back pay outcomes over time. Our study, in fact, supports this hypothesis. Figure 3 shows the percentage of reinstatement without back pay outcomes in the three 8-year increments spanning the years between 1982 and 2005, inclusively. From a 19.65 percent prevalence in the 1982-1989 set of decisions—not far below the range found in other contemporary studies—the Minnesota proportion of reinstatement without back pay outcomes fell to 16.69 percent in 1990-1997 and still further to 14.11 percent in 1998-2005. Although the identified association's chi square is not statistically significant, the overall 28.2 percent drop in reinstatements without back pay outcomes that occurred between the first and third periods is significant. Whether this finding foretells an ongoing shift in remedy outcomes remains to be seen.

Figure 3. Reinstatement Without Back Pay Over Time

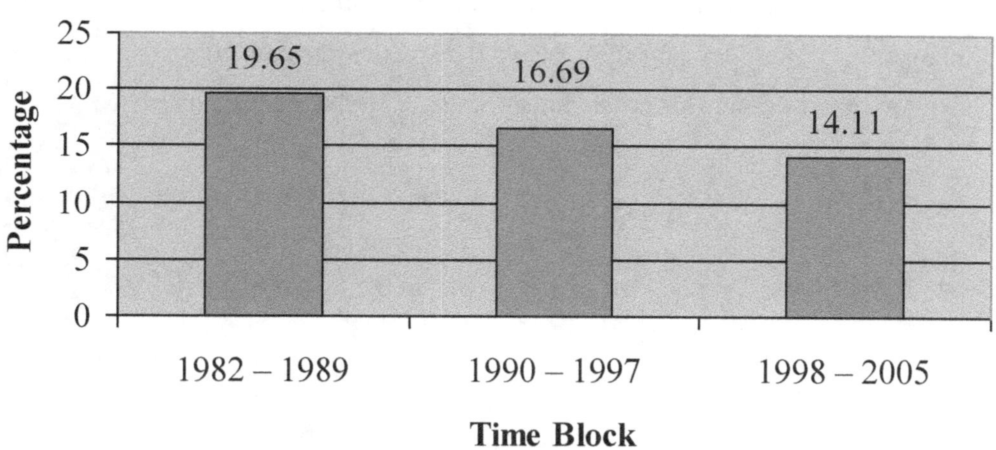

Chi-square(2) = 4.4708, p = .107

Reduction to Suspension

More than 10 percent of all discharge cases involved instances in which an arbitrator reinstated the grievant and reduced the discharge to a period of suspension without pay. This amounts to 22.2 percent of all reinstatement outcomes, representing the least prevalent of the three reinstatement options.

The two most likely offenses to result in a reduction to suspension were on-the-job misconduct and insubordination. With respect to these offenses, a plausible explanation for this high prevalence is that arbitrators are prone to concur in management's allegation that the grievant engaged in the alleged misconduct, while also concluding that management overreacted in selecting discharge as the appropriate level of discipline.

A most remarkable reduction to suspension finding concerns the length of the suspension period. The mean length of the arbitration-ordered suspension period was 61.04 work days. Even after deleting from the data an 849-day suspension outlier from the analysis, the mean length of the remaining suspensions was 55.57 days, or approximately 11 work weeks.[36] The mean suspension length by type of offense (depicted in Figure 4) ranged from a high of approximately 75 work days for on-the-job misconduct to a low of approximately 25 work days for dishonesty. The mode outcome, consisting of more than one-sixth of all reduction to suspension results, was a 30-day suspension period.

---

[36] We also removed four other reductions to suspension observations for this analysis because of the indeterminate nature of the suspension period. As a result, our figures are based on a data set consisting of the remaining 144 reduction to suspension outcomes.

Figure 4. Mean Length (in days) of Suspension Imposed by Offense Category and Total

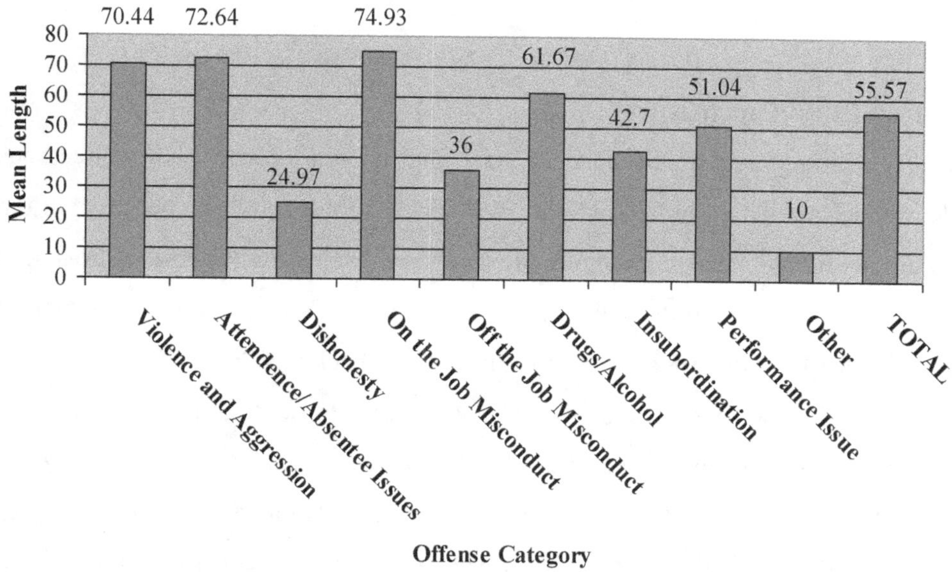

These findings demonstrate that the reduction to suspension outcomes also do not replicate employer-imposed suspension lengths. While the mean reduction to suspension period is less than one-third the length of the mean reinstatement without back pay period, it still is 11 times the length of the typical one week employer-imposed suspension. This suggests that many arbitrators are determining the length of the reduction to suspension period on the basis of personal notions of equity as opposed to conforming to employer practices. Therefore, we conclude that many arbitrators use the reduction to suspension option to craft a second type of compromise outcome similar to that for which the reinstatement without back pay option is so often criticized.

Entitlement to a Future Vacancy

Our survey encountered an unexpected third category of split decisions. Nine decisions, or 0.63 percent of all discharge cases, resulted in an order awarding the grievant, not reinstatement, but rather the opportunity to fill a future vacancy. Although this was a rare outcome, the surprising fact is that it happened as often as it did. This is neither an outcome that is referenced in the arbitration literature nor one that has been considered by prior studies. This remedy was most often invoked by arbitrators in cases involving violence or poor performance. Six of the nine instances were ordered by less experienced, non-NAA arbitrators.

Mitigation of Lost Earnings

The leading treatises in the field assert that most arbitrators will reduce back pay awards in discharge cases by the amount of compensation earned by the grievant through interim employment.[37] As an example, the *Common Law of the Workplace* treatise states, "with few exceptions, arbitrators, like the courts and the NLRB, will deduct actual interim earnings and willfully incurred losses from an order of back pay."[38]

The authorities are more equivocal with respect to the treatment of grievants who fail to mitigate their income losses pending the outcome of the arbitration process. The *Discipline and Discharge in the Workplace* treatise, for example, states that "back pay may be wholly or partially denied to employees who fail to make reasonable efforts to mitigate their damages."[39] Two leading lights of the labor arbitration field have espoused differing points of view on this issue. David Feller, in a 1981 article in the National Academy's *Proceedings*, stated that very few arbitrators address the duty to mitigate issue in the absence of evidence of actual earnings.[40] Anthony Sinicropi, in contrast, maintained that the view preferred by most arbitrators is that a grievant's failure to mitigate losses by seeking alternative employment reduces the employer's liability.[41]

---

[37] *Common Law of the Workplace*, § 10.17; *Discipline and Discharge in the Workplace*, 479; Hill & Sinicropi, *Remedies in Arbitration*, 207.

[38] *Common Law of the Workplace*, § 10.17.

[39] *Discipline and Discharge in the Workplace*, 478.

[40] David E. Feller, "Remedies in Arbitration: Old Problems Revisited," *Arbitration Issues for the 1980's: Proceedings of the 34th Annual Meeting of the National Academy of Arbitrators* (Washington, D.C.: Bureau of National Affairs, James L. Stern & Barbara D. Dennis, eds., 1982), 109, 123-124.

[41] Anthony V. Sinicropi, "Remedies: Another View of New and Old Problems," *Arbitration Issues for the 1980's: Proceedings of the 34th Annual Meeting of the National Academy of Arbitrators*

In an article published in 1997, Matthew Frankiewicz examined 90 discharge cases published in *Labor Arbitration Reports* that ordered back pay as a remedy. He found that 39 decisions, comprising 42.9 percent of his sample, specifically directed that interim earnings be deducted from the amount of gross back pay awarded. In five of these decisions, the arbitrators further ordered "that back pay also be reduced if the grievant failed to mitigate damages by seeking alternative employment."[42]

We reviewed each of the 432 discharge decisions in our data set that awarded either full or partial back pay and found that 204 of these decisions, or 47.22 percent, explicitly stated that the amount of back pay was to be reduced by interim earnings or by the grievant's failure to mitigate. Although a tally was not kept, very few cases, as Professor Feller suggested, referenced the presentation of evidence challenging the grievant's efforts to seek interim employment.

Somewhat surprisingly, mitigation adjustments varied markedly by the type of offense at issue. As Table 7.9 indicates, arbitrators were more than twice as likely to order back pay reductions in cases involving insubordination or performance issues than they were in cases involving off-the-job misconduct. Whether this difference in outcomes reflects perceived distinctions in culpability or actual distinctions in the availability of interim employment is unclear.

Based on our findings and the similar findings of Arbitrator Frankiewicz, the pronouncements of the leading treatises arguably should be modified in two respects. First, they should state that *many*, but not necessarily *most*, arbitration decisions explicitly reduce back pay awards by the amount of interim earnings received. Second, they should state that only a *minority* of arbitration decisions explicitly reduce back pay awards on the basis of a grievant's failure to obtain suitable interim employment.

It could be argued that the first of these suggested modifications is of little importance because the principle of deducting actual earnings is so widely accepted that no

---

(Washington, D.C.: Bureau of National Affairs, James L. Stern & Barbara D. Dennis, eds., 1982), 134, 150.

[42] Matthew M. Frankiewicz, "Back Pay Awards: Current Arbitral Patterns," 52 *Dispute Resolution Journal* (1997), 28.

overt reference to such a practice is necessary. Indeed, since arbitrators typically leave to the parties the task of calculating back pay, what arbitrators say or do not say about mitigation may not tell us much about arbitral commitment to the mitigation principle. While that may be so, the fact that arbitrators in almost one-half of all decisions feel the need specifically to direct the reduction of interim earnings casts some doubt about the existence of a universally accepted rule.

Table 7.9 Reduction for Lost Earnings Outcomes by Offense Categories*
(N-size and row % are the top and bottom value, respectively)

Offense Category	Reduction	No Reduction	Row Totals
Violence and Aggression	33 37.93[a]	54 62.07	87 100.00
Attendance/Absentee Issues	32 46.38	37 53.62	69 100.00
Dishonesty	49 47.57	54 52.43	103 100.00
On the Job Misconduct	15 39.47	23 60.53	38 100.00
Off the Job Misconduct	6 24.00[a]	19 76.00	25 100.00
Drugs/Alcohol	6 37.50[a]	10 62.50	16 100.00
Insubordination	51 51.52	48 48.48	99 100.00
Performance Issue	34 50.00	34 50.00	68 100.00
Other	5 71.43	2 28.57	7 100.00
Column Totals**	204 47.22	228 52.78	432 100.00

* The alphabetic index a indicates that the percentages in column 1 and column 2 are statistically different at the .05 level or lower.
** Multiple offenses may apply per case. The totals shown in the bottom row are the overall totals for each possible outcome, disregarding the multiplicity of motivating offenses.

Retention of Jurisdiction

The Code of Professional Responsibility for Arbitrators of Labor-Management Disputes provides that once an arbitrator issues an award, "no clarification or interpretation

. . . is permissible without the consent of both parties."[43] Because of this rule, some arbitrators, in order to retain authority to address issues that may arise following the issuance of a decision, expressly retain jurisdiction to reopen the award for a period of time. A 2007 amendment to the Code expressly sanctions this practice by providing that "an arbitrator may retain remedial jurisdiction in the award to resolve any question that may arise over application or interpretation of a remedy" unless otherwise prohibited by agreement of the parties or applicable law.[44]

In a 1996 article, Jack Dunsford presented a forceful argument in favor of arbitrators retaining post-award jurisdiction over remedial issues.[45] In that article, Professor Dunsford noted that many arbitrators do not retain jurisdiction due to the erroneous view that such a practice is unlawful, unethical, or that it interferes with the finality of the award. After debunking each of these concerns, Professor Dunsford concluded that arbitrators should routinely retain jurisdiction in any case in which a remedy is ordered.[46]

The Common Law of the Workplace asserts that arbitrators "usually" retain jurisdiction in their awards:

> Once it is determined that a back pay award is appropriate, an arbitrator may remand the task of computation to the parties. Such a remedy is *usually*, but not always, accompanied by retention of jurisdiction by the arbitrator in the event that there is a subsequent dispute over the amount.[47]

This contention, however, is not borne out in the empirical studies. Professor Dunsford himself reported a review of 254 decisions in volume 100 of *Labor Arbitration Reports*, with arbitrators retaining jurisdiction in 40 or 15.75 percent of those decisions.[48] It is not clear,

---

43 *Code of Professional Responsibility for Arbitrators of Labor-Management Disputes* § 6C.1 (2007).

44 *Code of Professional Responsibility for Arbitrators of Labor-Management Disputes* § 6E (2007).

45 John E. Dunsford, "The Case for Retention of Remedial Jurisdiction in Labor Arbitration Awards," 31 *Georgia Law Review* 201 (1996).

46 *Id.* at 279.

47 *Common Law of the Workplace*, § 10.14 (emphasis added).

48 Dunsford, "The Case for Retention of Remedial Jurisdiction," 205 n. 12.

however, whether this survey was limited to discharge cases or to those decisions calling for a remedy. Arbitrator Frankiewicz conducted a study that did look specifically at reported discharge cases and found that arbitrators retained jurisdiction in 49.5% of those decisions.[49]

Our examination focused on the 432 discharge cases in our data set in which arbitrators ordered reinstatement with either full or partial back pay. Operating under the assumption that arbitrators generally remand the task of computing back pay to the parties in these circumstances, we coded whether "the arbitrator's award explicitly retains jurisdiction to decide subsequent disputes . . . with regard to the remedy." We were somewhat surprised to learn that arbitrators expressly reserved jurisdiction in only 115, or 26.62 percent, of these decisions. With almost three out of four decisions not retaining jurisdiction, the quoted assertion from *The Common Law of the Workplace* may be questioned and is properly the subject for future research.

Professor Theodore J. St. Antoine, the editor of *The Common Law of the Workplace*, has questioned whether our data may undercount the actual prevalence of jurisdiction retention by not differentiating between ad hoc appointments and permanent panel appointments. In an article commenting on a preliminary analysis of our data that was later published, he stated:

> The CBB [Cooper, Bognanno, & Befort] empirical study indicated that in 432 cases where the employee was reinstated with full or partial back pay, the arbitrator did not retain jurisdiction in about 73 percent of the time. But, the precise question asked of the data was whether the arbitrator "expressly" retained jurisdiction to resolve any subsequent disputes. That is a big difference. Although I invariably retain jurisdiction in such situations in an ad hoc appointment, I do not feel any such need when I am handling a case as a permanent arbitrator or as a member of a board of arbitrators. There the understanding of everyone is that the issue will come back for a final ruling if the parties are not able to resolve it.[50]

---

49 Frankiewicz, "Back Pay Awards," 33.

50 Theodore J. St. Antoine, "How and Why Arbitrators Decide Discipline and Discharge Cases: An Empirical Examination – Comments," *Arbitration 2007, Workplace Justice for a Changing Environment: Proceedings of the 60th Annual Meeting of the National Academy of Arbitrators* (Washington, D.C.: Bureau of National Affairs, Stephen F. Befort & Patrick Halter, eds., 2008), 459, 461.

Recognizing the legitimacy of this query, we re-examined our data by segregating those cases with no listing agency. Presumably, the vast majority of such cases involve some type of ongoing appointment. We found that arbitrators expressly retained jurisdiction in 25 percent of these decisions. While this finding does not dispel the possibility that some of the arbitrators in the remaining 75 percent of decisions may have assumed that retention of jurisdiction was automatic, the substantial similarity in outcomes suggests that appointment status may have little effect on an arbitrator's decision to retain jurisdiction.

We also considered whether arbitral practices with respect to the retention of jurisdiction issue have changed over time, particularly in response to Professor Dunsford's 1996 article. As shown in Figure 5, no long term trend is documented by our data. While the proportion of cases in which arbitrators retained jurisdiction climbed from the first to second periods reviewed, the percentage declined during the most recent period.

Figure 5. Proportion of Cases with Jurisdiction Retained

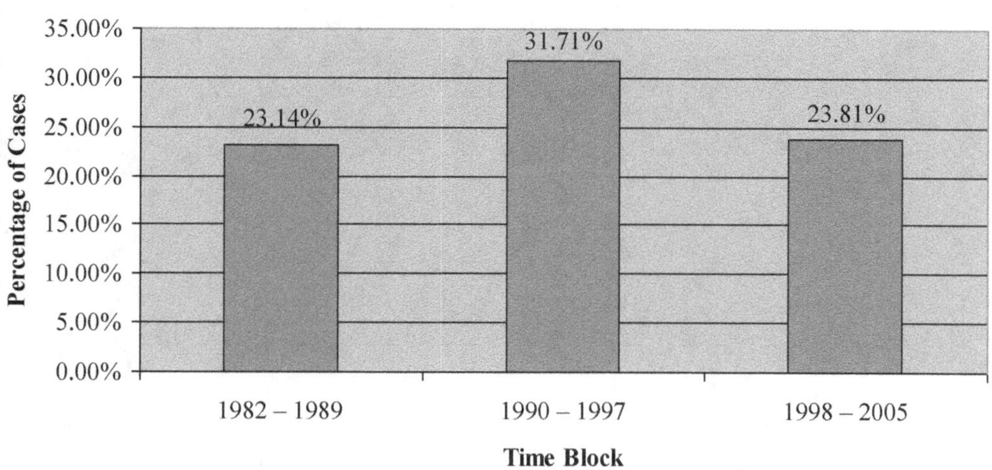

Demographic Factors

We also reviewed these discharge case remedial outcomes in terms of sector of origin (private or public) and in terms of two arbitrator characteristics, namely, whether the arbitrator has a J.D. degree, and whether the arbitrator was a member of the National Academy of Arbitrators (NAA) at the time the case was decided. The chi-square tests adjacent to the following tables show a strong relationship between remedial outcomes and each of these three variables.

Sector

Our data include nearly an equal number of discharge cases arising in the public (705) and private (727) sectors. Table 7.10 shows that arbitration outcomes generally are more favorable to public sector employers than to private sector employers. Public sector employers had a 56.17 percent win rate, while private sector employers prevailed in 48.83 percent of cases. This finding is contrary to an earlier study by Stieber, Block, and Corbitt that found no significant difference in outcomes by sector in discharge cases.[51]

In terms of offense categories, public sector employers do particularly well in cases involving performance or drug/alcohol issues, with win rates in these categories exceeding 67 percent. Private sector employers, on the other hand, have the most difficulty in cases involving dishonesty, violence or on-the-job misconduct, with employer win rates in each of those categories below 45 percent.

---

[51] Jack Stieber, Richard N. Block, & Leslie Corbitt, "How Representative are Published Decisions?" *Arbitration 1984: Absenteeism, Recent law, Panels, and Published Decisions: Proceedings of the 37th Annual Meeting of the National Academy of Arbitrators* (Washington, D.C.: Bureau of National Affairs, Walter J. Gershenfeld, ed., 1985), 172, 181 (finding no significant differences in denial rates in discharge cases originating in the two sectors). See also Debra J. Mesch, "Grievance Arbitration in the Public Sector: A Conceptual Framework and Empirical Analysis of Public and Private Sector Cases," 15 *Review of Public Personnel Administration* (Fall 1995), 22, 29, 31 (finding that employers prevailed 4.5% more often in public sector discipline and discharge cases, but concluding that this differential was not significant).

Table 7.10 Reinstatement Outcomes by Sector*
(N-size, row % and column % are the top, middle and bottom value, respectively)

Reinstatement Outcomes	Public Sector	Private Sector	Row Totals
Uphold the Discharge	396 52.73[1] 56.17[1a]	355 47.27[1] 48.83[1]	751 100.00 52.44[1]
Reinstate – Full Back Pay	119 42.05[a] 16.88[2a]	164 57.95 22.56[2]	283 100.00 19.76[2]
Reinstate – Partial Back Pay	75 50.34 10.64[3]	74 49.66 10.18[3]	149 100.00 10.41[3]
Reinstate – No Back Pay	109 45.42 15.46[4]	131 54.58 18.02[4]	240 100.00 16.76[4]
Entitlement to Future Vacancy	6 66.67 0.85[5]	3 33.33 0.41[5]	9 100.00 0.63[5]
Column Totals	705 49.23 100.00	727 50.77 100.00	1,432 100.00 100.00

Chi-square (4) = 12.0821, p = .017
* The numeric indexes 1, 2, 3, 4 and 5 indicate that the percentages in row 1 and row 2, row 2 and row 3, row 3 and row 4, row 4 and row 5, and row 5 and row 1, respectively, are statistically different at the .05 level or lower. The alphabetic index a indicates that the percentages in column 1 and column 2 are statistically different at the .05 level or lower.

As depicted in Figure 6, arbitrators in public sector cases tend to order longer periods without pay in split decisions than do arbitrators in private sector cases. In cases involving reinstatement without back pay outcomes, public sector grievants experienced a mean period of 195.96 work days (9.8 months) without pay, while the corresponding no-pay period for private sector grievants was 154.50 work days (7.7 months)–a difference that is statistically significant. A significant differential also occurs in reduction to suspension cases. Public sector grievants had a mean period of suspension without pay of 60.45 days, while private sector grievants had an average suspension without pay period of 50.55 days.

Figure 6. Mean Length of No Back Pay Period Totals and Suspension Totals by Sector

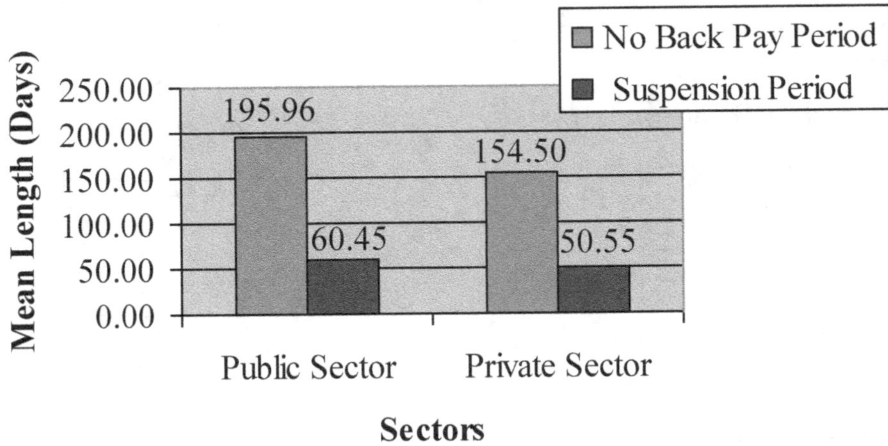

Chi-square (1) = 1.0055, p = 0.316
* The "no back pay period" and the "suspension period" inter-sector differences are statistically significant at the .01 level.

Arbitrator Characteristics

Table 7.11 depicts the relationship between remedial outcomes and whether an arbitrator is trained as an attorney. Significantly, employers prevailed in almost 60 percent of discharge cases (58.78 percent) before non-attorney arbitrators, while achieving that outcome in less than one-half of such cases (48.40 percent) before attorney arbitrators. Arbitrators who have earned a J.D. degree similarly ruled more favorably for unions in all three reinstatement categories. These differences are statistically significant and represent original findings.

Table 7.11 <u>Reinstatement Outcomes by Arbitrator's Attorney Status</u>*
(N-size, row % and column % are the top, middle and bottom value, respectively)

Reinstatement Outcomes	Non-Attorney Arbitrator	Attorney Arbitrator	Row Totals
Uphold the Discharge	328 43.68[1a] 58.78[1a]	423 56.32[1] 48.40[1]	751 100.00 52.44[1]
Reinstate – Full Back Pay	104 36.75[a] 18.64[2]	179 63.25 20.48[2]	283 100.00 19.76[2]
Reinstate – Partial Back Pay	40 26.85[a] 7.17[3a]	109 73.15 12.47[3]	149 100.00 10.41[3]
Reinstate – No Back Pay	81 33.75[4a] 14.52[4a]	159 66.25 18.19[4]	240 100.00 16.76[4]
Entitlement to Future Vacancy	5 55.56 0.90[5]	4 44.44 0.46[5]	9 100.00 0.63[5]
Column Totals	558 38.97[a] 100.00	874 61.03 100.00	1,432 100.00 100.00

Chi-square (4) = 29.5003, p = 0.000
* The numeric indexes 1, 2, 3, 4 and 5 indicate that the percentages in row 1 and row 2, row 2 and row 3, row 3 and row 4, row 4 and row 5, and row 5 and row 1, respectively, are statistically different at the .05 level or lower. The alphabetic index a indicates that the percentages in column 1 and column 2 are statistically different at the .05 level or lower.

NAA membership is often used as a proxy for arbitral experience because during our sampling period an arbitrator must have decided a minimum of 50 cases within a five-year period in order to qualify for NAA membership. As Table 7.12 and the chi-square suggest, the distribution of decisions issued by arbitrators and their status as members of the NAA are significantly associated. Although NAA and non-NAA arbitrators issued insignificantly different shares of outcomes favorable to management (54.15 percent v. 50.45 percent), they issued significantly different shares of reinstatement outcomes. Thus, NAA arbitrators (20.34 percent) were significantly more likely than non-NAA arbitrators (12.58 percent) to issue decisions ordering a reinstatement with no back pay remedy.

Table 7.12 Reinstatement Outcomes by Arbitrator's NAA Status*
(N-size, row % and column % are the top, middle and bottom value, respectively)

Reinstatement Outcome	Non-NAA Arbitrator	NAA Arbitrator	Row Totals
Uphold the Discharge	333 44.34[1a] 50.45[1]	418 55.66[1] 54.15[1]	751 100.00 52.44[1]
Reinstate – Full Back Pay	151 53.36 22.88[2a]	132 46.64 17.10[2]	283 100.00 19.76[2]
Reinstate – Partial Back Pay	87 58.39[3a] 13.18[a]	62 41.61[3] 8.03[3]	149 100.00 10.41[3]
Reinstate – No Back Pay	83 34.58[4a] 12.58[4a]	157 65.42[4] 20.34[4]	240 100.00 16.76[4]
Entitlement to Future Vacancy	6 67.67 0.91[5]	3 33.33 0.39[5]	9 100.00 0.63[5]
Column Totals	660 46.09[a] 100.00	772 53.91 100.00	1,432 100.00 100.00

Chi-square (4) = 29.4536, p = 0.000
* The numeric indexes 1, 2, 3, 4 and 5 indicate that the percentages in row 1 and row 2, row 2 and row 3, row 3 and row 4, row 4 and row 5, and row 5 and row 1, respectively, are statistically different at the .05 level or lower. The alphabetic index a indicates that the percentages in column 1 and column 2 are statistically different at the .05 level or lower.

In terms of offense categories, employers had disproportionately higher win rates (> 64 percent) before non-attorney arbitrators in cases involving attendance, dishonesty, drug/alcohol, or performance issues. Lawyer-arbitrators, in contrast, tended to be most sympathetic to unions in insubordination cases, upholding employer discharge decisions in less than 40 percent of those decisions. Few similar outliers exist in terms of the correlation with NAA membership, the two exceptions being that NAA arbitrators sustained employer discharge decisions in approximately 70 percent of cases involving drug/alcohol or performance issues.

Grievants experienced statistically significant and decidedly longer periods without pay in split decisions decided by NAA arbitrators. With respect to decisions directing the reinstatement without back pay remedy, grievants in cases decided by NAA arbitrators had a mean period without pay of 9.34 months, essentially two months longer than grievants with cases decided by non-NAA arbitrators, whose mean period without pay was 7.39 months. This differential may reflect, not necessarily a more punitive attitude by NAA arbitrators, but simply the fact that their dockets are more crowded. Indeed, the average length of time between discharge and decision in cases handled by NAA arbitrators was 2.2 months longer than for non-NAA arbitrators, a period that more than offsets the disparity in no-pay periods. The crowded-docket effect, however, does not explain the greater length of unpaid suspensions imposed by NAA arbitrators. In this regard, NAA arbitrators ordered a mean period of 66.81 unpaid days when reducing a discharge to a period of suspension, while the non-NAA group ordered a mean period of 47.99 unpaid days.

Whether an arbitrator has legal training does not affect the length of unpaid periods. While attorney-arbitrators imposed a mean no-pay period of 7.77 months in reinstatement without back pay outcomes, arbitrators without a law degree directed an insignificantly different 8.42 months without back pay. The gap also was smaller with respect to reduction to suspension outcomes where attorney-arbitrators ordered a mean suspension period of 60.64 days, while non-attorney arbitrators directed a mean suspension period of 53.88 days–a difference that is significant.

NAA membership also correlates with a decided difference in arbitral outcomes in two additional contexts. First, arbitrators who were NAA members were more inclined to impose a last chance arrangement as a condition of reinstatement. Among those discharge cases in which reinstatement was ordered, NAA arbitrators included a last chance condition in 15.10 percent of cases, while non-NAA arbitrators did so in only 9.03 percent of cases (significant at the .05 level).

Second, arbitrators with NAA membership exhibited a greater tendency to retain jurisdiction following the issuance of decisions calling for a back pay remedy. As noted above, arbitrators in our sample generally retained jurisdiction in approximately 26 percent of discharge decisions ordering full or partial back pay. However, arbitrators who were NAA members retained jurisdiction at a rate of 38.14 percent in such circumstances, which is more than double the 17.23 percent retention rate for non-NAA member arbitrators.

In considering the impact of arbitral experience, a fair question to ask is whether the data in our study are skewed by the disproportionate number of decisions issued by the most prolific of our 81 arbitrators.[52] In order to test for this possibility, we examined the decisions with reference to the total number of decisions issued by each arbitrator in our sample with benchmarks based upon the issuance of 25, 50, and 100 or more decisions, respectively. Four arbitrators in our sample each issued 100 or more decisions.

Our analysis, which appears in Table 7.13, provides several interesting results. First, employer win outcomes did not vary significantly by experience level. Second, arbitrators with less than 100 decisions also did not issue statistically different reinstatement outcomes by level of experience. On the other hand, the share of union wins and split outcomes issued by arbitrators with less than 100 decisions did vary significantly with those issued by arbitrators with more than 100 decisions. The more prolific arbitrators issued significantly fewer decisions ordering full union wins or split decisions that reduce a discharge to a suspension, while ordering significantly more reinstatement without back pay outcomes. The latter category represents the largest area of divergence with the more prolific arbitrators ordering reinstatement without back pay two-and-a-half times more frequently (26.01 percent) than arbitrators who issued 24 or fewer decisions (10.74 percent).

---

[52] In this regard, Nels Nelson, in commenting on an earlier summary of some of our findings, raised concerns that our sample "may not be representative of all arbitrators." Nels E. Nelson, "Comments on an Empirical Examination of How Labor Arbitrators Decide Discipline and Discharge Cases," *Arbitration 2007, Workplace Justice for a Changing Environment: Proceedings of the 60th Annual Meeting of the National Academy of Arbitrators* (Washington, D.C.: Bureau of National Affairs, Stephen F. Befort & Patrick Halter, eds., 2008), 465.

Table 7.13 Reinstatement Outcomes by Number of Decisions*
(N-size, row % and column % are the top and bottom value, respectively)

Reinstatement Outcomes	24 or Fewer Decisions	25 – 49 Decisions	50 - 99 Decisions	100 or More Decisions	Row Totals
Uphold the Discharge	134 17.84^{x} 55.37	166 22.10^{y} 55.52	192 25.57^{z} 49.74	259 34.49 52.22	751 100.00 52.78
Reinstate – Full Back Pay	53 18.73 21.90^{x}	67 23.67 22.41^{y}	93 32.86 24.09^{z}	70 24.73 14.11	283 100.00 19.89
Reinstate – Partial Back Pay	29 19.46 11.98	38 25.50 12.71^{y}	44 29.53 11.40	38 25.50 7.66	149 100.00 10.47
Reinstate – No Back Pay	26 10.83^{x} 10.74^{x}	28 11.67^{y} 9.36^{y}	57 23.75^{z} 14.77^{z}	129 53.75 26.01	240 100.00 16.87
Column Totals	242 17.01^{x} 100.00	299 21.01^{y} 100.00	386 27.13^{z} 100.00	496 34.86 100.00	1,423 100.00 100.00

Chi-square (9) = 61.5937, p = 0.000
* The alphabetic indexes x, y and z indicate that the percentages in column 1 and column 4, column 2 and column 4, and column 3 and column 4, respectively, are statistically different at the .05 level or lower. The reinstatement outcome "Entitlement to Future Vacancy" is omitted because of small sample size.

With reinstatement without back pay being the most controversial of all remedial outcomes, it is not clear why the most experienced arbitrators more frequently invoke that particular remedy. Perhaps, as discussed above, it represents an allocation of the costs of administrative delay to the party whose conduct triggered the need for discipline and arbitral review. In any event, the continuing selection of these more experienced arbitrators appears to belie the popular notion that the parties dislike the reinstatement without back pay outcome and the arbitrators who utilize that option.

Summary

Arbitrators generally have the authority to assess the reasonableness of employer disciplinary decisions and to modify the penalty imposed if such is unreasonable. Arbitrators upheld management discharge decisions in slightly more than one-half of the cases in our study (52.44 percent), with smaller percentage outcomes for full union wins (19.20 percent) and split decisions (28.35 percent). Our remedial outcome findings are similar to other reported studies in terms of full employer and full union wins, but they differ in finding a smaller proportion of reinstatement without back pay outcomes.

Our results are consistent with prior generalizations and studies that arbitrators tend to enforce last chance agreements. Our study shows management win rates more than 20 percent higher in discharge cases interpreting a last chance agreement as compared to cases without such an agreement. We also confirm the findings of other studies that split decisions, including reinstatement without back pay and discharges reduced to suspensions, result in suspensions without pay that are far longer in duration than would be imposed by employers as a disciplinary sanction.

In some respects, however, our findings take issue with conventional wisdom. For example, we question the assumption that arbitrators typically retain jurisdiction when they issue back pay awards. Our study found that arbitrators expressly retained jurisdiction in only 26.62 percent of decisions ordering reinstatement with full or partial back pay. Similarly, we show a higher employer win rate for public sector cases, a finding that contradicts an earlier study that found no significant difference in outcomes by sector.

With respect to the impact of delay on reinstatement outcomes, we found that the length of time between the employer's discharge decision and the arbitration award did not affect reinstatement without back pay outcomes. We also found that delay has a modest, but not statistically significant inverse correlation with the prevalence of reinstatement outcomes generally, with the percentage of reinstatements ordered by arbitrators dropping in cases decided eighteen months or more following the initial discharge decision.

Finally, employers prevailed more frequently in our study with arbitrators who are not attorneys and, to a lesser extent, with arbitrators who are members of the National Academy of Arbitrators (NAA). NAA arbitrators also ordered significantly more reinstatement without back pay awards than arbitrators who were not NAA members. In general, we found a continuing decrease in the prevalence of reinstatement without back pay awards over the time period of this study.

CHAPTER 8

REMEDIES IN CASES OF LESSER DISCIPLINE

Employers frequently impose discipline short of discharge. These lesser disciplinary actions are subject to the same just cause test in arbitration as discussed in Chapter 7.

In contrast to the discharge remedy where the employer's objective is to remove a poor performing employee from the workforce, the employer's goal in using lesser forms of discipline is to retain the employee's services while attempting to improve future work performance. As such, it is often stated that the objective of discipline short of discharge is to correct rather than to punish behavior.[1] These lesser forms of discipline, accordingly, should be designed "to convey the seriousness of the behavior and to afford employees an opportunity to improve."[2]

Employers generally attempt to correct behavior by progressive discipline. The purpose of progressive discipline is to impose sanctions in gradually increasing levels of severity to gain an employee's attention and to encourage the employee to correct behavior in order to avoid still harsher additional sanctions.[3] Some collective bargaining agreements explicitly provide for progressive disciplinary steps, but, even in the absence of such language, progressive discipline is generally required for other than the most serious of offenses,[4] an assertion for which we find support in Chapter 9.

Even with a system of progressive discipline, arbitrators require that the discipline imposed bear a proportional relationship to the offense in question. *The Common Law of the Workplace* describes the proportionality requirement as follows:

> The level of discipline permitted by the just cause principle will depend on many factors, including the nature and consequences of the employee's offense, the

---

[1] *Discipline and Discharge in the Workplace* (Washington, D.C.: Bureau of National Affairs, Norman Brand & Melissa H. Biren, eds., 2nd ed. 2008), 65; *The Common Law of the Workplace: The Views of the Arbitrators* (Washington, D.C.: Bureau of National Affairs, Theodore St. Antoine, ed., 2nd ed. 2005), § 6.7.

[2] *Discipline and Discharge in the Workplace*, 65.

[3] *Id.* at 57, 61.

[4] *Common Law of the Workplace,* § 6.7.

> clarity or absence of rules, the length and quality of the employee's work record, and the practices of the parties in similar cases. Discipline must bear some reasonable relation to the seriousness or the frequency of the offense.[5]

As with discharge cases, it is well-established that an arbitrator has the authority to modify lesser disciplinary sanctions where appropriate unless expressly restricted by the parties' collective bargaining agreement.[6] An arbitral reduction in remedy is most likely to occur when the arbitrator believes that the employer's sanction is disproportionately severe or where due process or mitigating circumstances warrant a lesser penalty,[7] as empirically demonstrated in Chapter 9.

Disciplinary measures that do not terminate the employment relationship generally fall into two categories. At the lower rung of severity are warnings and reprimands. These two terms are often used interchangeably to refer to a sanction that notifies an "employee that she has engaged in unacceptable behavior and that future misconduct will likely result in more severe discipline."[8] The disciplinary nature of warnings and reprimands, which is often defined by the parties' collective bargaining agreement, should be distinguished from communications that merely counsel or instruct employees as to desirable behavior. While the latter form of communication attempts to obviate the need for discipline, warnings and reprimands constitute ground level forms of discipline that may justify greater disciplinary sanctions in the event of future misconduct.[9] Warnings and reprimands typically are issued for initial and relatively minor offenses such as attendance problems and poor work performance. Some contracts utilize a ladder of disciplinary sanctions with oral warnings followed by written warnings or reprimands.[10]

---

5 *Common Law of the Workplace*, § 6.7.

6 Marvin F. Hill, Jr. & Anthony V. Sinicropi, *Remedies in Arbitration* (Washington, D.C.: Bureau of National Affairs, 2nd ed., 1991), 270-271; *Common Law of the Workplace*, § 10.6 Comment.

7 *Discipline and Discharge in the Workplace*, 490-501.

8 *Id.* at 62 (citing Koven, Smith, & Farwell, *Just Cause: The Seven Tests* (2nd ed. 1992), 403-404).

9 *Discipline and Discharge in the Workplace*, 67-69, 73-74.

10 *Id.* at 62-63. Under some collective bargaining agreements, warnings may not be challenged in arbitration.

Suspensions constitute the second and more severe form of non-discharge discipline. In general, a suspension results in the involuntary removal of an employee from work for a period of time accompanied with a loss of pay.[11] Employers typically utilize suspensions for infractions that are more serious than those addressed by warnings and reprimands or for repeat violations of lesser infractions. The length of the period of unpaid leave may be influenced by the parties' collective bargaining agreement, the employer's practices, or both. In any event, the written notice of suspension usually contains some warning as to the likely consequence of further problem behavior.[12]

Disciplinary Remedies in General

Other Studies

Few studies have compared remedial outcomes in discharge and non-discharge discipline cases. Most studies either look broadly at the universe of discipline cases or concentrate solely on discharge cases. Interestingly, as shown in Table 8.1, the two studies that have made such a comparison in recent years have reported divergent findings. While the Mesch and Dalton study found that employers had a greater proportion of successful outcomes in discharge as compared to other discipline cases, a study undertaken by Haber, Karim, and Johnson reported the opposite finding.

---

[11] *Discipline and Discharge in the Workplace*, 74.

[12] *Id.*

Table 8.1 Discharge and Other Discipline Outcomes by Study: Management Win Rates
(In Percent)

Study	Discharge Upheld	Other Discipline Upheld
Mesch & Dalton[1] (1988-1990)	45.5	42.0
Haber, Karim, & Johnson[2] (1990-1995)	40.1	44.4

[1] Debra J. Mesch & Dan R. Dalton, "Arbitration in Practice: Win, Lose, or Draw?" 4 *The Human Resources Professional* (Spring 1992), 37-45 (analyzing 443 discipline and discharge cases published in *Labor Arbitration Reports* between 1988 and 1990).
[2] Lawrence J. Haber, Ahmad R. Karim & J. Douglas Johnson, "A Survey of Published, Private-Sector Arbitral Decisions," 48 *Labor Law Journal* (1997), 431-436 (analyzing 1128 discipline and discharge private sector arbitration awards published in *Labor Arbitration Reports* between 1990 and 1995).

Our Study

Our results parallel those of Mesch and Dalton. As shown in Table 8.2, management win rates for non-discharge cases in our study are substantially and significantly lower than they are for discharge cases. And, while full management wins were 2.7 times more likely than full union wins in discharge cases, full union win rates (40.19 percent) virtually equal full management win rates (41.12 percent) in reprimand cases. These respective outcomes suggest that arbitrators are more likely to rule for unions as the stakes decline in importance.

Table 8.2 Comparison of Outcomes in Discharge, Suspension & Reprimand Cases*

(N-size, row % and column % are the top and bottom value, respectively)

Arbitration Outcomes	Discharge	Suspension	Reprimand	Row Totals
Arbitrator Found Just Cause for Discipline (Management Win)	751 73.48[1a] 52.44[1a]	227 22.21[1b] 43.99[1]	44 4.31[1c] 41.12[c]	1,022 100.00 49.73[1]
Arbitrator Found No Just Cause for Any Discipline (Union Win)	275 62.36[2a] 19.20[2a]	123 27.89[b] 23.84[2b]	43 9.75[1c] 40.19[2c]	441 100.00 21.46[2]
Arbitrator Found Just Cause for Lesser Discipline than that Imposed by Employer (Split Decision)	406 68.58[3a] 28.35[3]	166 28.04[3b] 32.17[3b]	20 3.38[c] 18.69[3c]	592 100.00 28.81[3]
Column Totals	1,432 69.68[a] 100.00	516 25.11[b] 100.00	107 5.21[c] 100.00	2,055 100.00 100.00

Chi-square (4) = 35.3025, p = 0.000

* The numeric indexes 1, 2 and 3 indicate that the percentages in row 1 and row 2, row 2 and row 3, and row 3 and row 1, respectively, are statistically different at the .05 level or lower. The alphabetic indexes a, b and c indicate that the percentages in column 1 and column 2, column 2 and column 3, and column 3 and column 1, respectively, are statistically different at the .05 level or lower.

A Closer Look at Suspensions

We coded a number of variables that provide a more in-depth view of suspension cases. First, we measured suspensions by length and divided them into two categories: those of one week (five work days) or longer in duration, and those of less than one week in duration. As shown in Table 8.3, the number of longer suspensions only slightly exceeded those in the shorter category. Moreover, we see that employers prevailed at a significantly higher rate in cases involving shorter suspensions than they did in cases with longer suspensions. This finding is somewhat surprising since, as noted above, the proportion of management wins generally declined along with decreases in discipline severity. The lower win rates for management in cases involving lengthier suspensions correspond with a sizable increase in split decision outcomes. The full union win rates, however, do not significantly vary with respect to length of suspension.

Table 8.3 <u>Comparison of Outcomes by Suspension Length</u>*
(N-size, row % and column % are the top and bottom value, respectively)

Outcomes	Long Suspension	Short Suspension	Row Totals
Management Win	105 46.26 38.75[1a]	122 53.74 49.80[1]	227 100.00 43.99[1]
Union Win	65 52.85 23.99[2]	58 47.15 23.67	123 100.00 23.84
Split Decision	101 60.84[3a] 37.27[a]	65 39.16[3] 26.53[3]	166 100.00 32.17[3]
Column Totals	271 52.52 100.00	245 47.48 100.00	516 100.00 100.00

Chi-square (2) = 8.1894, p = 0.017
* The numeric indexes 1, 2 and 3 indicate that the percentages in row 1 and row 2, row 2 and row 3, and row 3 and row 1, respectively, are statistically different at the .05 level or lower. The alphabetic index a indicates that the percentages in column 1 and column 2 are statistically different at the .05 level or lower.

As in Chapter 7, we also took a closer look at split outcomes in suspension cases. Two distinct types of split decisions are prevalent in suspension cases: (1) the arbitrator may reduce a suspension's duration (such as by reducing a suspension of five days to one or two days); or (2) the arbitrator may reduce a suspension to a reprimand or warning. In essence, the former remedy serves as a reduction with partial back pay, while the latter is a reduction with full back pay that still carries some lesser degree of disciplinary consequences. Since a reduction in the duration of a suspension invariably entails a corresponding reduction in the amount of lost pay,[13] there is no corresponding phenomenon in the realm of suspensions to the reduction without back pay remedy so commonly used in discharge cases.

Table 8.4 depicts the remedy outcomes in suspension cases once the split decisions were divided into these two categories. The table shows that the reduction to a lesser suspension option constitutes approximately 60 percent of the split decisions, while the reduction to a reprimand or warning option comprises the remaining 40 percent.

Table 8.4 Suspension Outcomes*
(N-size and column % are the top and bottom value, respectively)

Outcome	Row Totals
Suspension Upheld in Full	227 43.99[1]
Suspension Reduced in Length	98 18.99[2]
Suspension Overturned in Full	123 23.84[3]
Suspension Reduced to a Warning or Reprimand	68 13.18[4]
Column Totals	516 100.00

* The numeric indexes 1, 2, 3 and 4 indicate that the percentages in row 1 and row 2, row 2 and row 3, row 3 and row 4, and row 4 and row 1, respectively, are statistically different at the .05 level or lower.

Table 8.5 tabulates the same four outcome possibilities with respect to the type of offense at issue. The table shows that employers were most likely to be successful in cases addressing off-the-job misconduct and performance issues, with win rates exceeding 50

13 *Elkouri & Elkouri, How Arbitration Works* (Washington, D.C.: Bureau of National Affairs, Kenneth May, ed., 7th ed. 2012), 18-47.

percent in both categories. On the other hand, unions prevailed either in whole or part more often in all remaining offense categories. These outcomes are similar to our discharge findings with respect to performance (high employer win rate) and insubordination (low employer win rate) issues. They are dissimilar, however, with respect to attendance issues where employers won a significantly higher percentage of discharge cases (54.06 percent) than suspension (39.29 percent) cases.[14] Because offense categories are not mutually exclusive, no chi square tests are reported for this table.

[14] See Chapter 7 *supra*.

Table 8.5 Suspension Outcomes by Offense Categories*
(N-size and row % are the top and bottom value, respectively)

Offense Categories	Suspension Upheld in Full	Suspension Reduced in Length	Suspension Overturned in Full	Suspension Reduced to Warning or Reprimand	Row Totals
Off the Job Misconduct	11 52.38[a]	3 14.29	6 28.57	1 4.76[d]	21 100.00
Performance Issue	37 50.68[a]	12 16.44	14 19.18	10 13.70[d]	73 100.00
Dishonesty	26 44.07	14 23.73	12 20.34	7 11.86[d]	59 100.00
On the Job Misconduct	28 43.75[a]	15 23.44	12 18.75	9 14.06[d]	64 100.00
Insubordination	62 40.79[a]	35 23.03	35 23.03[c]	20 13.16[d]	152 100.00
Attendance/Absentee Issues	22 39.29	11 19.64	19 33.93[c]	4 7.14[d]	56 100.00
Violence and Aggression	60 40.00[a]	34 22.67	32 21.33	24 16.00[d]	150 100.00
Drugs/Alcohol	4 40.00	2 20.00	4 40.00[c]	0 0.00[d]	10 100.00
Other	1 12.50	2 25.00	5 62.50[c]	0 0.00	8 100.00
Column Totals**	227 43.99[a]	98 18.99[b]	123 23.84[c]	68 13.18[d]	516 100.00

* The alphabetic indexes a, b, c and d indicate that the percentages in column 1 and column 2, column 2 and column 3, column 3 and column 4, and column 4 and column 1, respectively, are statistically different at the .05 level or lower.

** Multiple offenses may apply per case. The totals shown in the bottom row are the overall totals for each possible outcome, disregarding the multiplicity of alleged motivating offenses.

A Closer Look at Reprimands

Unions in our study have a considerably better track record in reprimand cases than they do in either discharge or suspension cases. As shown in Table 8.6, the full union win rate in reprimand cases (40.19 percent) is not significantly different than that of full employer wins (41.12 percent). Split outcomes–where the reprimand is reduced to a lesser sanction such as an oral warning–constitute the remaining 18.69 percent. The fact that reprimand cases comprise only 4.13 percent of all decisions in our data suggests that the parties generally are disinclined to commit the resources necessary to process these low stakes cases to arbitration.

Table 8.6 <u>Outcomes in Reprimand Cases</u>*
(N-size and column % are the top and bottom value, respectively)

Arbitration Outcomes	Row Totals
Management Win	44 41.12
Union Win	43 40.19[2]
Split Decision	20 18.69[3]
Column Totals	107 100.00

* The numeric indexes 1, 2 and 3 indicate that the percentages in row 1 and row 2, row 2 and row 3, and row 3 and row 1, respectively, are statistically different at the .05 level or lower.

In terms of offense categories, outcomes in reprimand cases were similar to outcomes in suspension cases in two respects. First, employers prevailed most often in cases involving performance issues where reprimands were upheld in 50.00 percent of all cases. Second, employers prevailed least often—15.38 percent—in cases involving attendance issues. As illustrated in Table 8.7, employers had win rates above the norm in cases involving performance issues across all levels of discipline severity, while union win rates in attendance cases varied inversely with the severity of the sanction imposed. These findings suggest that arbitrators generally insist on progressive discipline for initial attendance problems, but, contrary to some popular perceptions, are less likely to excuse poor performance even at an early stage.

Table 8.7 Management Win Rates Per Offense Categories**
(In Percent)

Offense Categories	Discharges	Suspensions	Reprimands
Performance Issues	64.62[a]	50.68	50.00
Attendance Issues	54.06[a]	41.07	15.38[c]

* The alphabetic indexes a, b and c indicate that the percentages in column 1 and column 2, column 2 and column 3, and column 3 and column 1, respectively, are statistically different at the .05 level or lower.

Demographic Factors

Sector

A striking finding of our study is the significantly higher incidence of non-discharge decisions in the public sector as compared to the private sector. While the number of private sector discharge cases only slightly exceeded the number of such cases arising in the public sector,[15] the number of public sector suspension and reprimand cases exceeded those emanating from the private sector by more than a factor of four. As depicted in Table 8.8, this difference increased as the level of the sanction decreased, with public sector reprimand cases exceeding those in the private sector by a factor of almost 10 to 1. These results suggest that private sector unions are less likely to challenge discipline in a pre-discharge setting than are public sector unions. This distinction likely reflects larger public sector bargaining units where the parties have relatively greater access to resources.

---

[15] See Chapter 7 *supra.*

Table 8.8 Cases per Sector*
(N-size, row % and column % are the top, middle and bottom value, respectively)

Outcomes	Public Sector	Private Sector	Row Totals
Suspensions	416 80.62[1a] 81.09[1a]	100 19.38[1] 90.91[1]	516 100.00 82.83[1]
Reprimands	97 90.65[a] 18.91[a]	10 9.35 9.09	107 100.00 17.17
Column Totals	513 82.34[a] 100.00	110 17.66 100.00	623 100.00 100.00

Chi-square (1) = 6.1371, p = 0.013
* The numeric index 1 indicates that the percentages in row 1 and row 2 are statistically different at the .05 level or lower. The alphabetic indexes a, b and c indicate that the percentages in column 1 and column 2, column 2 and column 3, and column 3 and column 1, respectively, are statistically different at the .05 level or lower.

While the data for the two sectors vary greatly with respect to case numbers, they exhibit little difference with respect to case outcomes. As suggested by the chi-square tests, none of the inter-column differences in Table 8.9 are significant, which indicates essentially identical case outcomes for suspension cases in the two sectors. Since our data set of 107 reprimand cases included only 10 from the private sector, no meaningful comparison can be made on that level.

Table 8.9 Suspension Outcomes by Sector*
(N-size, row % and column % are the top, middle and bottom value, respectively)

Suspension Outcomes	Public Sector	Private Sector	Row Totals
Suspension Upheld in Full	185 81.50[a] 44.47[1]	42 18.50 42.00[1]	227 100.00 43.99[1]
Suspension Reduced in Length	81 82.65[a] 19.47	17 17.35 17.00[2]	98 100.00 18.99[2]
Suspension Overturned in Full	97 78.86[a] 23.32[3]	26 21.14 26.00	123 100.00 23.84[3]
Suspension Reduced to a Warning or Reprimand	53 77.94[a] 12.74[4]	15 22.06 15.00[4]	68 100.00 13.18[4]
Column Totals	416 80.62[a] 100.00	100 19.38 100.00	516 100.00 100.00

Chi-square (3) = 0.9269, p = 0.819
* The numeric indexes 1, 2, 3 and 4 indicate that the percentages in row 1 and row 2, row 2 and row 3, row 3 and row 4, and row 4 and row 1, respectively, are statistically different at the .05 level or lower. The alphabetic index a indicates that the percentages in column 1 and column 2 are statistically different at the .05 level or lower.

Attorney Arbitrators

Unions had a higher win rate in our study in non-discharge cases heard by arbitrators who are legally trained. As reflected in Table 8.10, this is particularly true for reprimands, where the union win rate significantly was more than twice as high in cases heard by attorney arbitrators as compared to non-attorney arbitrators. Relative outcomes in suspension cases are much closer, but, as shown in Table 8.11, unions still prevailed more often before attorney arbitrators than they did in cases before arbitrators without legal training (27.61 *versus* 17.37 percent). These results are consistent with those reported in Chapter 7 which show that attorney arbitrators also tend to rule more favorably for unions in discharge cases.[16]

[16] See Chapter 7 *supra*.

Table 8.10 Reprimand Outcomes by Arbitrator's Attorney Status*
(N-size, row % and column % are the top, middle and bottom value, respectively)

Reprimand Outcomes	Non-Attorney	Attorney	Row Totals
Reprimand Upheld	23 52.27[1] 60.53[a]	21 47.73[1] 30.43	44 100.00 41.12
Reprimand Ordered Rescinded	8 18.60[a] 21.05[a]	35 81.40 50.72	43 100.00 40.19[2]
Reprimand Reduced to a Lesser Sanction	7 35.00[a] 18.42	13 65.00 18.84	20 100.00 18.69[3]
Column Totals	38 35.51[a] 100.00	69 64.49 100.00	107 100.00 100.00

Chi-square (2) = 10.7668, p = 0.005
* The numeric indexes 1, 2 and 3 indicate that the percentages in row 1 and row 2, row 2 and row 3, and row 3 and row 1, respectively, are statistically different at the .05 level or lower. The alphabetic index a indicates that the percentages in column 1 and column 2 are statistically different at the .05 level or lower.

Table 8.11 Suspension Outcomes by Arbitrator's Attorney Status*
(N-size, row % and column % are the top, middle and bottom value, respectively)

Suspension Outcomes	Non-Attorney	Attorney	Row Totals
Suspension Upheld in Full	87 38.33[a] 45.79[1]	140 61.67 42.94[1]	227 100.00 43.99[1]
Suspension Reduced in Length	44 44.90[a] 23.16	54 55.10 16.56[2]	98 100.00 18.99[2]
Suspension Overturned in Full	33 26.83[a] 17.37[3]	90 73.17 27.61[3]	123 100.00 23.84[3]
Suspension Reduced to a Warning or Reprimand	26 38.24[a] 13.68[4]	42 61.76 12.88[4]	68 100.00 13.18[4]
Column Totals	190 36.82[a] 100.00	326 63.18 100.00	516 100.00 100.00

Chi-square (3) = 8.3062, p = 0.040
* The numeric indexes 1, 2, 3 and 4 indicate that the percentages in row 1 and row 2, row 2 and row 3, row 3 and row 4, and row 4 and row 1, respectively, are statistically different at the .05 level or lower. The alphabetic index a indicates that the percentages in column 1 and column 2 are statistically different at the .05 level or lower.

National Academy of Arbitrators Membership

The opposite holds true with respect to arbitrator membership in the National Academy of Arbitrators (NAA). That is, arbitrators in our study with NAA membership were more likely to rule for employers in non-discharge cases. This tendency is significantly pronounced in reprimand cases where, as shown in Table 8.12, the employer win rate was approximately 25 percentage points higher for cases heard by NAA members as opposed to nonmembers. As with legal training, the impact of NAA membership decreased in suspension cases, but still correlates positively with management win outcomes (Table 8.13). Here again, these outcomes are consistent with those reported in Chapter 7, which similarly show a higher win rate for employers before NAA arbitrators in discharge cases.[17]

[17] See Chapter 7 *supra.*

Table 8.12 <u>Reprimand Outcomes by Arbitrator's NAA Status</u>*
(N-size, row % and column % are the top, middle and bottom value, respectively)

Reprimand Outcomes	Non-NAA Member	NAA Member	Row Totals
Reprimand Upheld	19 43.18[1] 30.65[a]	25 56.81[1] 55.56[1]	44 100.00 41.12
Reprimand Ordered Rescinded	30 69.77[a] 48.39[2a]	13 30.23 28.89[2]	43 100.00 40.19[2]
Reprimand Reduced to a Lesser Sanction	13 65.00[3a] 20.97	7 35.00[3] 15.56[3]	20 100.00 18.69[3]
Column Totals	62 57.94[a] 100.00	45 42.06 100.00	107 100.00 100.00

Chi-square (2) = 6.8101, p = 0.033
* The numeric indexes 1, 2 and 3 indicate that the percentages in row 1 and row 2, row 2 and row 3, and row 3 and row 1, respectively, are statistically different at the .05 level or lower. The alphabetic index a indicates that the percentages in column 1 and column 2 are statistically different at the .05 level or lower.

Table 8.13 Suspension Outcomes by Arbitrator's NAA Status*
(N-size, row % and column % are the top, middle and bottom value, respectively)

Suspension Outcomes	Non-NAA Member	NAA Member	Row Totals
Suspension Upheld in Full	105 46.26 40.23[1]	122 53.74 47.84[1]	227 100.00 43.99[1]
Suspension Reduced in Length	47 47.96 18.01[2]	51 52.04 20.00	98 100.00 18.99[2]
Suspension Overturned in Full	73 59.35 27.97[3]	50 40.65 19.61[3]	123 100.00 23.84[3]
Suspension Reduced to a Warning or Reprimand	36 52.94 13.79[4]	32 47.06 12.55[4]	68 100.00 13.18[4]
Column Totals	261 50.58 100.00	255 49.42 100.00	516 100.00 100.00

Chi-square (3) = 5.2334, p = 0.155
* The numeric indexes 1, 2, 3 and 4 indicate that the percentages in row 1 and row 2, row 2 and row 3, row 3 and row 4, and row 4 and row 1, respectively, are statistically different at the .05 level or lower. The alphabetic index a indicates that the percentages in column 1 and column 2 are statistically different at the .05 level or lower.

The correlation between experience and outcomes favorable to employers is even more pronounced once the records of the most prolific arbitrators in our study are examined. As in Chapter 7, we compared the outcomes ordered by four arbitrators who each decided more than 100 discipline and discharge cases with the outcomes ordered by the remaining 77 arbitrators in our study. Table 8.14 shows that the more prolific arbitrators ruled in favor of employers in 60 percent of reprimand cases, while the remaining group of arbitrators ruled for employers in only 36.78 percent of such cases. Similarly, as shown in Table 8.15, employers experienced a win rate in suspension cases heard by the prolific arbitrators that was more than 10 percentage points higher than with respect to similar cases heard before the remaining group of arbitrators. Clearly, these more experienced arbitrators had a greater tendency than their counterparts to defer to employer decision-making in cases involving milder and progressive forms of discipline.

Table 8.14 Reprimand Outcomes by Number of Decisions Issued*
(N-size and column % are the top and bottom value, respectively)

Reprimand Outcomes	24 or Fewer Decisions	25 - 49 Decisions	50 - 99 Decisions	100 or More Decisions
Reprimand Upheld	8 26.67[x]	12 38.71	12 46.15	12 60.00
Reprimand Ordered Rescinded	13 43.33	13 41.94	11 42.31	6 30.00
Reprimand Reduced to a Lesser Sanction	9 30.00	6 19.35	3 11.54	2 10.00
Column Totals	30 100.00	31 100.00	26 100.00	20 100.00

Chi-square (6) = 7.6846, p = 0.262

* The alphabetic indexes x, y and z indicate that the percentages in column 1 and column 4, column 2 and column 4, and column 3 and column 4, respectively, are statistically different at the .05 level or lower.

Table 8.15 Suspension Outcomes by Number of Decisions Issued*
(N-size and column % are the top and bottom value, respectively)

Suspension Outcomes	24 or Fewer Decisions	25 - 49 Decisions	50 - 99 Decisions	100 or More Decisions
Suspension Upheld in Full	53 41.09	40 40.00	55 41.35	79 51.30
Suspension Reduced in Length	25 19.38	13 13.00	29 21.80	31 20.13
Suspension Reduced to a Warning or Reprimand	14 10.85	19 19.00	17 12.78	18 11.69
Suspension Overturned in Full	37 28.68[x]	28 28.00[y]	32 24.06	26 16.88
Column Totals	129 100.00	100 100.00	133 100.00	154 100.00

Chi-square (9) = 13.7498, p = 0.132

* The alphabetic indexes x, y and z indicate that the percentages in column 1 and column 4, column 2 and column 4, and column 3 and column 4, respectively, are statistically different at the .05 level or lower.

Summary

Management win rates for non-discharge cases in our data are substantially lower than they are for discharge cases. In general, the likelihood of a union win increased as the level of discipline decreased. As an example, union win rates approximated management win rates in reprimand cases. Employers prevailed most often in non-discharge cases involving performance issues, while they prevailed least often in attendance cases. Non-discharge cases were far more likely to arise in the public sector. Employers enjoyed more favorable outcomes in non-discharge cases heard by non-attorney arbitrators, arbitrators who belong to the National Academy of Arbitrators, and arbitrators with larger caseloads.

CHAPTER 9

MITIGATING AND PROCEDURAL FACTORS IN THE REDUCTION OF PENALTIES

Arbitrators primarily modify employer discipline for three broad categories of reasons. First, an arbitrator may vacate or reduce a penalty because the evidence does not support the alleged factual basis for discipline. Second, an arbitrator may modify an employer's choice of sanction due to procedural failings in the employer's disciplinary process. Third, an arbitrator may alter a disciplinary sanction due to mitigating factors.[1] In contrast to evidentiary and procedural reasons, mitigating factors refer to conduct and characteristics personal to an individual grievant that may warrant a reduction in penalty.[2] After a brief discussion of the relative prevalence of these three factors, this chapter will explore the mitigating circumstances and procedural fault categories in more detail.

Reasons for Reduction in Discipline

Prior Studies

Most, but not all, prior studies have found the lack of sufficient evidence to be the most frequently cited explanation for modifying penalties, with mitigating circumstances following close behind.[3] In contrast, a study by Morris Stone found these two factors to be reversed in terms of relative prevalence.[4] Meanwhile, Ahmad Karim and Thomas Stone found that explanations for modification varied depending on whether the arbitrator reversed

---

1 George W. Bohlander, "Why Arbitrators Overturn Managers in Employee Suspension and Discharge Cases," 23 *Journal of Collective Negotiations* 73, 76-82 (1995).

2 Richard Mittenthal & Howard S. Block, "The Ever Present Role of Arbitral Discretion," *Labor Arbitration Under Fire* (Ithaca, N.Y.: Cornell ILR Press, James L. Stern & Joyce M. Najita, eds., 1997), 231, 238.

3 George W. Bohlander & Donna Blancero, "A Study of Reversal Determinants in Discipline and Discharge Arbitration Awards: The Impact of Just Cause Standards," 21 *Labor Studies Journal* (Fall 1996), 41; Bohlander, "Why Arbitrators Overturn Managers," 73; Arthur Anthony Malinowski, "An Empirical Analysis of Discharge Cases and the Work History of Employees Reinstated by Labor Arbitrators, " 36 *The Arbitration Journal* (March 1981), 31.

4 Morris Stone, "Why Arbitrators Reinstate Discharged Employees," 92 *Monthly Labor Review* (October 1969), 47.

(union win) or reduced (split outcome) the employer's discipline. They found that due process considerations were most prevalent in the former context, while arbitrators most often cited "excess punishment" as the basis for reducing a penalty's severity.[5]

A striking aspect of these prior studies is the consistent share of outcomes found to be influenced by mitigating factors. Four of the five prior studies each reported that mitigating consequences were responsible for 18-20 percent of all arbitral reductions in discipline.[6] The consistency of these findings is all the more remarkable given the wide diversity of factors labeled as "mitigating" in the various studies.

Our Data

We examined 592 decisions in which arbitrators reduced discipline imposed by an employer to a lesser sanction. This set of cases includes those decisions that reduced discipline to a lesser sanction, but not those cases that reversed an employer's discipline by totally vacating the sanction imposed. For each examined decision, we coded the arbitrator's rationale in reducing discipline into one of eight categories. Table 9.1 depicts these results, showing that the impact of mitigating circumstances was by far the most common factor influencing arbitral reductions.

---

[5] Ahmad Karim & Thomas H. Stone, "An Empirical Examination of Arbitrator Decisions in Reversal and Reduction Discharge Hearings," 13 *Labor Studies Journal* (Summer 1988), 41, 47-48.

[6] Bohlander & Blancero, "A Study of Reversal Determinants," 8 tbl 1 (19.7 percent); Bohlander, "Why Arbitrators Overturn Managers," 81 (18 percent); Malinowski, "An Empirical Analysis of Discharge Cases," 35 tbl 3 (18.8 percent); Stone, "Why Arbitrators Reinstate Discharged Employees," 48 tbl 1 (19.7 percent).

Table 9.1 Number of Split Decision Cases Based on Reasons Given for Reduction*

(N-size and column % are the top and bottom value, respectively)

Reason Given for Reduction	Row Totals
Employee is Not Guilty of the Offense Alleged But Is Guilty of a Lesser Offense	59 9.97[1]
Employee Was Guilty of the Offense Alleged But There Were Mitigating Factors	254 42.91[2]
Employee Was Guilty of the Offense Alleged But There Were Procedural Faults	49 8.28[3]
Employee Was Guilty of the Offense Alleged and There Were Both Mitigating Factors and Procedural Faults	76 12.84[4]
Employee Was Guilty of the Offense Alleged But Rationale for the Reduction of Discipline is Not Explained	7 1.18[5]
Employee Was Guilty of a Lesser Offense and There Were Mitigating Circumstances	79 13.34[6]
Employee Was Guilty of a Lesser Offense and There Were Procedural Faults	23 3.89[7]
Employee Was Guilty of a Lesser Offense and There Were Both Mitigating Circumstances and Procedural Faults	45 7.60[8]
Column Totals	592 100.00

* The numeric indexes 1, 2, 3, 4, 5, 6, 7 and 8 indicate that the percentages in row 1 and row 2, row 2 and row 3, row 3 and row 4, row 4 and row 5, row 5 and row 6, row 6 and row 7, row 7 and row 8, and row 8 and row 1, respectively, are statistically different at the .05 level or lower.

By combining the appropriate categories from this list, we were able to identify the total number of decisions that were impacted by each of the three principal reduction motivations. This tabulation is depicted in Table 9.2.

Table 9.2. Factors Influencing Reduction Outcomes
(N-size and % of all reduction cases are the top and bottom value, respectively)

Reduction Factors	Decisions Impacted*
Mitigating Factors	454 76.69
Lack of Evidence	206 34.80
Procedural Faults	193 32.60

*592 decisions; multiple reduction factors may apply per case.

Table 9.2 demonstrates that our findings with regard to the factors influencing reduction outcomes are markedly different than those reported in the earlier studies. Table 9.2 shows a rank ordering of relative prevalence in which mitigating factors serve as the principal motivation for reducing disciplinary outcomes. The number of decisions impacted by mitigating factors was so widespread that these decisions amounted to slightly more than 76% of all reduction outcomes in our data, a prevalence that is approximately four times greater than that reported in the earlier studies.

The divergence of our data from earlier findings may be magnified by three design parameters. First, our analysis allowed for multiple influencing factors in a decision, while some of the earlier studies only recorded a single principal factor for each case.[7] Second, most of the prior studies based their findings on a combination of reversal and reduction outcomes, while we examined only outcomes in which discipline was reduced to a lesser sanction.[8] As noted by Karim and Stone, mitigating circumstances tend to play a larger proportionate role in reduction as compared to reversal outcomes.[9] Third, most of the prior studies used a longer list of potentially influential factors, while our study focused on the

---

[7] See, e.g., Bohlander & Blancero, "A Study of Reversal Determinants," 10 tbl 1 (noting that where multiple determinants for modifying a discharge penalty was stated, "only the principle (sic) reason for the reversal was classified).

[8] See, e.g., Malinowski, "An Empirical Analysis of Discharge Cases," 33 (analyzing all reported cases during the time period in which the arbitrator ordered the reinstatement of the grievant).

[9] Karim & Stone, "An Empirical Examination of Arbitrator Decisions in Reversal and Reduction Discharge Hearings," 48-49.

three principal umbrella categories.[10] To the extent that a study uses a longer list of potential factors, it tends to diminish the share of each individual factor.

Table 9.3 shows the prevalence of the three reduction factor categories by the type of discipline imposed. In general, the impact of mitigating factors tended to wane as the severity of discipline decreased. In contrast, the impact of the evidentiary and procedural factors generally tended to increase as the level of discipline decreased. This suggests that arbitrators were more likely to reduce cases of stringent discipline by considering factors that portray the individual grievant in a positive fashion than they were by looking at more impersonal factors such as the strength of the evidence and the presence of procedural faults.

Table 9.3 <u>Impact of Factors Influencing Reduction by Type of Discipline</u>*

(N-size, row % and column % of cases with specific discipline are the top, middle and bottom value, respectively)

Reduction Factors	Discharge	Suspension	Reprimand	Total
Mitigating Factors	323 71.15[a] 79.56	120 26.43[b] 72.29	11 2.42[c] 55.00	454 100.00 76.69
Lack of Evidence	127 61.65[a] 31.28	70 33.98[b] 42.17	9 4.37[c] 45.00	206 100.00 34.80
Procedural Faults	132 68.39[a] 32.51	52 26.94[b] 31.33	9 4.66[c] 45.00	193 100.00 32.60
Total Cases**	406 68.58[a] 100.00	166 28.04[b] 100.00	20 3.38[c] 100.00	592 100.00 100.00

* The numeric indexes 1, 2 and 3 indicate that the percentages in row 1 and row 2, row 2 and row 3, and row 3 and row 1, respectively, are statistically different at the .05 level or lower. The alphabetic indexes a, b and c indicate that the percentages in column 1 and column 2, column 2 and column 3, and column 3 and column 1, respectively, are statistically different at the .05 level or lower.

** 592 decisions; multiple reduction factors may apply per case.

[10] See, e.g., Bohlander, "Why Arbitrators Overturn Managers," 78-80 tbl. 1 (analyzing the prevalence of 17 reasons for overturning discipline); Stone, "Why Arbitrators Reinstate Discharged Employees," 48 tbl 1 (analyzing 19 reasons given by arbitrators for reversing management).

A Closer Look at Mitigating Factors

Discipline and Discharge in Arbitration recognizes that mitigating factors provide an appropriate basis for modifying the penalty imposed by an employer. The treatise states: "Most arbitrators will evaluate the discipline imposed by the employer to determine whether the penalty (or corrective measure) is excessive. Discipline may be considered excessive if it is disproportional to the degree of the offense . . . or if mitigating circumstances were ignored."[11] We broke the above analysis of reduction factors down a step further by measuring the relative influence of mitigating factors by sub-types. For this analysis, we identified eight specific types of mitigating factors plus a catch-all "other" category. As Table 9.4 demonstrates, the dominant mitigating reasons that arbitrators gave for reducing discipline were "punishment too severe for offense" (33.92 percent) and "good work record" (32.60 percent). Arbitrators also cited two other mitigating factors in more than twenty percent of our reduction cases: "lack of progressive discipline" (27.09 percent) and "length of service" (23.35 percent).

---

[11] *Discipline and Discharge in Arbitration* (Washington, D.C.: Bureau of National Affairs, Norman Brand & Melissa H. Biren, eds., 2nd ed. 2008), 103.

Table 9.4 Mitigating Factors for Reducing Employer Discipline

Mitigating Factors	Total*	Rank Order	% of Decisions	% of Mitigations Cited*
Punishment too severe for offense	154	1	33.92	19.01
Good work record	148	2	32.60	18.27
Lack of progressive discipline	123	3	27.09	15.19
Length of service	106	4	23.35	13.09
Other	84	5	18.50	10.37
Absence of serious harm caused by employee's conduct	65	6	14.32	8.02
Employee acted in good faith	59	7	13.00	7.28
Rehabilitation (i.e., drug, alcohol, mental health, and gambling addiction)	49	8	10.79	6.05
Provocation	22	9	4.85	2.72
Column Totals	810	N/A	N/A	100.00

*$\sum$ N = 810 as more than one mitigating factor is cited in some of the 454 case decisions.

Because prior studies have measured a wide divergence of what have been described as mitigating factors, a direct comparison with those studies in terms of percentage findings is not helpful. A comparison on a more targeted basis, however, is possible. In this regard, a number of studies have found that the most frequently invoked mitigating factor leading to a reduction in discipline is the grievant's past work record.[12] Two studies also concluded that arbitrators rely on the quality of an employee's work record approximately three to four

[12] Donna Blancero & George W. Bohlander, "Minimizing Arbitrator 'Reversals' in Discipline and Discharge Cases," 46 *Labor Law Journal* (1995), 616, 617; Ken Jennings, Barbara Sheffield, & Roger Wolters, "The Arbitration of Discharge Cases: A Forty-Year Perspective," 38 *Labor Law Journal* 33, 41 (1987); Stone, "Why Arbitrators Reinstate Discharged Employees," 47.

times more often than the length of an employee's tenure as a basis for reducing discipline.[13] Our data generally are consistent in demonstrating both the overall importance of an employee's "good work record" and the relatively greater importance given by arbitrators to a good record (32.60 percent) as opposed to a long record (23.35 percent).

We also attempted to discern whether employees with greater tenure generally had more success in challenging employer discipline. While some studies suggest such a correlation,[14] our data and the related chi-square test result do not. We divided our pool of discharge cases into two groups: 1) those involving grievants with ten or more years of tenure with the discharging employer, and 2) those involving grievants with fewer than ten years of tenure. Although not statistically significant, the data in Table 9.5, show that the grievants in the greater tenure group actually fared slightly worse than those with less tenure. This again suggests that a grievant's *good* work record was more important than a grievant's *long* work record.

---

[13] Jennings, Sheffield, & Wolters, "The Arbitration of Discharge Cases: A Forty-Year Perspective," 38, 41 (finding that arbitrators invoked a grievant's prior work record in 46 percent of discharge cases as compared to a grievant's seniority in 13 percent of cases); Ken Jennings & Roger Wolters, "Discharge Cases Reconsidered," 31 *Arbitration Journal* (September 1976), 164, 171 (finding that arbitrators invoked a grievant's prior work record in 42 percent of discharge cases as compared to a grievant's seniority in 10 percent of cases).

[14] Patricia A. Simpson & Joseph J. Martocchio, "The Influence of Work History Factors on Arbitration Outcomes," 50 *Industrial and Labor Relations Review* (1997), 252, 264; Robert C. Rodgers & I.B. Helburn, "The Arbitrariness of Arbitrators' Decisions," *Proceedings of the 37th Annual Meeting of the Industrial Relations Research Association* (Madison, WI.: Industrial Relations Research Association, Barbara D. Dennis, ed., 1985), 234.

Table 9.5 Reinstatement Outcomes by Tenure*
(N-size and column % are the top and bottom value, respectively)

Reinstatement Outcomes	Fewer than 10 Years of Service	10 Years or More of Service
Uphold the Discharge	480 51.67[1]	271 53.88[1]
Reinstate – Full Back Pay	197 21.21	86 17.10
Reinstate – Partial Back Pay	96 10.33	53 10.54
Reinstate – Without Back Pay	151 16.25	89 17.69
Entitlement to Future Vacancy	5 0.54	4 0.80
Column Totals	929 100.00	503 100.00

Chi-square (4) = 3.8497, p = 0.427
* The numeric indexes 1, 2, 3, 4 and 5 indicate that the percentages in row 1 and row 2, row 2 and row 3, row 3 and row 4, row 4 and row 5, and row 5 and row 1, respectively, are statistically different at the .05 level or lower. The alphabetic index a indicates that the percentages in column 1 and column 2 are statistically different at the .05 level or lower.

Further, as discussed in Chapter 8, progressive discipline is commonly utilized by both employers and arbitrators to correct employee behavior.[15] Indeed, *The Common Law of the Workplace* states:

> Because industrial discipline is corrective rather than punitive, *most* arbitrators require use of progressive discipline, even when the collective agreement or employment contract is silent on the subject.[16]

The fact that arbitrators reduced discipline in 27.09 percent of our cases for "lack of progressive discipline" appears to support the proposition that this is a major mitigating factor.

---

[15] See Chapter 8 *supra*.

[16] *The Common Law of the Workplace: The Views of Arbitrators* (Washington, D.C.: Bureau of National Affairs, Theodore J. St. Antoine, ed., 2d ed. 2005), § 6.7 Comment (emphasis added).

Offense Categories

Table 9.6 shows how frequently arbitrators relied on mitigating factors in modifying remedies for varying offense categories. This table shows that arbitrators who reduce penalties relied on mitigating factors in 80 percent or more instances with respect to discipline involving four offense categories: drug/alcohol; performance; insubordination; and off-the-job misconduct. Here again, it should be noted that this table analyzes only cases involving a reduction in penalty and not those in which the penalty has been wholly reversed.

Table 9.6 Reductions Based on Mitigating Factors by Offense Categories

Offense Category	Reductions Based on Mitigating Factors	Total Number of Cases where Offense was Committed	Percentage of Offense Cases where Mitigating Factor was Used
Drugs/Alcohol	18	21	85.71
Performance Issue	73	88	82.95
Insubordination	138	171	80.70
Off the Job Misconduct	16	20	80.00
Attendance/Absentee Issues	79	103	76.70
Dishonesty	70	95	73.68
Violence and Aggression	108	153	70.59
On the Job Misconduct	47	70	67.14
Other	2	5	40.00

An examination of mitigation sub-types in terms of offense categories reveals several interesting results. A number of commentators, for example, have suggested that some arbitrators may reduce discipline related to drug or alcohol use when a grievant presents evidence of successful participation in a rehabilitation program.[17] Our data support this hypothesis by showing that arbitrators invoked rehabilitation as a mitigating factor far more often in drug and alcohol cases as compared to other types of cases. The rehabilitation

[17] *Discipline and Discharge in the Workplace*, 273-275; *Common Law of the Workplace*, § 6.29; Helen Elkiss, "Employee Rights vs. Employer Concerns: Substance Abuse Off-Duty," 49 *Dispute Resolution Journal* (March 1994), 79, 81.

factor also played a significant role in reducing discipline imposed for attendance and off-the-job misconduct problems. Presumably, many of these cases involved underlying drug and alcohol problems as well. As shown in Table 9.7, these three categories, in total, accounted for approximately two-thirds (37 of 56) of all reductions influenced by rehabilitation efforts.

Table 9.7 <u>Reductions Based on Rehabilitation Factor by Offense Categories</u>

Offense Category	Reductions Based on Rehabilitation Factor	Reductions Based on Mitigating Factors	Percentage of Reductions Based on Mitigating Factors Where Rehabilitation was Cited
Drugs/Alcohol	6	18	33.33
Attendance/Absentee Issues	21	79	26.58
Off the Job Misconduct	4	16	25.00
Violence and Aggression	10	108	9.26
On the Job Misconduct	3	47	6.38
Dishonesty	4	70	5.72
Performance Issue	4	73	5.48
Insubordination	4	138	2.90
Other	0	2	0.00

Another mitigating factor that primarily targets a particular offense category is provocation. As several commentators have predicted,[18] arbitrators in our data set relied on evidence of provocation most often to mitigate discipline based on violence and aggression. Indeed, approximately 60 percent of all cases in which provocation played a mitigating role occurred in violence or aggression cases.

---

[18] *Discipline and Discharge in the Workplace*, 345; Margaret A. Lucero & Robert E. Allen, "Fighting on the Job," 53 *Dispute Resolution Journal* (August 1998), 50, 53-54.

Perhaps more surprising is the fact that arbitrators in our study seldom treated provocation as a basis for reducing discipline for insubordination.[19] This finding suggests widespread acceptance of the "obey now, grieve later" maxim.[20] Apparently, most arbitrators believed that abrasive supervisor behavior does not serve as a legitimate justification for an employee's self-help response.

Table 9.8 shows the impact of an employee's past work record with respect to each of our offense categories. Arbitrators relied on a grievant's good work record most often to mitigate discipline relating to off-the-job misconduct (43.75 percent) and dishonesty (42.86 percent). On the other hand, a grievant's past work record had the least mitigating impact on discipline resulting from drug/alcohol (16.67 percent) and attendance problems (17.72 percent). The apparent lesson from these data is that arbitrators are less likely to exercise leniency based on past work performance for offenses that are chronic in nature. Or, to put it another way, perhaps employees with chronic problems are less likely to have amassed a work record that is worthy of serving as a mitigating factor.

---

[19] While arbitrators relied on provocation as a mitigating factor in 4.85 percent of all disciplinary penalty reduction cases, arbitrators did so in only 3.62 percent of those cases where the discipline was premised on insubordination.

[20] *Common Law of the Workplace*, § 6.8.

Table 9.8 Reductions Based on Good Work Record Factor by Offense Categories

Offense Categories	Reductions Based on Good Work Record Factor	Reductions Based on Mitigating Factors	Percentage of Reductions Based on Mitigating Factors Where Good Work Record was Cited
Off the Job Misconduct	7	16	43.75
Dishonesty	30	70	42.86
Insubordination	50	138	36.23
On the Job Misconduct	16	47	34.04
Violence and Aggression	34	108	31.48
Performance Issue	20	73	27.40
Attendance/Absentee Issues	14	79	17.72
Drugs/Alcohol	3	18	16.67
Other	0	2	0.00

Table 9.9 provides a similar across-the-board look at the impact of a lack of progressive discipline on offense categories. Arbitrators most often cited a lack of progressive discipline to justify remedial reductions for discipline related to on-the-job misconduct (36.17 percent) and performance issues (35.62 percent). The areas of discipline least affected by a lack of progressive discipline were off-the-job misconduct (18.75 percent) and attendance (18.99 percent). These outcomes suggest that arbitrators tend to hold employers to higher notice responsibilities for visible conduct that happens at work than they do for conduct occurring outside the immediate workplace. That, of course, does not explain the low impact of this factor on attendance cases. A more plausible explanation here is that discipline for attendance problems—particularly under no-fault attendance policies—generally follows a considerable amount of employer-initiated counseling and corrective action such that a lack of progressive discipline seldom exists to excuse discipline in this context.[21]

[21] See generally K. Dow Scott & G. Stephen Taylor, "An Analysis of Absenteeism Cases Taken to Arbitration: 1975-1981," 38 *The Arbitration Journal* (September 1983), 61, 67-68 (finding a relatively weak relationship between attendance discipline case outcomes and progressive discipline).

Table 9.9 Reductions Based on Lack of Progressive Discipline Factor by Offense Categories

Offense Category	Reductions Based on Lack of Progressive Discipline Factor	Reductions Based on Mitigating Factors	% Reductions Based on Mitigating Factors – Lack of Progressive Discipline was Cited
Other	1	2	50.00
On the Job Misconduct	17	47	36.17
Performance Issue	26	73	35.62
Insubordination	42	138	30.43
Violence and Aggression	27	108	25.00
Dishonesty	17	70	24.29
Drugs/Alcohol	4	18	22.22
Attendance/Absentee Issues	15	79	18.99
Off the Job Misconduct	3	16	18.75

Demographic Factors

Sector

Table 9.10 depicts discipline reduction outcomes by sector. Although reduction factors and sector are not statistically correlated, this table shows that arbitrators reduce discipline due to a lack of evidentiary support significantly more frequently in public sector cases. Arbitral reliance on mitigating and procedural factors, on the other hand, does not vary significantly with regard to sector of origin.

Table 9.10 Reductions by Sector*
(N-size and column % are the top and bottom value, respectively)

Reduction Factors	Public Sector	Private Sector	Row Totals
Mitigating Factors	262 75.50	192 78.37	454 76.69
Lack of Evidence	136 39.19[a]	70 28.57	206 34.80
Procedural Faults	106 30.55	87 35.51	193 32.60
Column Totals**	347 100.00	245 100.00	592 100.00

* The alphabetic index a indicates that the percentages in column 1 and column 2 are statistically different at the .05 level or lower.
** 592 decisions; multiple reduction factors may apply per case.

Again, while mitigation sub-types and sector are not significantly related variables, Table 9.11 reveals two outlier results. First, arbitrators in public sector cases are significantly more receptive to reducing discipline on the basis of a grievant's good work record than those hearing private sector disputes. Arbitrators in our data set relied on past work record to reduce discipline in 38.93 percent of all public sector reduction cases as compared to 23.96 percent in private sector cases. Second, arbitrators are almost twice as likely to mitigate discipline on the basis of provocation in private sector cases as they are in the public sector. To a lesser extent, arbitrators also are more likely to mitigate discipline on the basis of rehabilitation in the public sector and on the basis of progressive discipline in the private sector.

Table 9.11 Reductions Based on Mitigating Factors by Sector*
(N-size and column % are the top and bottom value, respectively)

Mitigating Factor	Public Sector	Private Sector	Row Totals
Length of Service	65 24.81	41 21.35	106 23.35
Good Work Record	102 38.93[a]	46 23.96	148 32.60
Employee Acted in Good Faith	33 12.60	26 13.54	59 13.00
Absence of Serious Harm Caused by Employee's Conduct	38 14.50	27 14.06	65 14.32
Provocation	9 3.44	13 6.77	22 4.85
Punishment Too Severe for Offense	89 33.97	65 33.85	154 33.92
Lack of Progressive Discipline	66 25.19	57 29.69	123 27.09
Rehabilitation	32 12.21	17 8.85	49 10.79
Other	54 20.61	30 15.63	84 18.50
Column Totals**	262 100.00	192 100.00	454 100.00

* The alphabetic index a indicates that the percentages in column 1 and column 2 are statistically different at the .05 level or lower.

** 454 decisions; multiple mitigating factors may apply per case.

Attorney Status

The relative impact of legal training on our arbitral reduction outcomes is illustrated in Table 9.12. While none of these distinctions are statistically significant, arbitrators with J.D. degrees are somewhat more likely to reduce discipline due to a lack of evidence and mitigating factors. On the other hand attorney arbitrators are somewhat less likely to reduce discipline on the basis of procedural faults. At first blush, this may seem surprising since attorneys are often perceived as more process-oriented than non-attorneys. But, due to their legal training, it may be that attorney arbitrators are more likely to require that procedural faults result in actual prejudice to the grievant before reducing the level of discipline on that basis.

Table 9.12 <u>Reductions by Arbitrator's Attorney Status</u>*
(N-size and column % are the top and bottom value, respectively)

Reduction Factors	Non-Attorney Arbitrator	Attorney Arbitrator	Row Totals
Mitigating Factors	137 74.05	317 77.89	454 76.69
Lack of Evidence	57 30.81	149 36.61	206 34.80
Procedural Faults	63 34.05	130 31.94	193 32.60
Column Totals**	185 100.00	407 100.00	592 100.00

* The alphabetic index a indicates that the percentages in column 1 and column 2 are statistically different at the .05 level or lower.
** 592 decisions; multiple reduction factors may apply per case.

Legal training does not correlate with major effects on the relative prevalence of mitigating sub-types in our data. As shown in Table 9.13, attorney arbitrators are somewhat more prone to mitigate discipline on the basis of provocation and a finding that the employer's punishment was too severe. More non-lawyer arbitrators, meanwhile, are inclined to reduce discipline on the basis of length of service and a lack of progressive discipline. Here, again, these distinctions are not statistically significant.

Table 9.13 Reductions Based on Mitigating Factors by Arbitrator's Attorney Status*

(N-size and column % are the top and bottom value, respectively)

Mitigating Factors	Non-Attorney Arbitrator	Attorney Arbitrator	Row Totals
Length of Service	35 25.55	71 22.40	106 23.35
Good Work Record	44 32.12	104 32.81	148 32.60
Employee Acted in Good Faith	15 10.95	44 13.88	59 13.00
Absence of Serious Harm Caused by Employee's Conduct	23 16.79	42 13.25	65 14.32
Provocation	5 3.65	17 5.36	22 4.85
Punishment Too Severe for Offense	43 31.39	111 35.02	154 33.92
Lack of Progressive Discipline	42 30.66	81 25.55	123 27.09
Rehabilitation	14 10.22	35 11.04	49 10.79
Other	28 20.44	56 17.67	84 18.50
Column Totals**	137 100.00	317 100.00	454 100.00

* The alphabetic index a indicates that the percentages in column 1 and column 2 are statistically different at the .05 level or lower.

** 454 decisions; multiple mitigating factors may apply per case.

NAA Membership

Table 9.14 shows that arbitrators who are members of the National Academy of Arbitrators (NAA) are significantly less likely to lower discipline on the basis of any of the three principal reduction factors. This lower incidence is particularly pronounced for procedural faults which are relied upon by NAA arbitrators in less than 25 percent of those cases with reduced penalties, while non-NAA arbitrators are influenced by procedural faults in more than 40 percent of such decisions.

Table 9.14 Reductions by Arbitrator's NAA Status*
(N-size and column % are the top and bottom value, respectively)

Reduction Factors	Non-NAA Arbitrator	NAA Arbitrator	Row Totals
Mitigating Factors	221 81.25[a]	233 72.81	454 76.69
Lack of Evidence	98 36.16	108 33.64	206 34.80
Procedural Faults	113 41.70[a]	80 24.92	193 32.60
Column Totals**	271 100.00	321 100.00	592 100.00

* The alphabetic index a indicates that the percentages in column 1 and column 2 are statistically different at the .05 level or lower.
** 592 decisions; multiple reduction factors may apply per case.

According to our data, arbitrators who were NAA members tended to give more credit to length of service, but less credit to past work record in mitigating discipline. NAA arbitrators, as shown in Table 9.15, also were somewhat more likely to reduce discipline due to a lack of progressive discipline. These distinctions, however, are not statistically significant.

Table 9.15 Reductions Based on Mitigating Factors by Arbitrator's NAA Status*
(N-size and column % are the top and bottom value, respectively)

Mitigating Factor	Non-NAA Arbitrator	NAA Arbitrator	Row Totals
Length of Service	48 21.72	58 24.89	106 23.35
Good Work Record	77 34.84	71 30.47	148 32.60
Employee Acted in Good Faith	34 15.38	25 10.73	59 13.00
Absence of Serious Harm Caused by Employee's Conduct	31 14.03	34 14.59	65 14.32
Provocation	11 4.98	11 4.72	22 4.85
Punishment Too Severe for Offense	76 34.39	78 33.48	154 33.92
Lack of Progressive Discipline	54 24.43	69 29.61	123 27.09
Rehabilitation	25 11.31	24 10.30	49 10.79
Other	34 15.38	50 21.46	84 18.50
Column Totals**	221 100.00	233 100.00	454 100.00

* The alphabetic index a indicates that the percentages in column 1 and column 2 are statistically different at the .05 level or lower.
** 454 decisions; multiple mitigating factors may apply per case.

A Closer Look at Procedural Faults

The Common Law of the Workplace articulates two fundamental propositions about the role of an employer's procedural failings in arbitrators' determinations of whether there was just cause for an employee's discipline or discharge. First, the treatise states: "It is generally accepted that some level of procedural due process is owed by employers to employees in the imposition of discipline and discharge."[22] Second, however, it notes that "arbitrators hold a range of different views on what constitutes the appropriate remedy for violation of procedural protections inherent in the concept of just cause."[23] *The Common*

[22] *Common Law of the Workplace*, § 6.12.
[23] *Id.* at § 6.12 Comment.

Law of the Workplace makes further assertions about the nature of the debate about what should follow from a finding that an employer's conduct failed to satisfy standards of procedural fairness: "[*M*]*ost* arbitrators conclude that the violation will affect the degree of the penalty or other adverse employer action, and *some* arbitrators conclude that the violation will nullify the penalty entirely."[24]

Arbitrator Carroll R. Daugherty's "Seven Tests of Just Cause" includes four inquiries related to procedural fairness (notice, pre-discipline investigation, fair investigation, non-discriminatory enforcement).[25] Under Daugherty's formulation, an employer's failure to satisfy any one of the requirements should result in a finding of no just cause regardless of the seriousness of the employee's offense or the extent to which the defect prejudiced the employee.[26]

Our data base does not test the extent to which arbitrators generally found a lack of just cause due to procedural errors. Instead, we focused on when and why arbitrators reduce, rather than eliminate, disciplinary sanctions because of an employer's procedural failing. The very fact that we found a large number of cases in which arbitrators who found an employer procedural error reduced, rather than eliminated, the employer's disciplinary sanction is further proof, corroborating that presented in Chapter 6, that many arbitrators decline to follow the directive of the Seven Tests of Just Cause.

To explore the role of employer procedural error in reducing disciplinary sanctions, we focused upon the 592 cases in our data base in which the arbitrator reduced, but did not overturn in full, the discipline imposed by the employer. Table 9.2, presented previously in this chapter, showed that in approximately one-third of the cases in which the arbitrator reduced employee discipline the arbitrator pointed to the employer's procedural fault as at least one of the reasons for the reduction (32.60 percent of reduction outcomes). We were able to determine which procedural failings were most frequently associated with a decision to reduce the disciplinary sanction. Table 9.16 shows that the requirements of notice of

---

[24] *Id.* at § 6.19 (emphasis added).

[25] See, generally, Chapter 6.

[26] *Id.*

conduct's possible disciplinary consequences and imposition of evenhanded discipline were the two procedural factors most often identified when discipline was reduced. These two top categories each were referenced in nearly one-third of reductions for procedural reasons.

Table 9.16 Reasons for Due Process Reductions (In Order of Frequency)
(N-size and column % are top and bottom value, respectively)

Due Process Category	Outcomes
Lack of Notice of the Possible Disciplinary Consequences of the Employee's Conduct	80 31.13
Inconsistent or Discriminatory Meting Out of Discipline	74 28.79
Inadequate Factual Investigation	40 15.56
Lack of Notice that Employee's Conduct was Prohibited	30 11.67
Other	21 8.17
Employer's Refusal to Allow Union Representation at Disciplinary Interview	7 2.72
Absence of a Pre-Disciplinary Interview for the Charged Employee	5 1.95
Column Totals*	257 100.00

* Total number of cases = 193. Each case may have multiple outcomes.

Notice in Table 9.16 that the two procedural violations least frequently associated with a penalty reduction were failure to offer the employee a pre-disciplinary interview and refusal to permit union representation at a disciplinary interview. We surmise that these procedural failings uncommonly resulted in a penalty reduction, not because arbitrators declined to reduce discipline when these failings occurred, but rather because employers were least likely to fail to afford these most basic protections to employees.[27]

[27] Professor and arbitrator Christine D. Ver Ploeg considers an employee's opportunity to respond to an employer's accusation prior to discipline so fundamental to fairness that, alone among procedural errors, failure to afford such an opportunity should result in overturning discipline in all cases. Christine D. Ver Ploeg, "Investigatory Due Process and Arbitration," *Arbitration 1992: Improving Arbitral and Advocacy Skills, Proceedings of the 45th Annual Meeting of the National Academy of*

Table 9.17 correlates the frequency with which a procedural failing was cited by an arbitrator as a reason for reduction of discipline with the type of offense the employee was alleged to have committed. Table 9.17 shows that insubordination cases were most likely to have penalty reductions for procedural errors, alone accounting for slightly more than one-quarter of all cases in which an arbitrator reduced a disciplinary sanction for a procedural error. Procedural errors resulted in reduction of discipline least frequently when employees were being disciplined for drug or alcohol violations or for off the job misconduct.

Arbitrators (Washington, D.C.: Bureau of National Affairs, Gladys W. Gruenberg, ed., 1993), 220, 234-236. In NLRB v. J. Weingarten, Inc., 420 U.S. 251 (1975), the Supreme Court held that it was an unfair labor practice for an employer to refuse to permit an employee to be represented by her union at an employer's investigatory interview which she reasonably believed might result in disciplinary action.

Table 9.17 Reductions Based on Due Process Factors by Offense Category (In Order of Frequency)

N-size and column % are top and bottom value, respectively)

Offense Category	Reductions
Insubordination	62 25.51
Violence & Aggression	40 16.46
Attendance / Absentee Issues	34 13.99
Performance Issue	34 13.99
Dishonesty	33 13.58
On the Job Misconduct	25 10.29
Drugs / Alcohol	7 2.88
Off the Job Misconduct	7 2.88
Other	1 0.41
Column Totals*	243 100.00

* Total number of cases = 193. Each case may have multiple outcomes.

Table 9.10, earlier in this chapter, showed that there was an insignificant difference between the public and private sectors with regard to the frequency with which the employer's penalty was reduced for a procedural fault. We see in Table 9.18 a similar comparability in the public and private sectors in the relative frequency with which particular procedural errors resulted in disciplinary reductions. Table 9.18 lists the procedural violations in rank order of their frequency. Note that the offenses are in essentially the same rank order in the public and private sectors.

Table 9.18 Due Process Outcomes by Sector*
(N-size and column % are top and bottom value, respectively)

Due Process Category	Public Sector	Private Sector	Row Totals
Lack of Notice of the Possible Disciplinary Consequences of the Employee's Conduct	39 28.06	41 34.75	80 31.13
Inconsistent or Discriminatory Meting Out of Discipline	39 28.06	35 29.66	74 28.79
Inadequate Factual Investigation	21 15.11	19 16.10	40 15.56
Lack of Notice that Employee's Conduct was Prohibited	18 12.95	12 10.17	30 11.67
Other	14 10.07	7 5.93	21 8.17
Employer's Refusal to Allow Union Representation at Disciplinary Interview	4 2.88	3 2.54	7 2.72
Absence of a Pre-Disciplinary Interview for the Charged Employee	4 2.88	1 0.85	5 1.95
Column Totals**	139 54.09	118 45.91	257 100.00

* The alphabetic index a indicates that the percentages in column 1 and column 2 are statistically different at the .05 level or lower.
** Total number of cases = 193. Each case may have multiple outcomes.

Table 9.12, earlier in this chapter, suggested that attorney arbitrators may be modestly less likely than non-attorney arbitrators to reduce disciplinary penalties for employers' procedural failings. Table 9.19 allows us to examine whether attorney and non-attorney arbitrators differ in the specific procedural faults that they cite as a reason for reducing employee discipline. If one looks only at the rank order of the categories of procedural failings cited by attorney and non-attorney arbitrators respectively, we see remarkable commonality in the relative frequency with which both categories of arbitrators cite a procedural reason for reducing discipline. For both attorney and non-attorney arbitrators, the two most frequently found procedural problems affecting a reduction in discipline were inconsistent discipline and lack of notice of possible disciplinary consequences. Inconsistent discipline came in first among attorney arbitrators and lack of notice of disciplinary consequences came in first among non-attorney arbitrators. The remaining categories of procedural failings (ranking three to seven) appear with identical relative frequency as a reason for penalty reduction in the awards of both attorney and non-attorney arbitrators. Looking instead at percentages, however, differences between attorney and non-attorney arbitrators can be observed. On Table 9.19 we see differences of more than 10 percentage points in two categories. Attorney arbitrators were significantly more likely than non-attorney arbitrators to rely on the inadequacy of an employer's investigation as a basis to reduce discipline. Non-attorney arbitrators were more likely than attorney arbitrators to point to a lack of notice of possible disciplinary consequences as the reason for penalty reduction.

Table 9.19 Due Process Outcomes by Arbitrator's Attorney Status (In Order of Attorney Frequency)*

(N-size and column % are top and bottom value, respectively)

Due Process Category	Attorney Arbitrator	Attorney Rank	Non-Attorney Arbitrator	Non-Attorney Rank	Row Totals
Inconsistent or Discriminatory Meting Out of Discipline	24 28.92	1	50 28.74	2	74 28.79
Lack of Notice of the Possible Disciplinary Consequences of the Employee's Conduct	20 24.10	2	60 34.48	1	80 31.13
Inadequate Factual Investigation	19 22.89[a]	3	21 12.07	3	40 15.56
Lack of Notice that Employee's Conduct was Prohibited	11 13.25	4	19 10.92	4	30 11.67
Other	6 7.23	5	15 8.62	5	21 8.17
Employer's Refusal to Allow Union Representation at Disciplinary Interview	2 2.41	6	5 2.87	6	7 2.72
Absence of a Pre-Disciplinary Interview for the Charged Employee	1 1.20	7	4 2.30	7	5 1.95
Column Totals**	83 32.30		174 67.70		257 100.00

* The alphabetic index a indicates that the percentages in column 1 and column 3 are statistically different at the .05 level or lower.

** Total number of cases = 193. Each case may have multiple outcomes.

As depicted above in Table 9.14, arbitrators who are NAA members were significantly less likely than non-NAA members to reduce discipline on the basis of an employer's procedural misstep. Table 9.20 compares arbitrators who were members of the NAA with non-member arbitrators with respect to identification of categories of procedural error as a reason for reducing a disciplinary sanction. The differences between these two groups of arbitrators here are relatively modest, with no procedural category showing as much as a 10 percentage point difference between the two groups. However, non-NAA members used lack of notice of possible disciplinary consequences more often than NAA members to lessen a disciplinary sanction. Similar to our comparison of attorney and non-attorney arbitrators, for NAA members as well as non-members, the most frequently cited procedural reasons for a penalty reduction were inconsistent discipline and lack of notice of possible disciplinary consequences.

Table 9.20 Due Process Outcomes by Arbitrator's NAA Status (In Order of NAA Member Frequency)*

(N-size and column % are top and bottom value, respectively)

Due Process Category	NAA Member	NAA Member Rank	Non-NAA Member	Non-NAA Member Rank	Row Totals
Inconsistent or Discriminatory Meting Out of Discipline	34 34.69	1	40 25.16	2	74 28.79
Lack of Notice of the Possible Disciplinary Consequences of the Employee's Conduct	26 26.53[a]	2	54 33.96	1	80 31.13
Inadequate Factual Investigation	14 14.29	3	26 16.35	3	40 15.56
Lack of Notice that Employee's Conduct was Prohibited	11 11.22	4	19 11.95	4	30 11.67
Other	10 10.20	5	11 6.92	5	21 8.17
Employer's Refusal to Allow Union Representation at Disciplinary Interview	3 3.06	6	4 2.52	7	7 2.72
Absence of a Pre-Disciplinary Interview for the Charged Employee	0 0.00	7	5 3.14	6	5 1.95
Column Totals**	98 38.13		159 61.87		257 100.00

* The alphabetic index a indicates that the percentages in column 1 and column 3 are statistically different at the .05 level or lower.

** Total number of cases = 193. Each case may have multiple outcomes.

Summary

Three factors generally influence arbitrators to reduce penalties imposed by employers: mitigating factors, lack of evidence, and procedural faults. In our data set, arbitrators relied on mitigating factors more than twice as often as the other two factors in reducing discipline. The most prevalent mitigating factors cited by these arbitrators were punishment too severe, good work record, and lack of progressive discipline. While length of service was the fourth most frequently cited mitigating factor, grievants in our study with more than 10 years of tenure actually experienced slightly less favorable outcomes than those with less job tenure.

Arbitrators in our study most often relied on mitigating factors to reduce penalties in cases involving four offense categories: drug/alcohol, performance, insubordination, and off-the-job misconduct. Arbitrators frequently relied on evidence of provocation to reduce discipline based on violence, but seldom did so with respect to discipline based on insubordination. Arbitrators most often cited a lack of progressive discipline to justify reductions for discipline related to on-the-job misconduct and performance issues. On the other hand, arbitrators seldom invoked either a lack of progressive discipline or past work record as a basis for reducing discipline based on attendance problems.

The two procedural factors most frequently cited by arbitrators in reducing discipline were the lack of notice of the possible disciplinary consequences of employee conduct and the employer's lack of evenhandedness in the level of discipline imposed. Arbitrators in our study most often relied on due process factors to reduce discipline in cases involving insubordination, while doing so least frequently in cases in which employees were disciplined for drug/alcohol or off- the- job misconduct.

Arbitrator reliance on mitigating and procedural factors did not vary significantly with respect to sector of origin. Similarly, the relative frequency with which arbitrators cited various procedural factors as a basis for reducing discipline was relatively consistent when examined by sector, the arbitrator's legal training, and the arbitrator's membership in the National Academy of Arbitrators (NAA). On the other hand, arbitrators were more likely to reduce discipline on the basis of a grievant's good work record in cases arising in the public sector. In addition, arbitrators who were members of the NAA were less likely to reduce discipline generally, with the lower incidence being particularly pronounced with respect to the invocation of procedural grounds for reduction.

CHAPTER 10

FOUR MINNESOTA STATUTES

As discussed in Chapter 1, our data set of discharge and discipline awards somewhat over-represents public sector decisions. In part, this reflects the greater degree of union density in Minnesota's public sector as compared to other jurisdictions.[1] This over-representation also is fostered by four Minnesota statutes that encourage the arbitration of public sector employment disputes.

This chapter takes a close look at these four Minnesota statutes. The first portion of this chapter discusses some of the special attributes of the Public Employment Labor Relations Act which governs labor relations in Minnesota's public sector. The second portion examines three other Minnesota statutes that provide for the arbitration of discipline and discharge decisions affecting certain classes of public employees, namely veterans and teachers. This examination enables a comparison of arbitral outcomes in cases governed by labor contracts with those governed by these state statutes. Since arbitrators acting under these statutes generally apply a just cause analysis similar to that used in labor arbitration, cases decided under these statutes are included in our overall data set.

Minnesota's Public Employment Labor Relations Act

In the private sector, the National Labor Relations Act (NLRA)[2] and the federal common law relating to arbitration[3] provide a uniform set of governing principles applicable throughout the United States. A far different situation exists in the public sector, however. Given the NLRA's exclusion of governmental employers from the scope of its coverage,[4]

---

[1] See Chapter 1 *supra*.

[2] 29 U.S.C. §§ 159-169 (2006).

[3] See Laura J. Cooper, Dennis R. Nolan, Richard A. Bales, & Stephen F. Befort, *ADR in the Workplace* (St. Paul, MN: West Academic Publishing, 3rd ed. 2014), 41-134.

[4] See 29 U.S.C. § 152(2) (2006).

public sector labor relations, except with respect to federal employment,[5] are subject to state rather than federal regulation. While a majority of states have adopted legislation governing state and local government labor relations, they differ significantly with respect to both the scope of coverage and the contours of substantive regulation.[6]

The Public Employment Labor Relations Act (PELRA) governs public sector labor relations in Minnesota.[7] Unlike many states that have adopted statutes applicable only to certain specified groups of public employees (such as teachers),[8] PELRA comprehensively applies to all public employee occupational groups.[9] PELRA generally provides greater rights to unions and public employees than do most other public sector statutes, particularly in terms of its coverage of workers in supervisory positions, its mandate of a grievance arbitration process, and its recognition of a limited right to strike. Each of these features has existed throughout the period of our empirical study and likely contributes to the greater prevalence of public sector awards in our survey.

Protection of Supervisors

The NLRA excludes supervisors from its coverage, meaning that private sector supervisory personnel do not have a protected right to bargain collectively or to engage in concerted activity.[10] A number of public sector jurisdictions follow this approach as well.[11]

---

[5] Labor relations in the federal sector are governed by the Civil Service Reform Act of 1978, 5 U.S.C. §§ 7101-7135 (2006).

[6] See Martin H. Malin, Ann C. Hodges, & Joseph E. Slater *Public Sector Employment: Cases and Materials* (St. Paul, MN: West, 2nd ed. 2011), 292-94..

[7] Minn. Stat. §§ 179A.01 to .40 (2012). The Minnesota Legislature first enacted PELRA in 1971. See Note, "The Minnesota Public Employment Labor Relations Act of 1971: Another Public Employment Experiment," 57 *Minnesota Law Rev*iew 134 (1972).

[8] See Malin, Hodges & Slater, *Public Sector Employment* at 294.

[9] See Minn. Stat. § 179A.03, subd. 14 (2012); see also Deborah A. Schmedemann, "The Scope of Bargaining in Minnesota's Public Sector Labor Relations: A Proposal for Change," 10 *William Mitchell Law Rev*iew 213, 214 (1984).

[10] 29 U.S.C. § 152(3) (2006).

[11] See Malin, Hodges & Slater, *Public Sector Employment* at 359.

In contrast, PELRA provides that public employers "shall extend exclusive recognition to a representative of or an organization of supervisory . . . employees for the purpose of negotiating terms or conditions of employment."[12] As a result, supervisory employees enjoy all of the protections that PELRA extends to public employees in general except that supervisors are barred from membership in the same bargaining unit as non-supervisory employees,[13] may not be represented by an exclusive representative that is affiliated with a union that represents non-supervisory employees of the same employer,[14] and do not have the right to strike.[15] For purposes of our study, PELRA's coverage of supervisory employees likely results in an increase in the overall number of disputes submitted to arbitration along with a greater diversity in the types of issues and contexts presented.

Mandatory Grievance Arbitration Process

PELRA further provides that

> . . . all contracts must include a grievance procedure providing for compulsory binding arbitration of grievances including all written disciplinary actions. If the parties cannot agree on the grievance procedure, they are subject to the grievance procedure promulgated by the commissioner [of the Bureau of Mediation Services].[16]

---

[12] Minn. Stat. § 179A.06, subd. 2 (2012). Some other jurisdictions have adopted a similar approach, *see e.g.*, N.H. Rev. Stat. Ann. 273-1:1.IX, 273-A:8.II (New Hampshire); Wash. Rev. Code § 41.56.040 (Washington).

[13] See Minn. Stat. § 179A.09, subd. 2 (2012) (prohibiting the designation of an appropriate unit which includes essential employees with other employees). PELRA defines "essential" employees to include supervisors. Minn. Stat. § 179A.03, subd. 7 (2012).

[14] See Minn. Stat. § 179A.06, subd. 2 (2012).

[15] See Minn. Stat. § 179A.18, subd. 1 (2012). An exclusive representative or employer of a unit of essential employees has the right to submit bargaining disputes to binding interest arbitration. Minn. Stat. § 179A.16, subd. 2 (2012).

[16] Minn. Stat. § 179A.20, subd. 4(a) (2012). The grievance procedure promulgated by the Bureau of Mediation Services is set out in Minn. Rules 5510.5110 to .5190 (2007).

By mandating an arbitration process for disciplinary grievances even in the absence of a contract grievance procedure agreed upon by the parties, PELRA again likely expands the overall number of public sector disputes submitted to grievance arbitration.

Limited Right to Strike

PELRA authorizes a limited right to strike by some public sector units following an impasse in collective bargaining and the exhaustion of a mandatory mediation period.[17] The statute does not authorize strikes in any other circumstances and expressly bars confidential, essential, and supervisory employees from engaging in a strike under any circumstances.[18] Minnesota is unusual, although not alone, in allowing a limited right to strike. Nine other states have enacted legislation authorizing public employee strikes in certain specified circumstances.[19] Courts in an additional four states have interpreted state laws to allow some range of lawful public employee strikes.[20] The recognition of a right to strike may interject issues into disciplinary arbitration proceedings that might not arise in most jurisdictions such as discipline based on alleged striker misconduct.

Statutory Limitations on Public Sector Terminations

Minnesota also has two sets of statutory schemes that permit the use of arbitration to determine whether a public employer has sufficient cause to terminate a covered employee. One statute applies to veterans of military service employed by local government units. Two other statutes apply to tenured public school teachers. The existence of these

---

17 See Minn. Stat. § 179A.18 (2012).

18 See Minn. Stat. § 179A.18, subd. 1 (2012). Any strike beyond that specifically authorized by statute is illegal and subject to penalties. *See* Minn. Stat. § 179A.19 (2012).

19 See Joyce M. Najita & James L. Stern, *Collective Bargaining in the Public Sector* 13, 20 (Armonk, NY: M E Sharpe, 2001) (listing the following states as having statutes authorizing some type of lawful strikes in the public sector: Hawaii, Pennsylvania, Illinois, Ohio, Alaska, Minnesota, Montana, Oregon, Vermont, and Wisconsin).

20 *Id.* (listing the following states as having some degree of judicially recognized public employee strike rights: California, Colorado, Idaho, and Louisiana).

statute-based arbitration regimes provides yet another explanation for the over-representation of public sector decisions in our data base.

In the following sections, we first describe the substantive and procedural protections afforded by each of these statutes. We then examine case outcomes under the two systems. Although the smaller data sets generated with respect to these two systems limit the meaningful range of statistical analysis, the resulting data nonetheless provide an interesting comparison of arbitral systems grounded in statute with those grounded in contract.

The Veterans Preference Act

The Minnesota Veterans Preference Act (VPA) provides that no covered veteran "may be removed from [public employment] except for incompetency or misconduct shown after a hearing, upon due notice, [and] stated charges, [and] in writing."[21] The statute defines a "veteran" as a citizen or resident alien honorably discharged from any branch of the armed forces after either having served on active duty for at least 181 days, or having incurred a disability while serving on active duty.[22] The VPA covers veterans employed by any public sector employer other than the University of Minnesota.[23] The VPA expressly excludes several positions from coverage, including department heads, teachers, and confidential officers.[24]

---

[21] Minn.. Sat. § 197.46 (2012).

[22] Minn. Stat. § 197.447 (2012).

[23] See Minn. Stat. § 197.455 (2012); see also Winberg v. Univ. of Minn., 499 N.W.2d 799 (Minn. 1993).

[24] The complete list of exemptions includes: "private secretary, teacher, superintendent of schools, [the] chief deputy of any elected official or head of a department, [and] any person holding a strictly confidential relation to the appointing officer." Minn. Stat. § 197.46 (2012). This section places the burden on the employer to establish exempt status. Courts also have interpreted the VPA as inapplicable to occasional or temporary employees. See Crnkovich v. Indep. School Dist. No. 701, Hibbing, 142 N.W.2d 284 (Minn. 1966).

A covered veteran may be discharged only for "incompetency" or "misconduct."[25] The Minnesota Supreme Court has described these grounds as the equivalent of a "just cause" standard.[26] Courts have sustained terminations where an employee was unable to perform the essential duties of the job,[27] or where an employee sexually harassed subordinate employees.[28] On the other hand, courts have ruled that the incompetency or misconduct at issue must be related to the employee's actual job performance[29] and that difficulties resulting from personality problems are not sufficient to justify a termination.[30]

The VPA requires that the public employer give the veteran a written notice of intent to discharge that includes instructions on how the employee may request a hearing within 60 days.[31] If an employer fails to provide a veteran with this notice, the 60-day limitations period is tolled indefinitely,[32] subject only to a six-year statute of limitations.[33]

A notified veteran must submit a written request for a hearing within the 60-day period or the right to a hearing is waived.[34] Significantly, a veteran protected by the VPA is entitled to receive full compensation from the date of termination through the date of the

---

25 Minn. Stat. § 197.46 (2012). The VPA does not apply to lesser forms of discipline such as a suspension, Wilson v. City of Minneapolis, 168 N.W.2d 19, 23 (Minn. 1969), unless the disciplinary suspension immediately precedes a discharge, and both are for the same misconduct, Mitlyng v. Wolff, 342 N.W.2d 120, 121 (Minn. 1984).

26 See AFSCME Council 96 v. Arrowhead Reg'l Corrs. Bd., 356 N.W.2d 295, 297-298 (Minn. 1984).

27 See Myers v. City of Oakdale, 409 N.W.2d 848, 852-853 (Minn. 1987).

28 See Davila v. Ramsey County Cmty. Human Servs. Dep't, 374 N.W.2d 547 (Minn. Ct. App. 1985), aff'd in part, rev'd in part on other grounds, 387 N.W.2d 421 (Minn. 1986).

29 See Ekstedt v. Vill. of New Hope, 193 N.W.2d 821, 828 (Minn. 1972).

30 See State v. Civil Serv. Comm'n of Minnesota, 130 N.W.2d 143 (Minn. 1964).

31 Minn. Stat. § 197.46 (2012).

32 See Young v. City of Duluth, 386 N.W.2d 732, 738 (Minn. 1986). The court in *Young* ruled that the tolling occurs regardless of whether the veteran actually was aware of his or her VPA rights. *Id.*

33 Minn. Stat. § 541.05, subd. 1(2) (2012); Johnson v. County of Anoka, 536 N.W.2d 336, 339 (Minn. Ct. App. 1995).

34 See Minn. Stat. § 197.46 (2012).

hearing body's decision even if the termination is sustained.[35] Thus, a public employer may suspend a veteran pending the hearing panel's decision, but only with full pay.[36]

The VPA provides that a removal hearing is to be held either before a civil service commission, or, if none is available in that jurisdiction, before a three-member panel selected by the parties.[37] In practice, however, if the veteran is a member of a bargaining unit, it is common for the employer and the veteran to agree to have a single grievance arbitrator also serve as the VPA officer.[38] The proper role of the hearing body, however constituted, is to determine whether the public employer acted reasonably in terminating the veteran for incompetency or misconduct.[39] The public employer has the burden of proof to show that it acted reasonably in its decision to terminate.[40]

A veteran who is successful in challenging his or her termination may be entitled to reinstatement and damages, which can include back pay if the public employer wrongfully failed to continue wage payments over the interim period, as well as the reasonable value of

---

[35] See Johnson v. Vill. of Cohasset, 116 N.W.2d 692, 700 (Minn. 1962); State ex rel. Jenson v. Civil Serv. Comm'n of Minneapolis, 130 N.W.2d 143, 147 (Minn. 1964); Henry v. Metro. Waste Control Comm'n, 401 N.W.2d 401, 406 (Minn. Ct. App. 1987).

[36] See Leininger v. City of Bloomington, 299 N.W.2d 723, 731 (Minn. 1980); Kurtz v. City of Apple Valley, 290 N.W.2d 171, 173 (Minn. 1980).

[37] Minn. Stat. § 197.46 (2012).

[38] See Minnesota Counties Insurance Trust, Resource Briefing: Veterans' Preference Act, February 2001,t http://www.mdva.state.mn.us/VeteransPrefRBText.pdf..

[39] See Southern Minn. Mun. Power Agency v. Schrader, 394 N.W.2d 796, 801-802 (Minn. 1986); Myers v. City of Oakdale, 461 N.W.2d 242, 245 (Minn. Ct. App. 1990).

[40] See Schrader, 394 N.W.2d at 802; Johnson v. Vill. of Cohasset, 116 N.W.2d 692, 698 (Minn. 1962).

fringe benefits.[41] The hearing body also possesses the authority to determine whether extenuating circumstances justify reducing the termination to a lesser sanction.[42]

Teacher Tenure Act and Continuing Contract Act

The Continuing Contract Act and Teacher Tenure Act similarly provide procedural and substantive protections for Minnesota public teachers in employment terminations. The Teacher Tenure Act applies to teachers in "cities of the first class"[43] which include Duluth, St. Paul, and Minneapolis.[44] A "teacher" for purposes of the Teacher Tenure Act is defined to include "every person regularly employed, as a principal, or to give instruction in a classroom, or to superintend or supervise classroom instruction, or as placement teacher and visiting teacher."[45] The Teacher Tenure Act also covers those employed as counselors and librarians who are licensed as teachers or school librarians.[46] The Continuing Contract Act protects teachers in cities in Minnesota other than those of the first class.[47] The Continuing Contract Act defines a "teacher" for purposes of the statute as "a principal, supervisor, and

---

[41] Young v. City of Duluth, 410 N.W.2d 27, 30 (Minn. Ct. App. 1987). Despite the VPA's requirement that the public employer keep the veteran on the payroll pending the disciplinary hearing, the veteran has a duty to mitigate damages, and a back pay award should be reduced by the amount which, through the exercise of due diligence, the veteran could have earned in an employment of a like kind or grade. See Robertson v. Special School Dist. No. 1, 347 N.W.2d 265, 267 (Minn. 1984); Spurck v. Civil Serv. Bd., 42 N.W.2d 720, 726-27 (Minn. 1950).

[42] See Schrader, 394 N.W.2d at 801-02; *see also* State v. Gallagher, 527 N.W.2d 158, 161 (Minn. Ct. App. 1995) (holding power of hearing panel to modify disciplinary sanction is not dependent on whether the employer acted reasonably in removing veteran, but upon the existence of extenuating circumstances).

[43] Minn. Stat. § 122A.41 (2012).

[44] Minn. Stat. § 410.01 (2012); *Classification of Cities*, Information Brief (Minn. House of Rep. Research Dep't) Jan. 2007, at 2.

[45] Minn. Stat. § 122A.41, subd. 1(a) (2012).

[46] *Id.*

[47] Minn. Stat. §122A.40, subd. 18 (2012).

classroom teacher and any other professional employee required to hold a license from the state department."[48]

The Continuing Contract Act and Teacher Tenure Act provide similar protections to teachers. While a school board is granted wide discretion in choosing not to renew the contracts of probationary teachers,[49] both statutes provide that non-probationary teachers only may be dismissed for cause and only after heightened procedural requirements are met.

The Continuing Contract Act

The Continuing Contract Act provides two alternative sets of standards for the termination of continuing-contract teachers, one standard that applies to terminations effective at the end of the school year[50] and another for terminations effective during the school year.[51] As discussed more fully below, terminations effective at the end of the year are in response to behavior that is remediable. Such terminations only may be ordered after giving a teacher an opportunity to remedy deficiencies. Immediate terminations are reserved for more serious misconduct and do not require that the teacher have an opportunity to remedy deficiencies.

Terminations Effective at the Close of the School Year

Subdivision 9 of the Continuing Contract Act provides that a continuing contract may be terminated effective at the close of the school year, upon any of the following grounds:

> (a) Inefficiency;
>
> (b) Neglect of duty, or persistent violation of school laws, rules, regulations, or directives;

---

[48] Minn. Stat. §122A.40, subd. 1 (2012).

[49] Minn. Stat. §122A.41, subd. 2(a) (2012); Minn. Stat. §122A.40, subd. 5(a) (2012).

[50] Minn. Stat. §122A.40, subd. 9 (2012).

[51] Minn. Stat. §122A.40, subd. 13 (2012).

(c) Conduct unbecoming a teacher which materially impairs the teacher's educational effectiveness;

(d) Other good and sufficient grounds rendering the teacher unfit to perform the teacher's duties.[52]

Terminations made under Subdivision 9 require that the teacher be given the opportunity first to correct the deficiency within a reasonable time after receiving written notice.[53]

Cases for which the application of subdivision 9 is appropriate generally have involved incidents that have not resulted in physical or psychological harm to students. Most commonly, school boards pursue dismissal under this subdivision for deficiencies such as ineffective communication with parents or students, improper grading, poor recordkeeping, tardiness, and poor classroom management.[54] If a teacher has been provided with an opportunity to remedy deficiencies and fails to do so, a school board must give written notice of its intent to terminate prior to April 1, and such notice must state the ground for the

---

[52] Minn. Stat. § 122A.40, subd. 9 (2012).

[53] *Id.* The statute provides little guidance about what constitutes a reasonable amount of time to allow for remediation and about how remediation is assessed. In Cianflone v. Indep. Sch. Dist. No. 112 Chaska, No. CX-01-2269, 2002 WL 1364247 (Minn. Ct. App. June 25, 2002), the Minnesota Court of Appeals held that termination of a teacher who used inappropriate discipline techniques in 1998 was proper because he had been warned in 1993 for similar behavior. Though the teacher did not commit any violations within the five-year period, the court found that the warning given five years earlier began the time in which the teacher was required to remediate. The court stated, "If, as Cianflone asserts, the school board was required to wait a reasonable time after every additional deficiency occurred, no teacher could ever be terminated for improper conduct." *Id.*, at *3. The Minnesota Supreme Court has suggested that the longer a teacher has been teaching, the more time may be necessary to allow for remediation of certain classroom management practices. Ganyo v. Indep. Sch. Dist. No. 832, 311 N.W.2d 497, 502 (Minn. 1981) ("It seems harsh and unreasonable to accord [petitioner] only 5 weeks after the notice of deficiency . . . and 8 weeks before the notice of termination to remedy 25 years of teaching practice which was now labeled deficient for the first time.").

[54] See e.g., Ganyo, 311 N.W.2d 497 (poor classroom control, lack of clear directions to students, inappropriate record keeping, ineffective communication and student evaluation); Whaley v. Anoka-Hennepin Indep. Sch. Dist. No. 11 325, N.W.2d 128 (Minn. 1982) (poor rapport with teachers, insufficient communication, inappropriate use of class time, failure to be punctual).

proposed termination.[55] The board must alert the teacher of the right to request a hearing before the school board or an arbitrator within 14 days of receiving the written notice.[56]

The hearing before an arbitrator or school board may be held in public or private at the choice of the teacher.[57] The teacher may have counsel present, and counsel may examine and cross-examine witnesses, present arguments, and present rebuttal evidence.[58] If the proceeding is brought before an arbitrator, the arbitrator reviews the grounds for termination de novo to determine if the stated grounds exist and support the termination.[59] An arbitrator may impose a lesser penalty than termination only if a party proposes a lesser penalty at the hearing.[60]

Termination Effective During the School Year

Subdivison 13 provides that the board may discharge a teacher, effective immediately, upon the following grounds:

> (1) immoral conduct, insubordination, or conviction of a felony;
>
> (2) conduct unbecoming a teacher which requires the immediate removal of the teacher from the classroom or other duties;
>
> (3) failure without justifiable cause to teach without first securing the written release of the school board;

---

[55] Minn. Stat. § 122A.40, subd. 7 (2012).

[56] *Id.* See Zeller v. Prior Lake Pub. Sch., Indep. Sch. Dist. No. 719, 108 N.W.2d 602 (Minn. 1961) (holding that a letter stating that school board had not "re-elected" teacher for ensuing year, and that any hearing that teacher might request would be of no help to her, was not proper notice of proposed termination under former statute). Matter of Peterson, 472 N.W.2d 687 (Minn. Ct. App. 1991) (stating that a notice that attached a copy of statute and stated, "You will note that you have the right to select a private or public hearing" satisfied statute's requirement). Under the Teacher Tenure Act, the teacher has only ten days to request a hearing. Minn. Stat. §122A.41, subd. 7 (2012).

[57] Minn. Stat. § 122A.40, subd. 14 (2012).

[58] *Id.*

[59] Minn. Stat. § 122A.40, subd. 15(c) (2012).

[60] *Id.*

(4) gross inefficiency which the teacher has failed to correct after reasonable written notice;

(5) willful neglect of duty; or

(6) continuing physical or mental disability subsequent to a 12 months leave of absence and inability to qualify for reinstatement in accordance with subdivision 12.[61]

As with proposed terminations under subdivision 9 of the Continuing Contract Act, the school board must give written notice to the teacher of proposed termination and the teacher's right to request a hearing before an arbitrator or the school board.[62] However, a teacher notified of a subdivision 13 violation only has 10 days to request a hearing,[63] in contrast to the 14 day period provided by subdivision 9. As with terminations under subdivision 9, a school board acting under subdivision 13 may suspend a teacher only with pay until the conclusion of the hearing process.[64] A teacher whose termination is proposed under subdivision 13 is afforded the same rights during the hearing, including the same opportunities to present evidence, and must receive a written termination order if found to have engaged in the alleged misconduct.[65]

The Minnesota Supreme Court has ruled that an immediate discharge under subdivision 13 is appropriate only for conduct that is not remediable.[66] In determining whether or not conduct is remediable, courts have stated that the decision-maker should consider: "(1) the teacher's prior record; (2) the severity of the conduct in light of the teacher's record; (3) the threatened physical or psychological harm to students or other teachers; and (4) whether the conduct could have been corrected had the teacher been warned

---

[61] Minn. Stat. § 122A.40, subd. 13 (2012).

[62] Minn. Stat. § 122A.40, subd. 7 (2012).

[63] Minn. Stat. § 122A.40, subd 13 (2012).

[64] *Id.*

[65] Minn. Stat. § 122A.40, subd. 16 (2012).

[66] Kroll v. Independent School District No. 593, 304 N.W.2d 338, 345 (Minn. 1981).

by superiors."[67] The state Supreme Court acknowledged that some isolated conduct may be so outrageous and severe as to warrant immediate discharge despite a teacher's prior unblemished record, but nevertheless stated that the teacher's record must always be considered in assessing remediability.[68]

Cases of irremediable misconduct warranting an immediate discharge most commonly have involved instances of sexual or physical abuse of students.[69] These two circumstances, however, are not the exclusive basis for an immediate discharge. In *Downie v. Independent School District No. 141*,[70] for example, the Minnesota Court of Appeals upheld the immediate discharge of a junior high school counselor for engaging in a series of acts that included communicating confidential information revealed to him by a student. The Minnesota Court of Appeals also has upheld the immediate discharge of a teacher who stole funds from two co-teachers under circumstances that likely would result in "faculty disorder and an unsatisfactory learning environment."[71]

The Teacher Tenure Act

Under subdivision 6(a) of the Teacher Tenure Act, applicable to school districts in the cities of Minneapolis, St. Paul, and Duluth, a teacher may be discharged or demoted for the following reasons:

(1) immoral character, conduct unbecoming a teacher, or insubordination;

(2) failure without justifiable cause to teach without first securing the written release of the school board having the care, management, or control of the school in which the teacher is employed;

---

[67] In the Matter of Discharge of Peterson, 472 N.W.2d 687 (Minn. Ct. App. 1991).

[68] Kroll, 304 N.W.2d 338, 346. See also Russell v. Special Sch. Dist. No. 6, 366 N.W.2d 700, 705 (rejecting the argument that the issue of remediability can be addressed without looking at past conduct).

[69] See, e.g., In re Etienne, 460 N.W.2d 109 (Minn. Ct. App. 1990) (sexual relationship with a student); Russell v. Special School District No. 6, 366 N.W.2d 152 (Minn. Ct. App. 1985) (physical abuse of a student).

[70] 367 N.W. 2d 913 (Minn. Ct. App. 1985).

[71] In the Matter of Shelton, 408 N.W.2d 594, 598 (Minn.Ct.App. 1987).

(3) inefficiency in teaching or in the management of a school;

(4) affliction with active tuberculosis or other communicable disease; or

(5) discontinuance of position or lack of pupils.[72]

Unlike the Continuing Contract Act, the Teacher Tenure Act does not explicitly create separate standards for teachers fired during the school year and those fired at the end of the year. Instead the act provides for certain situations when a teacher must be discharged immediately, including a finding that the teacher is afflicted with a communicable disease[73] and upon notice that a teacher's license has been revoked due to a conviction for child abuse or sexual abuse.[74] The act also does not explicitly require that teachers terminated for remediable conduct receive an opportunity to remedy deficiencies, and the Minnesota Court of Appeals has held that no such requirement exists.[75] One commentator, however, has noted that courts and arbitrators in recent years generally have extended this protection to teachers covered by the act.[76]

As with the Continuing Contract Act, a school board choosing to discharge or dismiss a teacher must issue a written notice of the proposed action stating the grounds upon which the action is being taken.[77] The teacher also has a right to request arbitration for a proposed action stemming from causes 1-4 enumerated in subdivision 6(a) and must make a request within 10 days of receiving notice from the school board.[78] Unlike the Continuing Contract Act, the Teacher Tenure Act imposes no April 1st deadline for issuing termination

---

[72] Minn. Stat. § 122A.41, subd. 6(a) (2012).

[73] Minn. Stat. § 122A.41, subd. 6(a)(4) (2012).

[74] Minn. Stat. § 122A.41, subd. 6(b) (2012).

[75] *See* In Re the Proposed Termination of James E. Johnson's Teaching Contract with Indep. Sch. Dist. No. 709, 451 N.W.2d 343, 347 (Minn. Ct. App. 1990).

[76] Christine Ver Ploeg, "Terminating Public School Teachers for Cause Under Minnesota Law," 31 *William Mitchell Law Rev*iew 303, 320-321 (2004).

[77] Minn. Stat. § 122A.41, subd. 10 (2012).

[78] Minn. Stat. § 122A.41, subd. 7 (2012).

orders. Instead the act states that the order must be issued within 25 days of giving notice of the proposed termination.[79] As a further distinction, the Teacher Tenure Act gives school districts in cities of the first class discretion to determine whether a suspension pending decision is with or without pay.[80]

Data

Table 10.1 shows outcomes in statutory cases as compared to all discharges in our data set. The most interesting finding here is the fact that the percentage of employer wins is relatively uniform across all case categories, in the 52 to 57 percent range, with only an insignificantly higher rate in the teacher discharge cases.

---

[79] Minn. Stat. § 122A.41, subd. 10 (2012).

[80] Minn. Stat § 122A.41, subd. 12 (2012).

Table 10.1 Outcome by Case Type*
(N-size, row % and column % are the top and bottom value, respectively)

Outcomes	Veterans	Teachers	All Public Sector Discharges
Uphold the Discharge	23 47.92 52.27[1]	25 52.08 56.82[1]	396 100.00 56.17[1]
Reinstate – Full Back Pay	10 52.63 22.73	9 47.37 20.45	119 100.00 16.88[2]
Reinstate – Partial Back Pay	11 55.00 25.00[3]	9 45.00 20.45[3]	75 100.00 10.64[3]
Reinstate – No Back Pay	0 0.00 0.00	1 100.00 2.27	109 100.00 15.46[4]
Entitlement to Future Vacancy	0 0.00 0.00[5]	0 0.00 0.00[5]	6 100.00 0.85[5]
Column Totals	44 50.00 100.00	44 50.00 100.00	705 100.00 100.00

Chi-square (3) = 1.3360, p = 0.721
* The numeric indexes 1, 2, 3, 4 and 5 indicate that the percentages in row 1 and row 2, row 2 and row 3, row 3 and row 4, row 4 and row 5, and row 5 and row 1, respectively, are statistically different at the .05 level or lower. The alphabetic index a indicates that the percentages in column 1 and column 2 are statistically different at the .05 level or lower.

We had expected that the statutory cases would yield a higher win rate for employers for two reasons. First, since employers are required to keep veterans and most teachers on the payroll until the date of the hearing body's decision,[81] we assumed that more employees would challenge discharge decisions under these statutes even with relatively weaker cases. Second, since many of the teacher discharge cases, as noted above, involved claims of egregious misconduct,[82] we assumed that employers would more frequently be able to sustain a showing of cause for discharge.

---

[81] See note 64 *supra* and accompanying text.

[82] See notes 69-71, 74 *supra* and accompanying text.

Our findings, in contrast, evidence no significant difference in employer win outcomes when these two types of statutory cases are compared to all public sector discharge cases. The fact that employer win rates are substantially similar in all case categories suggests that the statutory- and contract-based cases also are substantially similar in nature. It is likely that representatives in both statutory and contract contexts weed out the sure winners and sure losers, thereby submitting a similar mix of close cases for arbitral resolution.

A second interesting finding is the near absence of reinstatement without back pay outcomes in statutory cases. This result is not surprising given the statutory procedures. Under both the VPA[83] and the Continuing Contract Act,[84] the affected employees experience no loss of back pay since both statutes require employers to provide pay until the date of decision. In addition, the teacher termination statutes expressly deny an arbitrator the authority to order a lesser penalty than termination except "to the extent that either party proposes such lesser penalty in the proceeding."[85] Only the Teacher Tenure Act applicable to teachers in cities of the first class permit school districts to suspend teachers without pay pending the hearing outcome.[86] Not surprisingly, Table 10.1's only reinstatement without back pay award arose under that act.

Given the statutory mandate of the VPA and the Continuing Contract Act to provide full pay until the date of decision, it is surprising to see that such a high proportion of the statutory decisions reinstate discharged employees with an award of partial back pay. Since such an award ostensibly requires a reinstated employee to forfeit pay already received and required by state law, it is questionable whether such an award is even consistent with the requirements of those two statutes.

Table 10.2 breaks the teacher cases into two categories: those terminations taken at the end of a school year, and those taken immediately during the school year. The table

---

[83] See note 21 *supra* and accompanying text.

[84] Minn. Stat. § 122A.40, subd. 13 (2012).

[85] Minn. Stat. §§ 122A.40, subd. 15(c), 122A.41, subd. 13(c) (2012).

[86] Minn. Stat. § 122A.41, subd. 12 (2012).

depicts employer win rates for the two categories that are not significantly different, but shows that full employee wins were more prevalent in end-of-year terminations while split decisions providing for reinstatement with a reduced level of discipline were more prevalent with respect to immediate discharges. Arbitrators apparently found that the more egregious types of misconduct alleged in immediate discharge cases almost invariably warranted at least some level of punishment.

Table 10.2 Outcomes in Teacher Termination Cases*
(N-size, row % and column % are the top, middle and bottom value, respectively)

Outcomes	End-of-Year Terminations	Immediate Terminations	Row Totals
Uphold the Discharge	18 72.00[a] 60.00[1]	7 28.00 50.00[1]	25 100.00 56.82[1]
Reinstate – Full Back Pay	8 88.89[2a] 26.67	1 11.11[2] 7.14	9 100.00 20.45
Reinstate – Partial Back Pay	4 44.44 13.33[3]	5 55.56 35.71	9 100.00 20.45[3]
Reinstate – No Back Pay	0 0.00 0.00	1 100.00 7.14	1 100.00 2.27
Entitlement to Future Vacancy	0 0.00 0.00[5]	0 0.00 0.00[5]	0 0.00 0.00[5]
Column Totals	30 68.18[a] 100.00	14 31.82 100.00	44 100.00 100.00

Chi-square (3) = 6.4273, p = 0.093
* The numeric indexes 1, 2, 3, 4 and 5 indicate that the percentages in row 1 and row 2, row 2 and row 3, row 3 and row 4, row 4 and row 5, and row 5 and row 1, respectively, are statistically different at the .05 level or lower. The alphabetic index a indicates that the percentages in column 1 and column 2 are statistically different at the .05 level or lower.

The size of the data set of veteran and teacher cases was too small to provide a meaningful analysis of outcomes by offense categories. The data, however, do show a pattern in the types of offenses at issue in the statutory cases. In VPA cases, allegations of poor performance (31.8 percent of all cases) and insubordination (27.3 percent) were most common. Meanwhile, allegations of violence (45.5 percent) and insubordination (34.1 percent) predominated in teacher termination cases. Taken in combination, employers asserted claims of insubordination in 30.7 percent of all statutory cases as compared to 19.0 percent in non-statutory discharge cases.

As shown in Table 10.3, employers fare considerably better in VPA cases decided by non-attorney arbitrators than they do in cases decided by arbitrators with legal training. While attorney arbitrators sustained discharge decisions in 38.71 percent of VPA cases, non-attorney arbitrators did so in a hugely significant 84.62 percent of VPA cases. Indeed, the non-attorney arbitrators favored employers to the extent that no employee fully prevailed in any of the thirteen VPA cases decided by a non-attorney arbitrator.

Table 10.3 Veterans Preference Act Outcomes by Arbitrator's Attorney Status*
(N-size, row % and column % are the top, middle and bottom value, respectively)

Reinstatement Outcomes	Non-Attorney Arbitrator	Attorney Arbitrator	Row Totals
Uphold the Discharge	11 47.83[1] 84.62[1a]	12 52.17[1] 38.71	23 100.00 52.27[1]
Reinstate – Full Back Pay	0 0.00 0.00[a]	10 100.00 32.26	10 100.00 22.73
Reinstate – Partial Back Pay	2 18.18[a] 15.38	9 81.82 29.03[3]	11 100.00 25.00
Reinstate – No Back Pay	0 0.00 0.00	0 0.00 0.00	0 100.00 0.00
Entitlement to Future Vacancy	0 0.00 0.00[5]	0 0.00 0.00[5]	0 100.00 0.00[5]
Column Totals	13 29.55[a] 100.00	31 70.45 100.00	44 100.00 100.00

Chi-square (2) = 8.5683, p = 0.014
* The numeric indexes 1, 2, 3, 4 and 5 indicate that the percentages in row 1 and row 2, row 2 and row 3, row 3 and row 4, row 4 and row 5, and row 5 and row 1, respectively, are statistically different at the .05 level or lower. The alphabetic index a indicates that the percentages in column 1 and column 2 are statistically different at the .05 level or lower.

The outcomes relating to legal training in teacher tenure cases are far different. As shown in Table 10.4, attorney arbitrators more frequently ruled for employers than did non-attorney arbitrators by a slight, albeit insignificant, margin.

It is interesting to note the high prevalence of attorney arbitrators hearing these statutory cases. While arbitrators with legal training decided 64.32 percent of all discharge cases in our data set, attorney arbitrators decided more than 70 percent of both types of statutory claims. While this difference is not statistically significant, it does suggest that the parties view legal training as comparatively more important when selecting arbitrators to hear cases implicating statutory issues, such as the complex remediability issues presented by the teacher termination statutes.

Table 10.4 Teacher Termination Outcomes by Arbitrator's Attorney Status*
(N-size, row % and column % are the top, middle and bottom value, respectively)

Reinstatement Outcomes	Non-Attorney Arbitrator	Attorney Arbitrator	Row Totals
Uphold the Discharge	6 24.00[a] 54.55	19 76.00 57.58[1]	25 100.00 56.82[1]
Reinstate – Full Back Pay	3 33.33 27.27	6 66.67 18.18	9 100.00 20.45
Reinstate – Partial Back Pay	2 22.22 18.18	7 77.78 21.88[3]	8 100.00 20.45[3]
Reinstate – No Back Pay	0 0.00 0.00	1 100.00 3.03	1 100.00 2.27
Entitlement to Future Vacancy	0 0.00 0.00[5]	0 0.00 0.00[5]	0 100.00 0.00[5]
Column Totals	11 25.00[a] 100.00	33 77.00 100.00	44 100.00 100.00

Chi-square (3) = 0.7170, p = 0.869
* The numeric indexes 1, 2, 3, 4 and 5 indicate that the percentages in row 1 and row 2, row 2 and row 3, row 3 and row 4, row 4 and row 5, and row 5 and row 1, respectively, are statistically different at the .05 level or lower. The alphabetic index a indicates that the percentages in column 1 and column 2 are statistically different at the .05 level or lower.

As shown in tables 10.5 and 10.6, arbitrators who were members of the National Academy of Arbitrators (NAA) tended more often to rule in favor of employers in statutory discharge cases. While this tendency also prevailed in discharge cases generally (54.15 percent full employer wins) the tendency was even more pronounced in statutory cases where the employer win rate equalled or exceeded sixty percent in both VPA and teacher termination decisions.

Table 10.5 Veterans Preferance Act Outcomes by Arbitrator's NAA Status*
(N-size, row % and column % are the top, middle and bottom value, respectively)

Reinstatement Outcomes	Non-NAA Arbitrator	NAA Arbitrator	Row Totals
Uphold the Discharge	11 47.83 45.83	12 52.17 60.00[1]	23 100.00 52.27[1]
Reinstate – Full Back Pay	6 60.00 25.00	4 40.00 20.00	10 100.00 22.73
Reinstate – Partial Back Pay	7 63.64 29.17[3]	4 36.36 20.00[3]	11 100.00 25.00[3]
Reinstate – No Back Pay	0 0.00 0.00	0 0.00 0.00	0 100.00 0.00
Entitlement to Future Vacancy	0 0.00 0.00[5]	0 0.00 0.00	0 100.00 0.00
Column Totals	24 54.55 100.00	20 45.45 100.00	44 100.00 100.00

Chi-square (2) = 0.9055, p = 0.636
* The numeric indexes 1, 2, 3, 4 and 5 indicate that the percentages in row 1 and row 2, row 2 and row 3, row 3 and row 4, row 4 and row 5, and row 5 and row 1, respectively, are statistically different at the .05 level or lower. The alphabetic index a indicates that the percentages in column 1 and column 2 are statistically different at the .05 level or lower.

Table 10.6 <u>Teacher Termination Outcomes by Arbitrator's NAA Status</u>*
(N-size, row % and column % are the top, middle and bottom value, respectively)

Reinstatement Outcomes	Non-NAA Arbitrator	NAA Arbitrator	Row Totals
Uphold the Discharge	4 16.00[a] 40.00	21 84.00 61.76[1]	25 100.00 56.82[1]
Reinstate – Full Back Pay	4 44.44 40.00	5 55.56 14.71	9 100.00 20.45
Reinstate – Partial Back Pay	2 22.22 20.00	7 77.78 20.59[3]	9 100.00 20.45[3]
Reinstate – No Back Pay	0 0.00 0.00	1 100.00 2.94	1 100.00 2.27
Entitlement to Future Vacancy	0 0.00 0.00[5]	0 0.00 0.00[5]	0 100.00 0.00[5]
Column Totals	10 22.73[a] 100.00	34 72.27 100.00	44 100.00 100.00

Chi-square (3) = 3.3567, p = 0.340
* The numeric indexes 1, 2, 3, 4 and 5 indicate that the percentages in row 1 and row 2, row 2 and row 3, row 3 and row 4, row 4 and row 5, and row 5 and row 1, respectively, are statistically different at the .05 level or lower. The alphabetic index a indicates that the percentages in column 1 and column 2 are statistically different at the .05 level or lower.

We also examined the mean length of time from date of discharge to date of decision in statutory cases. Our hypothesis was that employers would seek earlier hearing dates in statutory cases (under the VPA and the Continuing Contract Act) because of their obligation to provide pay throughout the hearing process regardless of case outcomes. Although Table 10.7 shows that statutory cases were decided almost one month earlier than non-statutory discharge cases in general, this difference is not statistically significant.

Table 10.7 Mean Length of Time from Discharge to Arbitration Decision*
(N = months)

Case Type	Length of Time
VPA	8.23
Teacher Termination	8.54
All Non-Statutory Discharge Cases	9.26

* The numeric indexes 1, 2 and 3 indicate that the percentages in row 1 and row 2, row 2 and row 3, and row 3 and row 1, respectively, are statistically different at the .05 level or lower.

Summary

Four Minnesota statutes likely contribute to a greater prevalence of public sector arbitration decisions in Minnesota. One of these statutes—PELRA—promotes public sector arbitration by granting organizational rights to supervisors and mandating provisions in all public sector labor contracts that provide for the submission of grievances to binding arbitration.

Minnesota also has adopted statutes that permit arbitrators to determine whether veterans employed by local government units and tenured public school teachers have been terminated for cause. Public employer win rates in these statutory cases generally are quite similar to those in public sector discharge cases. On the other hand, arbitrators in statutory cases seldom reinstated employees without back pay, but were twice as likely to reinstate employees with partial back pay as compared to decisions involving non-statutory public sector discharges.

The parties in statutory cases more frequently selected arbitrators with legal training to hear their disputes. Non-attorney arbitrators were far more likely than attorney arbitrators to rule for employers in VPA cases, but these two groups had very similar win rates with respect to teacher termination cases. In general, arbitrators resolved statutory cases in a more expeditious fashion than non-statutory discharge cases.

CHAPTER 11

SUMMARY OF FINDINGS

In this chapter we highlight some of our most interesting and significant findings. At the end of each entry, the number in parentheses indicates the chapter in which details and analysis of the findings can be found.

A. Comparing Outcomes in Discharge and Discipline Cases

1) Most of the arbitrated cases involved discharges (69.68 percent), followed by suspensions (25.11 percent) and, lastly, reprimands (5.21 percent). (2)

2) In round numbers, management's discipline and discharge decisions were fully sustained by arbitrators in 50 percent of cases, arbitrators reduced employer sanctions in 29 percent of cases, and *fully* reversed them in 21 percent of cases. (3)

3) Distribution of discipline and discharge decisions across employer win, union win, and split decision outcomes was relatively stable over the 1982-1989, 1990-1997 and 1998-2005 clusters of years. (2)

4) Management's chances of *fully* winning in arbitration were greatest in discharge cases (52.44 percent), followed by suspension cases (43.99 percent), and then reprimand cases (41.12) percent. (3, 7)

5) Union's chances of *fully* winning in arbitration were greatest in reprimand cases (40.18 percent), followed by suspension cases (23.84 percent), and then discharge cases (19.20 percent). (3, 8)

B. Comparing the Public and Private Sectors

1) The proportion of all arbitrated discipline and discharge cases arising from the public sector steadily increased between 1982 and 2005. (2)

2) The employers' win rate was significantly higher for public sector discharges (56.17 percent) than for private sector discharges (48.83 percent). (3, 7)

3) Sexual harassment and off-duty misconduct were more frequently arbitrated in the public sector. Arbitrations concerning absenteeism were more common in the private sector. (4)

4) Arbitrators were more likely to rely on the Seven Tests of Just Cause in private sector cases than in public sector cases. (6)

5) Arbitrated non-discharge discipline cases arose four times more frequently from the public sector than the private sector. (8)

6) There was no significant difference in arbitrator reliance on mitigating and procedural factors between the public and private sectors. (9)

7) Arbitrators were more likely to reduce discipline on the basis of a grievant's good work record in the public sector. (9)

8) Outcomes in public sector statutory cases arising under laws requiring just cause for the discharge or discipline of veterans and teachers were similar to outcomes in public sector cases arising under collective bargaining agreements. (10)

9) Arbitrators in public sector statutory cases seldom ordered reinstatement without back pay, but were twice as likely to order reinstatement with partial pay (suspension). (10)

C. Arbitrator Characteristics

1) Arbitrator gender bore no relationship to suspension and reprimand outcomes. (3)

2) In discharge cases, the percent of employer win decisions issued by female arbitrators (60.17 percent) significantly exceeded the percent of employer win decisions issued by male arbitrators (51.88 percent). (3)

3) In discharge cases, male arbitrators issued significantly more split decisions (29.81 percent) than female arbitrators (21.16 percent). (3)

4) Arbitrator age was not systematically related to award outcomes, regardless of the type of discipline imposed by the employer. (3)

5) Relatively few arbitrators decided a proportionately large share of awards. Approximately 14 percent of arbitrators decided slightly more than 59 percent of awards. (2)

6) Arbitrators with the heaviest caseloads (e.g., 50 or more cases in our data base) were more likely than arbitrators with lighter caseloads (fewer than 50 cases) to issue split decisions in discharge cases (31.22 percent vs. 23.72 percent) but not in discipline cases. Further, in matters of discharge, arbitrators with the heaviest caseloads were far more

likely to issue a management win (51.02 percent of awards) than a split decision (31.22 percent). (2)

7) In discipline cases, there was no significant relationship between the arbitrator's educational background and case outcome. In discharge cases, however, arbitrators with master's, law and doctorate degrees were significantly more likely to issue employer win decisions over union win decisions. Arbitrators with master's (60.56 percent) and Ph.D. degrees (59.64 percent) were more likely to issue employer win decisions than were those with law degrees (48.75 percent). (3)

8) In discipline cases, arbitrators who were academics were significantly more likely to favor the employer (50.42 percent) than were arbitrators who were practicing attorneys (38.98 percent). In discharge cases, arbitrators who were neither practicing attorneys nor academics had the highest management win rate of 62.50 percent, followed by academics (57.51 percent) and, lastly, by arbitrators who were both practicing attorneys and academics (50.87 percent). Arbitrators who were both practicing attorneys and academics issued the most union win outcomes (26.09 percent). (3)

9) Non-attorneys and NAA members ruled for employers relatively more often in both discharge and discipline cases. (3, 7, 8)

10) Non-attorney arbitrators were more likely than attorney arbitrators to rule in favor of employers in cases in which employees were disciplined or discharged because of either insubordination or absenteeism. (4)

11) NAA members were more likely than non-members to rule in favor of employers in cases in which employees were disciplined or discharged for unsatisfactory performance. (4)

12) Attorney arbitrators were more likely, and NAA members less likely, to state explicitly that they were applying a "preponderance of the evidence" proof standard. (5)

13) NAA members were more likely than non-members to employ the "clear and convincing" standard of proof and less likely than non-members to require proof "beyond a reasonable doubt." (5)

14) NAA arbitrators were more likely to order reinstatement without back pay. (7)

15) NAA members were less likely to reduce discipline on the basis of procedural faults. (9)

16) Attorney arbitrators were more frequently selected for public sector statutory cases. (10)
17) Non-lawyers more frequently ruled for employers in public sector statutory cases involving veterans. (10)

D. Grievant Characteristics

1) A female grievant's chances of having her suspension revoked or having her reprimand rescinded was significantly 1.36 times higher than for a male grievant. In discharge arbitrations, female and male grievants were equally likely to prevail. (3)
2) Whether the gender of the arbitrator and grievant matched did not significantly affect the
3) For alleged insubordination, property damage and sexual harassment, the grievants were more likely to be men, while women were more likely to arbitrate discipline or discharge for unsatisfactory performance and theft. (4)
4) Regardless of the type of discipline imposed, there is no statistical evidence that arbitrators treated a grievant's length of service (looking at employees with fewer than 10 years of service and those with 10 or more years of service) as a mitigating factor. (3, 9)
5) Arbitrators cited to mitigating factors more than twice as often as due process factors in reducing discipline. (9)
6) The most commonly invoked mitigating factors leading to a reduction in penalty were punishment too severe, good work record, and lack of progressive discipline. (9)
7) The most commonly invoked procedural factors leading to a reduction in penalty were lack of notice of possible disciplinary consequences and lack of evenhandedness in the level of discipline imposed. (9)

E. Party Advocates

1) The share of disciplinary cases that did *not* involve representation by legal counsel has steadily declined from 1982-1989 to 1998-2005. (2)
2) There was no correlation between a party's representation by an attorney and outcomes in discipline cases, but there was in discharge cases. In discharge cases, when *both* or *neither* party used an attorney the odds that either party would win were unchanged, but a party's odds of winning increased when it was the only party with an attorney. (3)

3) The offenses for which both sides were most likely to be represented by counsel were sexual harassment, drug use and off-duty misconduct. Employers were represented by attorneys in more than 80 percent of the cases involving threats and assaults of supervisors, threats to co-workers and sexual harassment. (4)

F. Offenses

1) Grievants charged with having committed more than one offense were significantly less likely to prevail fully in arbitration than were grievants charged with only one offense, regardless of the type of offense. (3)

2) Three offense categories (unsatisfactory performance, absenteeism and insubordination) individually accounted for more than 10 percent of all discharge offenses arbitrated and together these three categories accounted for more than 45 percent of all discharge offenses arbitrated. (4)

3) The only offense categories that continuously declined in relative frequency over the 24-year period of the study were attendance and absenteeism. (4)

4) Absenteeism was much more commonly arbitrated in discharge cases than in cases of lesser discipline. (4)

5) Among offense categories with at least 25 employer wins, employers were most successful in cases alleging drug offenses and least successful in cases alleging sexual harassment and abuse of students, patients, or inmates. In offense categories with at least 25 union wins, unions were most successful in cases alleging theft. In offense categories with at least 25 split decisions, sexual harassment was most likely to yield a split decision. (4)

6) Employers prevailed most often in discharge cases involving drug and performance allegations and least often in cases involving insubordination, on-duty misconduct, and off-duty misconduct. (7)

7) Employers prevailed most often in suspension cases involving performance and off-duty misconduct allegations and least often in cases alleging insubordination and attendance problems. (8)

8) Employer win rates in attendance cases were highest in discharge cases, lower in suspension cases, and still lower in reprimand cases. Employer win rates in performance cases were high across all levels of discipline. (8)

9) Arbitrators relied on mitigating factors most frequently to reduce discipline in cases involving drug, performance, insubordination, and off-duty misconduct allegations. (9)

10) Arbitrators frequently cited provocation as a basis to reduce discipline based on allegations of violence, but did so less frequently when discipline was based on allegations of insubordination. (9)

11) Arbitrators relied on a lack of progressive discipline to reduce discipline based on on-the-job misconduct and performance allegations, but did so less frequently when discipline was based on allegations of off-the-job misconduct and poor attendance. (9)

12) Arbitrators relied on procedural factors most frequently to reduce discipline in cases involving allegations of insubordination. (9)

G. Assessing Conventional Wisdom

1) The Seven Tests of Just Cause were argued by advocates and utilized by arbitrators much less frequently than most of the arbitration literature would suggest. We found no mention of an advocate's reliance on the Seven Tests in more than 95 percent of cases. In more than 90 percent of cases arbitrators did not rely upon the Seven Tests. Of the arbitrators in our data base, two-thirds never used the Seven Tests. (3, 6)

2) Arbitrators rarely referred in their awards to an explicit quantum of proof standard (proof by a "preponderance of the evidence," "clear and convincing evidence," or proof "beyond a reasonable doubt"). An explicit standard was articulated in only 16.22 percent of discipline awards and only 24.1 percent of discharge awards. There was no evidence that there was a relationship between an articulated standard of proof and outcomes in either discipline or discharge cases. (3)

3) Even in cases in which employees were disciplined or discharged for conduct that would be considered a crime or a matter of moral turpitude, heightened standards of proof, such as "clear and convincing" or "beyond a reasonable doubt" were rarely used. (5)

4) If a grievant was working under a last chance agreement when discharged, the odds of a full union victory fell by approximately 50 percent, and the odds of a split decision fell by about 40 percent. In contrast, employer win rates increased from 49.92 percent to 72.22 percent. (3, 7)

5) Arbitrators imposed longer no-pay periods with respect to discharges reduced to suspensions (11 weeks) or to reinstatement without back pay (37 weeks) than did employer-imposed sanctions (1 week). (7, 8)

6) Tenure was not a significant mitigating factor in most cases; employees with 10 or more years of service had slightly less favorable outcomes than those with fewer than 10 years of service. (9)

7) Arbitrators retained jurisdiction in only 26.62 percent of discharge cases in which reinstatement was ordered. (7)

8) Most decisions (52.78 percent) did not explicitly require discharged grievants awarded either full or partial back pay to mitigate lost earnings. (7)

H. Other Unique Findings

1) Delay had an insignificantly discernable effect on award outcomes. (3, 7)

2) Arbitral insistence on proof "beyond a reasonable doubt" has declined over time to the point of near disappearance in the more recent years of our study. (5)

3) More experienced and more prolific arbitrators were least likely to rely upon the Seven Tests in crafting their awards. (6)

4) The prevalence of decisions ordering reinstatement without back pay decreased significantly between 1982 and 2005. (7)

APPENDIX

Discharge & Discipline Project: Case Question and Coding

Please use a "1" instead of an X for items 13, 24 and 26

1. Case No. — Unique number assigned to each case by Excel. (caseno)

2. Case ID — Eight-digit field. Case ID assigned by MN Labor Arbitration Awards Summaries. Up to five-numeric digits followed by a decimal and two-digits in numeric or alphabetic. (caseid)

3. Arbitrator Name — Please enter last name, first name. In the case of panel arbitration use the neutral, if there are multiple neutrals use the chair. (arbitratorname)

   (Arbitratorcode is the variable with each arbitrator identified as 1-81)

4. Date of Decision MM/DD/YYYY) — Eight-digit field (with format

   Note single digit days and months are ok, the leading zero is dropped by Excel.
   Source: summary and decision (dateofdecision)

   (Two new variables created for the month and year: monthdateofdecision & yeardateofdecision)

   Dummy codes for year for decision created: DecisionYear_1 – DecisionYear_24

5. Employer Counsel — "Did the employer use legal counsel at the hearing?"

   One-digit field. Number assigned by RA.
   Source: decision

   1 = Yes

0 = No

(employercounsel)

(Three new dummy variables created: onlyemployercounsel, NoCounsel, & bothhavecounsel)

6.	Union Counsel	"Did the employee or union use legal counsel at the hearing?" One-digit field. Number assigned by RA. Source: decision 1 = Yes 0 = No (unioncounsel) (Three new dummy variables created: onlyunioncounsel, NoCounsel, & bothhavecounsel)
7.	Winner	One-digit field. Note that the numbers assigned to this field are published in MN Labor Arbitration Awards Summaries. The latter were pre-coded by the BNA and/or LRP Publications and do not strictly correspond to the kindred numbers assigned in item 20 below. 1 = Management 2 = Union 3 = Split 4 = Multiple issues coded as split, but management upheld on discipline 5 = Multiple issues coded as split, but union upheld on discipline (winner) (WINNERNEW is a new variable created from winner which combines selection 4 with

selection 1 and selection 5 with selection 2. Thus 1= Management, 2 = Union, & 3 = Split.)

8. Sector

One-digit field. Number assigned by RA.

1 = Public sector
2 = Private sector
(sector)

(2 dummy codes were created for each response: Sector_1 which corresponds to Public & Sector_2 which corresponds to Private)

9. Listing Agency

One-digit field. Number assigned by RA. From Summary's case caption or decision.

1 = Bureau of Mediation Services - BMS
2 = Federal Mediation & Conciliation Service - FMCS
3 = American Arbitration Association - AAA
4 = Other or Unknown
5 = Veteran's Preference (any source). Only includes discharge and suspensions.
6 = Teacher's Immediate Discharge
7 = Teacher's End of Year
(listingagency)

10. Gender of Grievant

One-digit field. Number assigned by RA. Source: summary & decision

1 = Male(s)
2 = Female(s)

(genderofgrievant)

(A dummy code was created: GoG where 1 = Female)

11.	Date of Discipline	Eight-digit field (with format MM/DD/YYYY). The date used is the date the employer imposed discipline or discharged the employee. If there was more than one disciplinary incident at issue then the date used is the date of the most serious disciplinary event. If the month is known, but the exact date cannot be determined, then the date is entered as the 15th of the month. Source: decision (dateofdiscipline) (Two new variables were created for the month and year: monthdateofdiscipline & yeardateofdiscipline)
12.	Years of Service	Number of years the employee had been employed by this employer on the date discipline was imposed. Source: decision 1=Less than 1year 2=1 year or more, but less than 5 years (1-5) 3=Five years or more, but less than 10 years (5-10) 4=Ten years or more, but less than 20 years (10-20) 5=20 years or more (20+) 6=Unknown or more than one grievant disciplined (yearsofservice) (A dummy was created: GrievantTenure where 1=10 years or more)
13.	Alleged Offense	The best classification for each offense is coded using the following two-digit fields. Number assigned by R.A. Source: summary and decision. (Categories modified from Elkouri & Elkouri)

Dummy codes were created for each offense.

01	Absenteeism (absenteeism)
02	Verbal or physical abuse of customers, or other members of the public (abuseofcustomerspublic)
03	Verbal or physical abuse of students, patients or inmates (abuseofstudentspatientsinmates)
04	Abusive Language to Supervision (abusivelanguagesupervisor)
05	Assault and fighting among employees (assaultfighting)
06	Computer misuse (other than obscenity, immoral conduct, or pornography) (computermisusenotobscenity)
07	Property damage (propertydamage)
08	Disloyalty to employer (e.g. competition with employer or conflict of interest) (disloyaltytoemployer)
09	Distribution of drugs (distributionofdrugs)
10	Falsifying company records (including time & production records) (falsifyingcompanyrecords)
11	Falsifying employment application (falsifyingemploymentapplication)
12	Gambling (gambling)
13	Horseplay (horseplay)
14	Insubordination (use 43 if not contemporaneous) (insubordination)
15	Leaving post (includes leaving work as a result of a dispute) (leavingpost)
16	Leaving work early (leavingworkearly)
17	Lying (not on company records or employment application) (lying)
18	Misconduct during strike (misconductduringstrike)
19	Moonlighting (excluding competition with employer) (moonlighting)
20	Negligence (negligence)

21	Obscene or immoral conduct or pornography with a computer (obsceneimmoralconductwcomputer)
22	Obscene or immoral conduct or pornography without a computer (obsceneimmoralconductwocomputer)
23	Off-duty misconduct (offdutymisconduct)
24	Possession or use of alcohol (possessionuseofalcohol)
25	Possession or use of drugs, positive drug test result, or refusal to take drug test (possessionuseofdrugsrefusaltotak)
26	Profane or abusive language (toward coworkers not including supervisor) (profaneabusivelanguagetocoworker)
27	Prohibited strike (prohibitedstrike)
28	Racial/Religious slur (racialreligiousslur)
29	Refusal to cross picket line (usually that of another union) (refusaltocrosspicketline)
30	Refusal to accept job assignment (refusaltoacceptjobassignment)
31	Refusal to accept overtime (refusaltoacceptovertime)
32	Sexual harassment (sexualharassment)
33	Sleeping on job or loafing (sleepingonjobloafing)
34	Slowdown (slowdown)
35	Tardiness (tardiness)
36	Theft from coworker or customer (theftfromcoworkerorcustomer)
37	Theft from employer (theftfromemployer)
38	Threat or assault of supervisor (threatassaultofsupervisor)
39	Threat to co-worker (threattocoworker)
40	Union activities (unionactivities)
41	Unsatisfactory performance (includes incompetence, poor productivity, & poor job performance) (unsatisfactoryperformance)

42	Other (other_allegedoffense)
43	Failure to follow a policy of a type not described above (not including reasonably contemporaneous insubordination that employer claims has been clearly articulated.) (failuretofollowapolicyofatypenot)

9 Super Offense Categories

Violence & Aggression (#2, 3, 4, 5, 26, 28, 32, 38, 39): 467 cases (ViolenceAggression)

Attendance/Absentee Issues (#1, 15, 16, 35): 352 cases (Attendance)

Dishonesty (#7, 8, 10, 11, 17, 36, 37): 377 cases (Dishonesty)

Drugs/Alcohol (#9, 24, 25): 96 cases (DrugsAlcohol)

On the Job Misconduct (#6, 12, 13, 18, 20, 21, 22): 175 cases (OntheJobMisconduct)

Off the Job Misconduct (#19, 23): 94 cases (OfftheJobMisconduct)

Insubordination (#14, 29, 30, 31, 43): 469 cases (InsubordinationRefusal)

Performance Issue (#33, 34, 41): 370 cases (Performance)

Other (#27, 40, 42): 24 cases (Other)

A continuous, count variable was created in case a record had more than one offense: (TotalOffenses)

Thus,

```
TotalOffenses |      Freq.     Percent        Cum.
------------+-----------------------------------
          1 |      1,737       84.53       84.53
          2 |        276       13.43       97.96
          3 |         34        1.65       99.61
          4 |          7        0.34       99.95
          5 |          1        0.05      100.00
------------+-----------------------------------
      Total |      2,055      100.00
```

14. Crime I

"Was the employee charged with a crime in the criminal justice system for the conduct that formed the basis of the employer's disciplinary action?"

One-digit field. Number assigned by RA.
Source: summary & decision

1 = Yes
2 = No
3 = Not Known

(crimei)

(A dummy variable was created where the "Not Known's" were assumed as a "No." This variable is named CrimeI_1).

15. Crime II

"If the answer to #14 was 2 or 3, did the Arbitrator describe the employee's conduct as a crime or an instance of moral turpitude?"

One-digit field. Number assigned by RA.
Source: summary & decision

1 = Yes
2 = No

(crimeii)

16. Last Chance

"Was the employee, at the time of the discipline, working under a "last chance" condition, either imposed by an agreement or by the award of a prior arbitrator?"

One-digit field. Number assigned by RA.
Source: summary & decision

1 = Yes, imposed by agreement
2 = Yes, imposed by arbitrator
3 = No

(lastchance)

(A dummy variable was created to indicate if last chance was imposed by anyone: NEWLASTCHANCE _0706)

17. Discipline

"What was the nature of the discipline imposed by the employer?"

One-digit field. Number assigned by RA. If more than one disciplinary action is at issue, then only the most serious discipline imposed is coded. If there are multiple actions of equal seriousness, then the disciplinary sanction that was imposed last is coded. Source: summary & decision

1 = Discharge
2 = Suspension of one week or more
3 = Suspension of less than one week
4 = Oral or written reprimand

(discipline)

(For regression purposes, category 2 and 3 were combined: DisciplineSuspension. Discipline_1 and Discipline_4 remained as is.)

18. Seven Tests I

"Does the employer or the union invoke Daugherty's Seven Tests?

One-digit field. Number assigned by RA. Source: decision

1 = The employer does, but not the union
2 = The union does, but not the employer
3 = Both parties invoke the Seven Tests
4 = Neither party invokes the Seven Tests

(seventestsi)

19.	Seven Tests II	"Does the arbitrator explicitly draw on Daugherty's Seven Tests in reaching the arbitrator's "guilt" and/or "just cause" determinations? One-digit field. Number assigned by RA. Source: decision 1 = Yes 2 = No (seventestsii) (For regression purposes, four dummy variables were created that incorporated #18 and # 19: NoSevenTest: Seven Tests were not invoked by anyone; PartiesSevenTest: Seven Tests invoked by at least one of the parties; ArbitratorSevenTest: Seven Tests invoked by the arbitrator only; BothSevenTest: Seven Tests invoked by at least one party and the arbitrator)
20.	Outcome	"What was the outcome of the award?" One-digit field. Number assigned by RA. (If the grievance considered more than one disciplinary action for a single grievant, then only the abritrator's decision with respect to the disciplinary action indicated at question 17 is coded. Source: summary & decision 1 = Arbitrator found just cause for discipline imposed (OutcomeMgmt) 2 = Arbitrator found no just cause for any discipline (OutcomeUnion) 3 = Arbitrator found just cause for lesser discipline than that imposed by employer (OutcomeSplit)

(outcome) This is the variable created originally and is utilized for the MNL regression analyses.

21. Guilt

"Does the arbitrator conclude that the grievant engaged in the misconduct alleged by the employer as the basis for the discipline?"

One-digit field. Number assigned by RA.
Source: summary & decision

1 = Yes
2 = No
3 = Different conclusion reached with regard to different offenses of the single grievant; guilty of some but not all offenses.
4 = Different conclusion reached with regard to different incidents constituting the same offense.
(guilt)

22. Proof

"What quantum of proof" does the arbitrator apply?"

One-digit field. Number assigned by RA.
Source: decision

1 = Preponderance of the evidence
2 = Clear and convincing evidence
3 = Evidence beyond a reasonable doubt
4 = No specific standard is articulated by the arbitrator

(proof)

(4 dummy variables were created: Proof_1, Proof_2, Proof_3, & Proof_4 [Correspond to the above])

23. Reduction

"If the answer to Question 20 (Outcome) is "3" (arbitrator imposed lesser discipline than employer), what reason is given for the reduction in discipline?"

One-digit field. Number assigned by RA.
Source: decision

1 = Employee is not guilty of the offense alleged but is guilty of a lesser offense
2 = Employee was guilty of the offense alleged but there were mitigating factors
3 = Employee was guilty of the offense alleged but there were procedural faults
4 = Employee was guilty of the offense alleged and there were both mitigating factors and procedural faults
5 = Employee was guilty of the offense alleged but rationale for the reduction of discipline is not explained
6 = Employee was guilty of a lesser offense and there were mitigating circumstances
7 = Employee was guilty of a lesser offense and there were procedural faults
8 = Employee was guilty of a lesser offense, there were mitigating circumstances, and there were procedural faults

(NEW_reduction)

24. Mitigation I

"If the answer to Question 23 (Reduction) was "2," "4," "6," or "8," what kinds of mitigation factors did the arbitrator rely upon?"

One-digit fields for each applicable factor.
Source: decision

Dummy codes were made for each of these items because cases could be classified as more than one.

1 = Length of service (NEW_lengthofservice)
2 = Good work record (NEW_goodworkrecord)
3 = Employee acted in good faith (NEW_eeactedingoodfaith)
4 = Absence of serious harm caused by employee's conduct (NEW_absenceofseriousharm)
5 = Provocation (NEW_provocation)
6 = Punishment too severe for offense (NEW_punishmenttoosevere)
7 = Lack of progressive discipline (NEW_lackofprogressivediscipline)
8 = Rehabilitation (i.e. drug, alcohol, mental health, & gambling addiction) (NEW_rehabilitation)
9 = Other (NEW_other)

25. Mitigation II

If the answer to Question 24 (Mitigation I) was "9" (Other), describe any other mitigating factor(s) considered by the arbitrator.

Memo field. Filled in by RA. Source: decision

(NEW_mitigationii)

26. Due Process I

"If the answer to Question 23 (Reduction) was "3," "4," "7," or "8" (procedural fault), what kinds of procedural factors did the arbitrator rely upon?"
One-digit fields for each applicable factor. Source: decision

Dummy codes were made for each of these items because cases could be classified as more than one.

1 = Lack of notice that the employee's conduct was prohibited (NEW_lackofnoticeconductprohib)

		2= Lack of notice of the possible disciplinary consequences of the employee's conduct (NEW_lackofnoticediscipline) 3 = Absence of a pre-disciplinary interview for the charged employee (NEW_absenceofpredisciplinary) 4 = Inadequate factual investigation (NEW_inadequatefactual) 5 = Employer's refusal to allow union representation at employee's disciplinary interview (NEW_employerrefusal) 6 = Inconsistent or discriminatory meeting out of discipline (NEW_inconsistentdiscriminatory) 7 = Other (NEW_other_dpi)
27.	Due Process II	If the answer to Question 26 (Due Process I) was "7" (Other), describe what other due process problem(s) was/were considered by the arbitrator. Memo field. Filled in by RA. Source: decision (NEW_due_processii)
28.	Reprimand Remedy	"If the answer to Question 17 (discipline) was "4" (reprimand), what was the arbitrator's decision? 1 = Reprimand was upheld 2 = Reprimand was ordered rescinded 3 = Reprimand was reduced to a lesser sanction (includes oral warnings) (reprimandremedy)
29.	Suspension Remedy	"If the answer to Question 17 (discipline) was "2" or "3" (suspension), what was the arbitrator's decision? 1 = Suspension was upheld in full 2 = Suspension was reduced in length

3 = Suspension was overturned in full
4 = Suspension was reduced to a warning or reprimand

(NEW_suspensionremedy)

30.	Reinstatement	"If the answer to Question 17 (discipline), was "1" (discharge), did the arbitrator:" One-digit field. Filled in by RA. Source: summary & decision 1 = Uphold the discharge 2 = Reinstate with full back pay 3 = Reinstate with partial back pay (reduced to a suspension) 4 = Reinstate with no back pay 5 = Entitlement to future vacancy (NEW_reinstatement)
31.	Last Chance	"If the answer to Question 30 (Reinstatement) was "2," "3," or "4," (employee was reinstated), did the arbitrator state that the reinstatement included 'last chance' conditions?" One-digit field. Filled in by RA. Source: summary & decision 1 = Yes 2 = No (NEW_lastchance)
32.	Back Pay I	"If the answer to Question 30 (Reinstatement) was "4" (employee was reinstated with no back pay), for how many months was the employee in 'no back pay status'?"

		Two-digit field. Filled in by RA. (NEW_backpayinobackpaymonths)
33.	Back Pay II	"If the answer to Question 30 (Reinstatement) was "3" (reinstatement with partial backpay), how long of a suspension was imposed (days)?" (Use 999 if the number of days is not known.) Three-digit field. Filled in by RA. (NEW_backpayiisuspensiondays)
34.	Back Pay III	"If the answer to Question 30 (Reinstatement) was "4" (no back pay), what reason does the arbitrator provide for not awarding full back pay?" Memo field. Filled in by RA. Source: decision. (If no reason is given, write "None.") (NEW_backpayiii)
35.	Jurisdiction	"If the answer to Question 30 (Reinstatement) was "2" or "3" (full or partial back pay), does the arbitrator's award explicitly retain jurisdiction to decide subsequent disputes between the parties with regard to the remedy? One-digit field. Filled in by RA. Source: decision 1 = Yes, jurisdiction retained 2 = No, jurisdiction not retained or no mention made of retention of jurisdiction. (NEW_jurisdiction)

36.	Reduction	"If the answer to Question 30 (Reinstatement) was "2" or "3" (full or partial back pay), does the arbitrator's award explicitly state that the amount of back pay is to be reduced by the employee's interim earnings or the employee's failure to mitigate by seeking employment?" One-digit field. Filled in by RA. Source: decision 1 = Yes 2 = No (NEW_reduction_q36)
37.	Arbitrator Practicing Lawyer	1 = Yes 0 = No (ArbitratorLawyer)
38.	Arbitrator Practicing Academic	1 = Yes 0 = No (ArbitratorAcademic) Four dummy variables were created: Arbitrator Practicing Attorney: JustPracLawyer Arbitrator Practicing Academic: JustPracAcademic Arbitrator is Both: Both Arbitrator is Neither: Neither
39.	Arbitrator Education	Categorical Variable 1=No College 2=Undergraduate 3=Master's Degree 4=JD

	5=PhD (Education) Dummy codes were created for the following: Education_1 = No College Education_2 = Undergraduate Education_3 = Master's Degree Education_4 = JD Education_5 = PhD
40. Arbitrator Experience	Dummy code that designates NAA Membership. 1 = Yes (if Year of Decision is equal to or greater than Year of Admittance). 0 = No (NAAExperienceDummy)
41. State of Residence	Categorical variable. 1 = MN 2 = WI 3 = IA 4 = FL 5 = NV 6 = ND (State) Dummy coded variables were created: State_1 = MN State_2 = WI State_3 = IA State_4 = FL State_5 = NV State_6 = ND

42. Arbitrator Gender

Dummy coded.
1 = Female
0 = Male

(arbitratorgender1iffemale)

43. Date of Decision (Not a String)

Converts string variable "dateofdecision" to Stata date variable.

(Ddateofdecision)

Date fields were merged initially into Stata as text. This new field allows the date to be numeric.

44. Date of Discipline (Not a String)

Converts string variable "dateofdiscipline" to Stata date variable.

(Ddateofdiscipline)

Date fields were merged initially into Stata as text. This new field allows the date to be numeric.

45. Months from Discipline to Decision

Elapsed time in months (rounded to the nearest month) between the date of discipline and the date of decision.

(disciplinetodecision_months)

46. (D) – Dummy coding for Q45

Months between discipline and decision
0 = -5 thru -1 (D0)
1 = 0 – 3 (D1)
2 = 4 – 6 (D2)
3 = 7 – 9 (D3)
4 = 10 – 12 (D4)
5 = 13 – 17 (D5)
6 = 18 – 23 (D6)
7 = 24+ (D7)

47. Age at Time of Decision	Year Decision Made – Birthyear = ageattimeofdecision Squared age: ageattimeofdecision_squared
48. Time Lag	Difference between Discipline and Decision Date (timedifference2; this contains 2047 cases because 8 cases have a missing date value) The variable timelag was created using imputation. The mean (291.7303) was entered for missing values.)
49. Sequence of Case	Arbitrator Case Sequence (CaseNoSequential)
50. Year Dummies	Dummy coded. Block1 = 1982 – 1989 Block2 = 1990 – 1997 Block3 = 1998 – 2005

* The variables listed above are the core variables used in the analyses. Additional variables were created to supplement these variables (e.g. dummy variables) and are listed exclusively within Stata.

INDEX

References are to pages

www.ingramcontent.com/pod-product-compliance
Lightning Source LLC
LaVergne TN
LVHW080020210926
848481LV00011B/3066
9781600422423